BEYOND CONSTRUCTIVE ENGAGEMENT:
UNITED STATES FOREIGN POLICY TOWARD AFRICA

The Washington Institute for Values in Public Policy is an independent, nonprofit research and educational organization that provides nonpartisan analyses exploring the ethical values underlying public policy issues. The Washington Institute seeks to promote democratic principles which affirm the inherent value, freedom, and responsibility of the individual, the integrity of the family and the interdependence of the community of man. The Institute researches a broad range of public policy options, recognizing that the individual, the government and privat social institutions share the responsibility for the common welfare—including the maintenance of a strong national defense. Policy options are generally viewed in light of their impact on the individual and the family. To encourage more informed decision-making on public policy issues, the Institute offers its research and resources to scholars, policymakers and the public.

ADDITIONAL TITLES

Human Rights in East Asia: A Cultural Perspective
Edited by James C. Hsiung (1986)

The Nuclear Connection: A Reassessment of Nuclear Power and Nuclear Proliferation
Edited by Alvin Weinberg, Marcelo Alonso and Jack N. Barkenbus (1985)

Central America in Crisis
Edited by Marcelo Alonso (1984)

Global Policy: Challenge of the 80's
Edited by Morton A. Kaplan (1984)

BEYOND CONSTRUCTIVE ENGAGEMENT:
UNITED STATES FOREIGN POLICY TOWARD AFRICA

Edited by
Elliott P. Skinner

A Washington Institute Book

Paragon House Publishers
New York

Published in the United States by
Paragon House Publishers
2 Hammarskjold Plaza
New York, New York 10017

A Washington Institute for Values in Public Policy book.

Library of Congress Cataloging-in-Publication Data

Beyond Constructive Engagement.

   "A Washington Institute book."
   Bibliography:
   Includes index.
   1. Africa—Foreign relations—United States—
Congresses. 2. United States—Foreign relations—
Africa—Congresses. 3. Africa—Foreign relations—
1960-   —Congresses. 4. United States—Foreign
relations—1981-   —Congresses. I. Skinner,
Elliott Percival, 1924-   .
DT38.7.B48   1986   327.7306   86-4899
ISBN 0-88702-209-X
ISBN 0-88702-210-3 (pbk.)

CONTENTS

PREFACE

The original essays in this book were especially prepared for a conference on United States Policy toward Africa, held on September 19–20, 1984, in Washington, D.C. At the time of their presentation, they were commented upon by selected individuals and were the subject of extended discussion. The conference was sponsored by The Washington Institute for Values in Public Policy, and was designed to examine in detail the conduct of United States foreign policy toward Africa against the backdrop of four years of the Reagan administration. While the original intent of the convenors was to review United States initiatives in Africa and to respond to all the salient issues facing peoples of that continent, it soon became apparent that in almost all of the papers, the commentators and the participants kept returning to the issue of South Africa and the United States' controversial policy of "constructive engagement." Carefully crafted to take a novel approach to the intractable problem of apartheid in South Africa, that policy soon assumed continent-wide dimensions as part of Reagan's global anti-Soviet strategy. The result has created a great deal of debate and concern among many Americans, especially Afro-Americans, about the implications of that policy for the United States and for the countries of Africa. The tragic events that have taken place in South Africa since the conference, and before its proceedings had gone to press, indicate quite clearly that the participants were justified in their fear that constructive engagement might fail. There was a widespread feeling that the United States needed a policy toward Africa that went beyond constructive engagement if it hoped to pursue its national interests in a rapidly changing world.

The conference also attempted to focus the attention of Americans on a continent which had never assumed the importance that many believe it warranted. Thus, the aim was to provide for those persons interested in Africa, an arena in which they could exchange their often contrasting views. The presenters and commentators were selected from the still rather small group of persons with a long interest in African affairs. The academic community is therefore well represented, and so are those government and philanthropic agencies and associations known for their activities related to Africa. My hope was that when the experiences of these persons were added to those of the many governmental officials who are involved with Africa on a daily basis, the resulting mix would provide the kind of insights into United States policy toward Africa so seldom achieved.

True to their commitment to provide an opportunity for specialists to organize conferences and to provide a forum for independent examinations of policies of importance to the American people, Neil A. Salonen, Director of The Washington Institute and President of the International Cultural Foundation and the Board of Trustees, welcomed my desire to organize the conference. Many members of the Board of Trustees of the Institute attended the conference, chaired sessions, and participated in the discussions. Professor Richard L. Rubenstein and David Carliner, Esq., were among those who were kind enough to chair sessions and to give their comments. Daniel Stein, the program officer for the conference, was especially helpful. He understood and sympathized with the pressures and the hustle and bustle involved in preparing a conference. Robert Sullivan, Mary Rand, and Colette Caprara, joined by other able staff members of the Institute, were there when help was needed to get the conference underway.

Finally, I want to express my deep gratitude to all those who attended the conference and to those who lent their emotional support for making it an intellectually stimulating and rewarding experience.

Introduction

Africa has been deemed so unimportant by most American leaders that in the 1984 presidential campaign the continent and its manifold problems were all but ignored by the two major candidates for the presidency of the United States. The Reverend Jesse Jackson attempted to engage his rivals for the Democratic Party's nomination in a serious debate about United States foreign policy toward Africa, but failed to do so. During a televised debate on America's foreign policy between Republican incumbent Ronald Reagan and his Democratic challenger Walter Mondale, the President insisted that his administration supported America's friends who were challenged by their enemies and detractors. Former Vice President Walter Mondale did not rise to the challenge, and ignored any reference to Africa in his response, although he had circulated a position paper on African affairs.

The propensity of Americans to ignore the problems of most countries until suddenly forced to intervene militarily or to provide economic relief is now widely admitted. Nevertheless, the lessons have not been learned. Americans heard little about either Korea or Vietnam, and knew even less about those countries, until they found themselves fighting there. Seemingly in vain did former Secretary of State Henry Kissinger subsequently warn that: "By establishing a pattern of response *in advance* of crisis situations, strategic doctrine permits a power to act purposefully in the face of challenges. In its absence, a power will constantly be surprised by events. An adequate strategic doctrine is therefore a basic requirement of American security." [1]

It is therefore with a sense of *déjà vu* that one notes that even before the victorious Ronald Reagan was inaugurated for his second term, events in Africa made the headlines and forced themselves on his attention. A disastrous famine, resulting in part from a calamitous drought, caught the attention of the world. The news shocked and alarmed the American people, and obliged the President to act by increasing food aid to Africa. Second, on Thanksgiving Eve, 1984, a number of black Americans mobilized by *TransAfrica* (a black American lobby for Africa), staged a sit-in at the South African embassy in Washington, D.C. This dramatic act ignited a protest movement against apartheid in South Africa which quickly assumed continental proportions. Coinciding as this movement did with Bishop Desmond Tutu's being awarded the Nobel Peace Prize, the President could not ignore the global recognition of the struggle against apartheid. He felt constrained to invite the bishop to the White House to discuss American policy toward South Africa.

President Reagan's attitude toward Africa is not new; rather, it is part of a centuries-long propensity of America's leaders to ignore conditions on that continent or to see them through the prism of European primacy. Then when it appeared that this point of view had to be modified, the United States substituted another prism, that of Soviet Communism, with which to deal with changes that were taking place in Africa. The reluctance to look Africa fully in the face continues today. This process was clearly enunciated by George McGhee, the Assistant Secretary of State for Near Eastern and African Affairs (there was no separate African bureau until 1958), when he attempted to explain to the members of the Foreign Policy Association in Oklahoma City on May 8, 1950, why the United States still had a Eurocentric policy toward Africa. He declared: "All of the so-called colonial powers represented on the continent of Africa are our friends and allies in the world-wide contest between the Free and the Communist worlds." He cautioned his listeners to bear in mind that the United States was "not in a position to exercise direct responsibility with respect to Africa." He stressed that the country had "no desire to assume the responsibilities borne by other powers, and indeed, our principles, our existing commitments, and our lack of experience all militate against our assumption of such obligations." The best that McGhee could hope for was that the Africans would not turn against the United States. He suggested:

> Advantage must be taken of this period of grace to further the development within Africa of healthy political, economic and social institutions, to create understanding on the part of the Africans of the forces of Communism which are disturbing the peace and security of hundreds of millions of people elsewhere in the world, and to inspire a determination to resist these forces . . .[2]

In addition to warning the African nationalists about the dangers of Communism, the United States sent mixed signals about its attitudes regarding African insistence upon independence. It warned about "the dangers of premature independence," but insisted that the United States really supported the goal of self-government or independence for all people, while adding the proviso that this referred to those people who "have the desire and capacity for it."[3] For their part the Africans did not halt their drive to end colonialism. Ghana achieved independence in 1957, and to combat the expected Soviet efforts to profit from this event, the incumbent President Dwight D. Eisenhower sent Vice President Richard M. Nixon to attend that country's celebration as well as to report on the state of other independent African countries. Clearly recognizing a need for a serious American approach to Africa, Nixon reported:

> The leaders and peoples of the countries I visited in Africa have many things in common. They cherish their independence, which most of them have only recently acquired, and are determined to protect it against any form of foreign domination. They rightfully expect recognition from us and others of their dignity and equality as individuals and peoples in the family of nations. They want economic progress for their underdeveloped econo-

mies.... There must be a corresponding realization throughout the executive branches of the Government; throughout the Congress and throughout the nation of the growing importance of Africa to the Free World, and the necessity of assigning higher priorities to our relations with that area.[4]

Echoing Nixon's appeal, the thirteenth American Assembly composed of leaders in almost all sectors of American life, meeting at Arden House (Harriman, New York) May 1– 4, 1958, declared in a preamble to its final report on "The United States and Africa":

Africa has entered upon the stage of world affairs in a role that demands the attention of the American people. The United States is involved in every corner of the globe; what this nation does or fails to do will affect Africa. In turn, events in Africa will have an impact on the United States.[5]

Except for creating a full-fledged Africa Bureau, United States policy toward Africa did not change during the remaining years of the Eisenhower administration. The United States simply followed France's lead with respect to our policies to both Guinea and Algeria. A more forward-looking John F. Kennedy toyed with Belgian primacy in the Congo, thereby courting disaster involving both the Soviets and the United Nations. The President showed concern when blacks started opposing apartheid in South Africa, but Kennedy took no serious measures to bring about change there or in Portugal's African colonial territories. The Johnson administration followed Britain's lead in the Rhodesian crisis and in the subsequent Nigerian civil war. Even when it was clear that the Nigerian federal government had won the war, the incoming Nixon administration (1969) scurried around consulting with France and other European countries, seeking to aid starving Biafrans who were even then rapidly coming under the control of the central government. Kissinger's ill-fated NSSM 39, which reemphasized the United States' belief in the primacy of

European interests in southern Africa, fell victim to the end of the Portuguese empire. He found himself shuttling throughout southern Africa in an attempt to prevent the expected domino effect to benefit the Soviet Union. The Carter administration did manage to assist Britain to decolonize Rhodesia, but retreating to a more traditional United States policy, it failed to exert itself to bring about meaningful changes in either Namibia or South Africa. The Reagan administration's adoption of Chester Crocker's views of "constructive engagement" toward South Africa absolutely affirmed United States views of the primacy of the European element in that area and appears to view the rest of Africa with "benign neglect."[6]

From 1960 onwards, the independent African states and Africans struggling for equality with dominant resident European-derived populations, wanted a more active United States policy toward Africa, but remained suspicious of its motives. Much to the Africans' surprise and chagrin, they experienced great difficulties in their attempts to build new institutions to cope with the realities of decolonization and the demands of statehood in a rapidly changing world. The European-derived political institutions failed to work in almost all the independent African societies, and the ensuing military regimes have not met the task of maintaining political stability. The political culture suitable for contemporary Africa has probably not yet emerged, and the process by which it will indeed come into being may well be long and hard.

In southern Africa this process has been complicated by wars of liberation and opposition to apartheid. Meanwhile, throughout the continent, ethnic competition for the strategic resources of the societies has escalated, resulting in civil wars and pogroms with the almost inevitable flight of millions of refugees. These problems are exacerbated by droughts and famines which have plagued large regions of the continent. Moreover, with few exceptions the economic policies promulgated by the African states, whether socialist, capitalist, or mixed, have succumbed to local mismanagement and global economic dislocations.

Most commentators largely agree that the United States has failed to react in a meaningful way to the crises in Africa.[7] Jennifer Seymour Whitaker, program director for Africa at the

Council on Foreign Relations and associate editor of *Foreign Affairs,* states in a book entitled, *Africa and the United States: Vital Interests,* that: "From the mid-1960s until the mid-1970s, developments on the continent of Africa were largely ignored by higher level foreign policy makers." She gives as the reasons for this attitude the Congo crisis, the consolidation of one-party states, and the rash of military coups. The result, according to Whitaker, was that: "Black Africa came to be perceived as merely a collection of small, poor, authoritarian states, without much importance to international politics."[8] Nevertheless, she felt that events throughout the continent, especially in southern Africa, did call for an "informed analysis of U.S. foreign policy toward Africa. . . ."[9]

African problems are indeed many and varied, but the major concerns of its people are economic development and the seemingly intractable problem of eliminating white racism and economic exploitation in the Republic of South Africa. Significantly, these are the issues that have come under the scrutiny of President Reagan, and have forced him to take some action. The problem of political instability, the search for ethnic harmony, the surviving problems of territorial boundaries, and the need to adapt socio-cultural systems to the modern world still plague most African societies. However, these issues are less the source of tension between the United States and African countries than are economic concerns and the policy of apartheid in South Africa. After four years of false hopes, very few accomplishments, and now escalating violence, it seems apparent that the United States needs a policy that goes beyond constructive engagement.

Long convinced that a Eurocentric United States policy toward Africa was doomed to failure, and anxious to provide a forum in which some of the best-informed persons on African affairs might shed fresh light on the problems I saw looming there, I obtained the support of The Washington Institute for Values in Public Policy to organize a conference on Africa. The Institute, for its part, hoped that out of this conference would come some recommendations for a more effective United States policy toward Africa. My feeling was that the time had come for the United States to elaborate a policy toward Africa which is frankly Africa–specific, or "Afro-spective" in character.[10] This is the only way that we can perceive what is really happening in Africa and deal with events there in a way to serve our national interests and help that continent realize its potential. During the conference the contributors, discussants, and participants presented their independent views on United States policy toward Africa, and in some cases there were strong disagreements. This book attempts to reflect faithfully all of these views.

Robert S. Browne places United States economic policy toward Africa in its complex historical, strategic, political, and psychological context. He understands why the United States places so much emphasis on those countries whose strategic minerals are vital to our military-industrial complex, but he raises questions as to whether our concern for safeguarding the sources of these minerals as the basis of our policy is not short-sighted. Browne calls attention to the low incidence of trade between the United States and most African countries, and the meager amount of private investment in the continent despite the continued emphasis in the United States of trade over aid. He notes that emergency food to meet the ravages of famine is often provided, but he suggests this aid is a source of disincentive for food production. Alarmed that the United States has not done very much to help the African states to solve their debt problem, Browne also calls attention to a general deterioration in the African economies, a condition he terms "negative growth."

Finally, Browne believes that our reaction to the Berg Report and the Lagos Plan of Action will be crucial to America's relationship to the future of African economic development. The plans take contrasting approaches to Africa's long-term development. Although still dependent upon exports to meet most of their economic needs, the Africans are increasingly striving for continental integration. Their need to increase food production along with their need for skills, capital, and technology will pose serious problems for the future.

William Foltz places United States strategic concerns in Africa in a sophisticated theoretical as well as operational model. He examines such factors as: African areas viewed as strategic obstacles; the availability of sea lanes around the continent; the potential use of African countries as a launching pad in the East-West conflict; the control of African commodities as strategic resources; and the wisdom of using African territories as "surrogate terrains" for local conflicts with global implications. Analyzing all of these factors in their strategic as well as political perspectives, Foltz wonders whether diplomacy might not be a more effective means for the United States to deal with its strategic concerns in Africa than relying on military force. He also suggests that it might be very important to help the African states police the continent, thereby obviating a number of United States strategic concerns.

William Lewis believes that the United States' major foreign policy concern, "to maintain order and stability in an increasingly disorderly world," is seriously challenged in Africa because of that continent's regional, cultural, and political diversity. He feels that the United States' tendency to react to African problems on an *ad hoc* basis, with no fixed pattern in mind, has not worked. Moreover, this has mainly served to reveal a flawed strategy. Lewis suggests that turbulence might well be the norm in contemporary African societies. This being the case, the United States may well not have the resources to deal with problems on that continent. Our attempt to use surrogates or allies to further our interests may not work because these may have other agendas. A sounder approach may well be one in which the United States recognizes that constant change is the African norm, and devises a policy to deal with it. In Lewis's opinion, aggressive stances and blustering do not help, and they fail to deal with Africa's diversity and turbulence.

Noting that while there are social and political problems in all the regions of Africa, Robert Rotberg finds that those in southern Africa, and especially in the Republic of South Africa, have proven the most intractable to United States policy. He observes that the African Bureau of the State Department has been devoting so much time and effort to southern Africa that it has largely ignored problems in the rest of the continent. Rotberg explores the relationship between apartheid and the inability of South Africa to resolve the issue of Namibia. He questions whether South Africa's struggle against SWAPO (South West Africa Peoples Organization) is justified either economically or politically, given the improbability of any non-SWAPO group emerging in Namibia to make peace on Afrikaner terms. Meanwhile, Rotberg shows how the conflict in Namibia spilled over into Angola, where the presence of Cuban troops engaged the United States on the side of South Africa. Nevertheless, he does not believe that South Africa's actions, such as forcing the beleaguered Mozambicans to sign the Nkomati Accord, have helped. In fact, the effects have left smoldering conflicts in the surrounding states, and almost no change in the fundamental conflicts within that Republic.

Finally, Rotberg believes that the Reagan administration's policy of constructive engagement has failed to help South Africa solve its domestic problems. Even though the President has indicated personal abhorrence of apartheid, his administration has established a greater sense of bonhomie with South Africa. This has made the Republic stronger and more resolute in its policies. Rotberg gives his own prescriptions for a more effective United States policy toward the southern African region.

Mabel Smythe discusses how economic, social, and political conflicts in Africa resulted in more than five million refugees on the continent by 1981. The number of refugees is now estimated to be about four million, and the help available to these persons is declining. Smythe notes, while historically the United States was generous toward refugees, there has been an increasing decline in refugee assistance. Equally as disturbing is the insufficient aid to countries which receive refugees. The resulting economic and development problems of the "asylum countries" could be rectified if United States policy encouraged the integration of refugee assistance programs into the economic development schemes for Africa. Smythe notes the intention of the Reagan administration to shift refugee assistance to the private sector (albeit with some government support). She also raises questions about the low level of immigration of Africans to the United States and notes that the majority of these persons seeking asylum in the United States have come from Ethiopia. Smythe's major concern is that the United States policy of attempting to restrain the rate of resettlement of refugees in an effort to oblige their countries of origin to take them back, may be in error. She presents some suggestions which she believes could facilitate United States aid in ending the suffering inherent in the African refugee problem.

Marie Davis Gadsden emphasizes the need for the United States to maintain an adequate level of educational and cultural activities in Africa. An early and still active participant in these activities over the years, she believes that a consistent involvement is especially important at this time when the Africans are moving toward a more comprehensive policy of attention to all phases of human development. This new approach stresses continued emphasis on primary school education, a new concern with the education of women, and an emphasis on the retention of Afro–centric values.

Of major concern to Gadsden is that our African education and cultural activities are minimal, *ad hoc,* and now burdened with a number of new restraints (such as decentralization of administration and financing of local school systems) so that the private sector could become more involved; and the candid and unequivocal official position of the administration that its educational-cultural contribution will be "small, whether compared to the magnitude of the problem or to the programs of other donors." This policy is affirmed in the face of the limited response of both the public and private sectors of the United States to crisis in Africa (as contrasted to those in Europe and the Middle East). She notes the decrease in the number of Peace Corps volunteers in Africa under the present United States administration. Gadsden laments the failure to recognize that education and culture are imperative for African development, and are very much part of our foreign policy.

Gwendolyn Carter observes that, after being largely ignored by most Americans for years, both South Africa and Namibia are now of major concern. She sees this new development as the result of a conscious policy of the Reagan administration to link the problems of South Africa and Namibia to the overriding conflicts of the cold war. Reacting to this new development, both the Democratic and Republican Parties addressed the problem of South Africa in their party platforms. Whereas the Democrats emphasized the need for more pressure to bring about changes there, the Republicans were self-congratulatory about what they considered to have been the positive results of constructive engagement. What surprised and alarmed Carter was that while the Republicans advocated a concern with the "rights of all South Africans," they have apparently decided to retreat from a long-term bipartisanship in United States foreign policy. Carter has also been alarmed by the growing instability she has noted in the region during the last sixteen years. She believes that Reagan's embracing of Crocker's policy of constructive engagement has complicated the matter, as has the linking of the withdrawal of Cuban troops from Angola to the solution of the Namibian issue. Moreover, she feels that by placing South Africa's security at the center of United States policy in the region, the administration played into the hands of South African Prime Minister Botha.

Carter expresses skepticism about whether the United States-backed Nkomati Accord has brought peace to the region. While ANC (African National Congress) attacks have been frustrated, MNR (Mozambique National Resistance Movement) assaults continue. She questions why the United States should recognize the legitimate role of SWAPO in dealing with Namibia, but deny the right of the ANC, to play a comparable role in attempting to resolve the conflict in South Africa itself. Carter does believe that the administration can influence South Africa's policy of denationalizing most of the blacks in that country. She suggests a number of changes for a viable policy toward South Africa and Namibia.

NOTES

1. Henry Kissinger, "Strategy and Organization," *Foreign Affairs* (April 1975), 375.

2. George McGhee, *Department of State Bulletin,* Vol. 22, No. 572, June 19, 1950, 999–1003.

3. Waldemar A. Nielsen, *The Great Powers and Africa* (New York: Praeger Publishers, 1969), 263; cf. Vernon McKay, *Africa in World Politics* (New York: Harper and Row, 1963), 320–324.

4. Richard M. Nixon, "The Emergence of Africa, Report to the President by Vice President Nixon on his Trip to Africa," White House Release, April 7, 1957.

5. "The United States and Africa," report of the American Assembly, Columbia University (June 1958), 241.

6. References to all of these policy positions will be found in the citations of the various articles in the body of the book.

7. See Elliott P. Skinner, *Afro-Americans and Africa: The Continuing Dialectic,* A Publication of The Urban Center, Columbia University, 1973; Hugh H. Smythe and Elliott P. Skinner, "Black Participation in U.S. Foreign Relations," *The Encyclopedia of the Black American,* Mabel M. Smythe, ed. (Englewood Cliffs, NJ: Prentice-Hall, 1978), 638–647.

8. Jennifer Seymour Whitaker, ed., *Africa and the United States: Vital Interests* (New York: New York University Press, 1978), 11.

9. Ibid., 4.

10. Many analysts have bemoaned the lack of an Africa-specific policy of the United States. Henry Jackson complained that "no other continent has been so consistently ignored by our policy makers.... A greater tragedy has occurred in the sphere of foreign policy, because American leaders noticed Africa only in the context of cold war competition with the Soviet Union." Henry F. Jackson, *From the Congo to Soweto: U.S. Foreign Policy Toward Africa Since 1960* (New York: William Morrow and Co., 1982), 18. (See also pages 283ff.)

CHAPTER 1

UNITED STATES ECONOMIC POLICIES TOWARD AFRICA

Robert S. Browne

I. INTRODUCTION

Having nurtured, at various epochs, civilizations far in advance of those then extant elsewhere on the globe, Africa has in the modern era fallen behind many other regions in terms of its contributions and its role in global affairs. Sometime during the Middle Ages, Africa was reduced to a relative backwater of human civilization. Even without speculating on the myriad possible reasons, world powers cannot deny that contemporary Africa is once again becoming an entity with which to be reckoned. Second only to Asia both in area and in population, the African continent offers a wealth of proved and unproved resources. Indeed, it was the early exploitation of these resources by the major European powers (and by the United States slave trade) which provided much of the economic base for the industrial economies of today's Western alliance.

The restraint of what had become a rapacious exploitation of the African continent was one of the more salutory consequences of World War II, for that conflict effectively undermined the imperial system which for so long had kept Africa under the political control of European powers.

For the past quarter century, we have been witnessing the first unsteady steps of this newly liberated continent, whose fifty independent political units are contained within boundaries more reflective of the political realities of late nineteenth-century Europe than of late twentieth-century Africa. Whether as a continental unit or as fifty independent nations, Africa constitutes a new and as yet largely unknown quantity in global political and economic affairs; and the manner in which the United States relates to it, and vice versa, will have significant implications for both.

In this paper we will examine some of the factors which are shaping this relationship and consider their implications. In Part II we will examine the United States government's perspectives on Africa and the concerns of the current administration relative to Africa. In Part III we will take a look at how these concerns correlate with our Africa policy. Part IV provides us an opportunity to note the specific economic programs which the United States is conducting in Africa. Finally, in Part V we identify some of the contemporary economic problems confronting Africa and explore the implications of two contrasting approaches to Africa's economic development.

II. HISTORICAL PERSPECTIVES AND UNDERLYING CONCERNS

Africa has never ranked high on America's scale of priorities, not culturally, not politically, and not economically. In addressing an audience in Boston recently, Secretary of State George Shultz observed that "many Americans have images of Africa that are anachronistic, partial, and often inaccurate. The perception of Africa that most of us grew up with—unknown lands somehow exotic and divorced from the rest of the world—has unfortunately persisted in some quarters despite the last 25 years of

African independence and increasing presence on the world stage. It is a misperception that ignores compelling realities."[1]

Among the compelling realities which Secretary Shultz might have enumerated is the fact that Africa, with a population seventy percent greater than the United States and a territory considerably more than twice the size, now consists of fifty sovereign nations which, owing to their voting cohesion, constitute the largest unified voting bloc in the United Nations. It is a repository of mineral resources of considerable strategic importance to the United States and is our second–largest supplier of petroleum.

Despite these impressive factors, Washington has never ranked Africa high among its priorities. This is evidenced not only by such indices as the travel itineraries of American officials and the topics to which administration spokespersons direct their attention, but also by the issues upon which Congress is asked to focus. It is implicit in policy statements of government officials, and of course in fund allocations which, while not an infallible guide to national priorities, can usually serve as a crude indicator of where national interest is believed to lie. On virtually all of these indicators, Africa appears to score below the other continents, although precise measurement and meaningful interpretation are admittedly difficult.

This low priority for Africa may be attributed variously to America's innate racism, to a lingering Eurocentered colonial view which perceives Africa as an extension of the European sphere of influence, or to the relatively low level of cold war confrontation centering on Africa. The fact that prior to the 1960s our State Department housed no Africa bureau but chose to handle African affairs through the European Bureau is an eloquent indication of our official attitude toward the continent during the period of colonial control. So we have a long history of viewing Africa as a region of only marginal concern, and of concern mainly in the perception that it is somehow linked to Washington's primary area of concern, the East-West confrontation.

Secretary of State Kissinger was the first American leader to take serious note of the absence of a clear Africa policy. His infamous National Security Study Memorandum (NSSM) 39, published in 1969, set forth a number of policy options for the

United States in southern Africa. The option selected, to retain a good working relationship with white minority regimes of the region, was fully in keeping with traditional American practice with regard to Africa. It was, however, quickly proved to be ill-chosen, inasmuch as the revolutionary movements in Mozambique and Angola displaced minority white regimes even before Kissinger's tenure ended, and the Zimbabwe struggle as well was essentially won by then.

With the arrival of the Carter administration we began to see some movement away from the traditional tendency to allow the lead in African affairs to be a European preserve. Even the long-established tendency to perceive African issues almost exclusively in terms of the East-West conflict was subjected to some reexamination under the prodding of Andrew Young. As a result, some effort was made to view Africa as a political entity meriting consideration on its own terms and not solely with reference to whatever scenario might be unfolding contemporaneously between Washington and Moscow. Although the Carter opening toward Africa was a fairly limited one, it nevertheless appeared to constitute a significant reappraisal of how the United States should relate to Africa. The forthright leadership which the United States took in the later stages of negotiations for Zimbabwe's independence, as well as in the search for a peaceful resolution of the Namibia impasse, seemed to presage an end to the traditional practice of leaving the initiative for resolving Africa's problems to the former metropolitan powers.

Before this shift of focus had an opportunity to take root, however, a new administration had assumed power in Washington, and Africa policy once again became a prisoner of European cultural bias and an adjunct to cold war policy. In southern Africa, the Carter tilt toward the impoverished and oppressed black majority was replaced by the pro-white policy of constructive engagement, epitomized by Assistant Secretary of State Chester Crocker's statement that, "in South Africa, the region's dominant country, it is not our task to choose between black and white"[2] — between oppressed and oppressor. Continent-wide, the bellicose anti-Sovietism which quickly became the trademark of the Reagan administration, emerged predictably as the primary focus of policy. Here is Secretary Shultz providing the rationale for United States policy in Africa in a speech delivered in January 1984:

> First, we have a significant and geopolitical stake in the security of the continent and the seas surrounding it. Off its shores lie important trade routes, including those carrying most of the energy resources needed by our European allies. We are affected when Soviets, Cubans, and Libyans seek to expand their influence on the continent by force, to the detriment of both African independence and Western interests.

> Second, Africa is part of the global economic system. If Africa's economies are in trouble, the reverberations are felt here. Our exports to Africa have dropped by 50 percent in the last three years; American financial institutions have felt the pinch of African inability to repay loans. And Africa is a major source of raw materials crucial to the world economy.

> Third, Africa is important to us politically because the nations of Africa are now major players in world diplomacy. They comprise nearly one-third of the membership of the United Nations, where they form the most cohesive voting bloc in the General Assembly.

> Finally, Africa is important to us, most of all in human terms. Eleven percent of America's population traces its roots to Africa; all of us live in a society profoundly influenced by this human and cultural heritage.[3]

Of these four concerns, it is the second which occupies our major attention in this paper inasmuch as we are addressing ourselves to American economic policy in Africa. Nevertheless, military and political concerns are so intimately linked with and provide so much of the rationale for our economic policy that they can hardly be ignored. Secretary Shultz's fourth concern, black America and its relationship to Africa, although a highly significant factor, does not appear to have played any visible role

7

in the shaping of United States policy toward Africa. It should (see Note).

III. EFFECTS OF AMERICAN CONCERNS ON AFRICA POLICY

The concern which Secretary Shultz expressed for protecting trade routes and for containing Soviet and Libyan influence in Africa is clearly evident from the manner in which American aid is allocated. Leaving aside Egypt, which received more economic aid from the United States than all the rest of the continent combined because it is the key Arab player in our Middle East scenario, the largest African recipient of United States economic aid is Sudan ($194 million for 1984) followed by Kenya ($84 million) and Somalia ($77 million).[4] These are countries which touch on the Red Sea and Indian Ocean, through which transit the vital oil tankers carrying their cargoes to Europe and beyond. These countries also surround Ethiopia, probably the Soviet Union's closest ally in Africa; Sudan is additionally important because it lies astride Chad and serves as somewhat of a counter to the Libyan involvement in that country. The $355 million given to these *three* countries should be compared with the $588 million which was allotted to the 42 other countries of black Africa.

Six out of these 42 managed to obtain $209 million, or well over one-third of the total. These favored six were Niger, Senegal, Liberia, Zaire, Zimbabwe, and Cameroon. Overt strategic and cold war considerations are less evident in the favoring of these six countries, although in the cases of both Niger and Senegal the shadow of Libya's Colonel Qadaffi unquestionably played a major role in determining their aid allocation. Both countries claim to feel threatened by Libyan expansionism, and uranium-producing Niger is having a portion of its territory claimed by the Libyan colonel. The substantial size of the Liberian aid program is an expression of the United States' special historic role in that country as well as a reflection of the severe economic difficulties which Liberia has faced as a result of the 1980 coup. Zaire can be considered an American cold war child in that the United States chose to support the right-wing faction in the civil war which racked that country soon after independence; and fallout from that decision continues some twenty years later. President Mobutu's inability to bring economic growth to his country or to win over dissident elements of his population has obliged the United States to continue pouring in large sums of money in order to maintain a measure of stability. The country also contains minerals strategically important to the United States. The Zimbabwe aid figure was part of a three-year commitment which the United States made at the time of independence. Zimbabwe, like Cameroon, is perceived by Washington as one of Africa's most promising places for private investment.

Having noted the high degree of correlation between American aid dollars and our military and political interests, we will turn our attention to Africa's mineral resources. The actual importance of these mineral resources to the United States is a somewhat controversial topic. The United States Bureau of Mines identifies 27 minerals as critical;[5] we rely on imports for 75 percent or more of our supply of eight of the 27. Africa supplies over half of the United States' consumption of chromite, cobalt, manganese, and the platinum group minerals, led by platinum and palladium. South Africa is the principal supplier of three of these four.

Chromite and the platinum group minerals are especially critical, because over half of our imports of both of these items come from South Africa and the Soviet Union. In the case of chromite, South Africa and Zimbabwe contain the world's major known reserves, although Zimbabwe is not currently a major supplier of chromite to the United States.

For the platinum group, South Africa and the Soviet Union are the only major sources of extensive known reserves. Inasmuch as the Soviet Union could hardly be considered to be a reliable supplier of strategic minerals to us in times of emergency, the importance of South African platinum sources is self-evident and probably goes far to explain why the United States has persistently demonstrated such reluctance to make a major assault on the offensive apartheid system practiced in that country. This timidity can hardly be justified, however, because South Africa relies on its mineral sales to help meet its very substantial foreign exchange needs as it attempts to become a major industrial nation. The country is not likely to find non-Western buyers for its minerals, and it cannot afford to forego the earnings they produce. Taking a longer-range perspective, majority rule will inevitably come to South Africa within the next decade or two, and a black-ruled South Africa favorably disposed toward the United States is certainly preferable to one harboring hostile memories. A black government in South Africa, however, probably would be obliged to sell its output to the United States and Europe regardless of its political leanings, just as the apartheid government would be. So we should feel free to follow our conscience on the apartheid question without fear of retaliation in the form of a minerals cut-off. Insofar as the chromite is concerned, Zimbabwe appears eager to expand its production and sales; therefore, a South African minerals squeeze would in any case apply only to the platinum group metals. The United States has unexploited platinum reserves in Montana which, together with expanded recycling efforts, could greatly reduce our dependence on imported suppliers. There is also work in progress on alternative technologies which could phase out the biggest single use of platinum—in catalytic converters—by the year 2000.

Cobalt is imported into the United States principally from Zaire (42 percent) and Zambia (13 percent). The United States has its own extensive reserves which are not being tapped at this time, and there are extensive supplies in nodular form on the ocean bottom.

The United States currently has a 97 percent dependence on imported manganese, with Gabon, South Africa, and Brazil serving as major suppliers. Australia has extensive reserves and is positioning itself to expand its output. There are also extensive undersea deposits. About 10 percent of South African manganese originates in Namibia.

In addition to these four, there are numerous other minerals which we import from Africa but on which our degree of dependence is substantially less. These include bauxite, iron, copper, gold, diamonds, mica, titanium, and phosphate. Clearly Africa is a major source and supplier of several minerals of great importance to our economic growth and to our security, although alternative sources exist for most of them—often within the United States itself—but at considerably higher prices. South Africa is by far the most important African supplier of these crucial minerals. This factor may explain why the United States and other major Western powers have limited themselves to verbal condemnation and mild slaps on South Africa's wrist for such outrageous international behavior as the illegal occupation of Namibia and the aggressive bombing and invasion of neighboring Angola and Mozambique, and domestically, for the institutionalization of apartheid and the use of terror as a means of retaining state power.

Our continuing access to these minerals is not likely to be threatened by the producing nations' making a political decision to deny them to us. Far more likely is the threat posed by a collapse of their internal economies, leading to domestic instability and chaos.

The salient fact which emerges from the foregoing survey is the unevenness with which the United States treats African nations. Although Africa is a continent of fifty nations, the United States focuses its bilateral assistance on only a handful of them, showering resources generously on three or four, somewhat less liberally on another half dozen, and virtually ignoring the rest. Security concerns clearly outweigh economic and other concerns and constitute the *raison d'être* for our foreign aid program. The matter of the continent's general economic development is either rejected or left to be addressed by multilateral aid or by other donors. Let us then look briefly at the various components of our economic programs in Africa.

IV. AMERICAN ECONOMIC PROGRAMS

The major components of our economic program in Africa are the following:

- Bilateral economic assistance

- Multilateral economic assistance

- Trade expansion initiatives

- Encouragement of private investment

- Emergency food aid

- Refugee assistance

The bilateral assistance program amounts to about $1 billion for sub-Saharan Africa ($944 million in 1984; $1063 million requested for 1985) and is divided into three categories: development assistance, economic support, and food programs, with respective fund allocations of roughly 40 percent, 40 percent, and 20 percent. Development assistance encompasses financing specific projects, strengthening African institutions, and myriad training programs. Economic support programs provide general financial assistance to countries in which the United States has special security interests. It often takes the form of providing dollars to permit the importation of goods which the country cannot afford to purchase but without which the country's stability would be endangered. The food programs consist of sales of American food in exchange for local currency, the proceeds of which are applied to long-term agricultural development, and of United States food donations to meet emergencies, of which Africa has many. For 1985 the administration proposed a new program, the Economic Policy Initiative (EPI), to provide funds to a limited number of African countries contingent upon their adopting policy reforms recommended by the United States, especially in the agricultural production and marketing areas. Seventy-five million dollars was requested for 1984 (but the Senate Appropriations Committee denied the funds at its first hearing on the foreign aid bill).

Multilateral assistance programs are essentially American contributions to the IDA (International Development Association), the soft loan window of the World Bank, and contributions to the regional development institutions for Africa, the African Development Bank and its soft loan window, the African Development Fund. The Reagan administration has openly stated its preference for bilateral over multilateral aid and has inflicted drastic cuts in the level of funding for the IDA. It has been only marginally more generous with the African regional development institutions.

Trade expansion has long been touted by both donor and recipient countries as the most important facet of the development relationship. Despite this, however, the level of United States-Africa trade is relatively meager compared with that of other regions of the world. In 1981 the United States exported some *$16 billion* of food, merchandise, and manufactured goods to sub-Saharan Africa (excluding South Africa) and purchased goods amounting to a somewhat larger sum from the region. This represented less than 5 percent of the United States' total foreign trade. Nine billion dollars of these imports consisted of petroleum from Nigeria, which is our largest supplier after Saudi Arabia. Both imports and exports dropped precipitously in 1982 and 1983 due to global recession and the decline in commodity prices. The United States trading deficit came to $6 billion, mainly from our trade with oil-producing Nigeria.

American business has not demonstrated notable aggressiveness in attempting to penetrate the African market, and our government has made only modest efforts at promoting American exports. Currently the strong United States dollar has naturally priced many of our products out of the market so that promotion at this time would be futile. Of equal or greater importance to the Africans would be the expansion of African exports, and there is much that could be done in this regard. The generalized system of preferences (GSP) legislation, which relieves developing countries of some of the onerous international trade regulations, needs to be extended and amended to provide developing countries greater access to American markets. It comes up for extension and revision in 1985. Similarly, the GATT (General Agreement of Trade and Tariffs) agreements should be further liberalized and some of the escape clauses closed. Tariff escalation provisions, which place higher tariffs on processed goods than on unprocessed ones, should be eliminated because they serve as a disincentive to primary goods producers to move to higher stages in the production process. Stated succinctly, the United States and other industrialized countries can both expand global trade and assist Africa by removing all vestiges of the protectionist policies which still inhibit Africa's export ability.

Private American investment in Africa is even more meager than our volume of trade. In 1981 Africa received only $6.8 billion or three percent of total American private direct investment abroad. Of this sum, one-third, or $2.2 billion, was in South Africa.[6] Perhaps another third was invested in North Africa, including Egypt, so sub-Saharan black Africa probably received no more than one percent of the total American private direct foreign investment. Here again, despite considerable rhetoric on the part of our spokespersons regarding the need for more private sector involvement, both private sector and government have demonstrated an amazing lack of aggressiveness in pushing for American investment in Africa. We have helped some countries draft investment codes and have exhorted them to become more receptive to foreign investors, but few American firms have attempted to follow up on such openings. The programs of the OPIC (Overseas Private Investment Corporation) and of the Export Import Bank have also been used sparingly in Africa. Our aid programs have generally included initiatives designed to assist African entrepreneurs, largely through the funding of prefeasibility studies.

Our emergency food aid and refugee assistance programs are large in scope (although still inadequate for what has proved to be two never-ending emergency situations) and are widely appreciated for their humanitarian aspects. However, food assistance is not an unmixed blessing for the continent; far too often it serves as a disincentive to food production. Cheap imported food frequently undersells local products and causes them to remain unsold. Because American food programs are designed to distribute foods which happen to be in surplus in the United States, humanitarian considerations are of only secondary importance to us. Rice and wheat are the surplus foods Africa craves, and our gifts and local currency sales of these items have resulted in millions of Africans' acquiring a taste for them. Rice grows well in only a few places in Africa and wheat in even fewer. Consequently, our ever-expanding food exports to Africa are creating demand for foods that Africa may never be able to produce widely for herself. This will probably exacerbate the very dependency syndrome against which Africans have been struggling so vigorously.

Is the package of economic programs an effective one for achieving our objectives in Africa? Probably not, although much of the package is useful and deserving of support. It is Secretary Shultz's view that the security of the continent and of the seas surrounding it is our top priority, followed by the growth, development, and solvency of Africa's economies, the maintenance of access to her raw materials, and the winning of African cooperation in international diplomatic forums. If we accept that view, then our short-run and piecemeal approach to the continent is not the most effective path to follow.

It is true that every country in sub-Saharan Africa (except Nigeria) receives *something* under our aid program, even Ethiopia and Angola, to whose governments we are openly hostile. However, the reality is that a select few countries are in effect being "bought" by the United States through very generous assistance programs while the overall allocation is quite inequitable on both a per-country and per-capita basis. Nor do the allocations correspond to need. Given the volatility of African governments, it is indeed short-sighted to attempt to buy allies and to shore up their economies in exchange for political or military favors to the United States. In the case of the Sudan, for example, where our aid program is twice that allocated to any other African country, the ruling government is extremely shaky and has a growing civil war on its hands largely brought on by its own heavy-handedness. That Sudan is thus likely to be a center of instability constitutes the greatest threat to security in a region such as Africa. The Economic Support Funds are the major culprits in creating this inequity. Although providing general support monies to afflicted economies can, if properly administered, be a real boon to an unbalanced or impoverished economy, limiting such funds to countries having some special security value for us is likely to be destabilizing from a continental perspective.

Our tilt toward bilaterial over multilateral aid also appears to be contrary to our best interests, especially when combined with the trend toward introducing conditionality into bilateral aid as we propose to do in the new Economic Policy Initiative. Although there is no question that aid donors, and especially lenders, have every right to attach conditions to their loans, it is a right which should be exercised with great circumspection. When the conditions are in fact demands that governments undertake major policy changes—changes which despite their being well intended could turn out to be disastrous errors—circumspection is especially desirable. A multilateral institution can absorb the backlash from such a mistake; an individual country is wise to avoid such risks. Because the IDA is by far the largest institutional lender in Africa, and a highly effective leverager of funds, American efforts to shrink the IDA program can only do damage to all of our objectives there.

One of the more serious deficiencies in our economic package for Africa is the absence of any major effort to address the growing burden of Africa's foreign indebtedness. This debt is running about $100 billion now, much less than in Latin America, but nevertheless much more than Africa will be in a position to service in the foreseeable future. Some Scandinavian countries have recognized this fact and have forgiven their share of the debts. The United States, on the other hand, continues to support the endless rescheduling of the debt even in the face of Africa's plunging export revenues. There can hardly be a more certain formula for creating future instability of a sort to threaten the very security which we claim to be seeking for the continent.

Having looked at some of the specifics of the United States effort in Africa, it is now useful to view the overall direction in which Africa is moving and how American policies relate to that. There is some basis for questioning the effectiveness of the entire global effort which has been made for Africa's economic development. Growing evidence seems to indicate that Africa's economic condition has been deteriorating for several years, and that on a per capita basis the continent is actually experiencing negative growth. After a growth spurt in the 1960s, the first decade of independence for most of Africa, the economies mostly stagnated in the 1970s and began to slip backward in the

1980s. This is evidenced not only by statistical data and budgetary deficits but also by the testimony of growing numbers of travelers within Africa, and of Africans themselves, who recount endless tales of breakdowns in the system—in every system: roads that have become unusable, schools without books, teachers without pay, health clinics without medicines, factories without raw materials, vehicles without fuel, machinery without spare parts, farms without crops, marketing boards without money, central banks without foreign exchange, plumbing without water, power lines without power. Although no place is yet besieged by all of these ills, many places in Africa are suffering with several of them, and their incidence is growing.

Overhanging it all is the expanding drought, which initially plagued the Sahel region but which is currently devastating some 22 countries extending eastward from the western Sahel to the Red Sea and Indian Ocean and south to Lesotho, Swaziland, and South Africa. In many places the drought is in its third year, and in the western Sahel and Ethiopia this drought follows closely behind a similiar diaster during the early 1970s. The possibility that drought may be becoming a permanent condition in parts of Africa is already acquiring credibility in some circles, although there appears to be little hard evidence on which to base such a conclusion. Unsound pricing and marketing policies have contributed to declines in production of a range of agricultural products, and per capita food production is actually on the decline.

The economic recession which gripped virtually the entire globe during the late 1970s, and which has dragged on into the 1980s, has certainly been a major contributor to Africa's hardships—perhaps *the* major contributor, for the African economies are more sensitive to the vagaries of their trading partners than are most economies. This derives both from their unparalleled openness—Africa exports a higher percentage of its GNP than does any other region—and from the fact that the African economies tend to be one-product, two-product, or at best three-product economies. That is, the bulk of their earnings comes from the export of a very limited number of items, rendering their economies highly susceptible to any changes in the price of, or the demand for, these items. Furthermore, many African countries produce similar products so that the number of different commodities exported in large volume is not very great. In fact, from 39 sub-Saharan nations only 32 major resource commodities accounted for about 70 percent of their non-fuel exports during 1976–1978.[7]

Africa's susceptibility to the ebbs and flows of the industrial economies is further intensified by the fact that many of Africa's exports suffer from low income elasticities. What this means in practice is that, while sales volume may not drop precipitously during a recession, nor rise dramatically during recovery, prices are likely to fluctuate widely—which they have. It also means that as consuming countries emerge from their prolonged recession, they are not likely to expand greatly their purchases of Africa's output, although prices may be expected to rise (toward ceilings which are determined by the production costs of substitute goods, of which modern technology is producing ever greater varieties). Rising prices attract new producers and cause expanded output, pushing prices downward and in the long run benefiting only the buyers.

This suggests that there are very real limits to what Africa can hope to achieve by focusing on expanding its production of traditional exports. Indeed, an argument can be made that restriction rather than expansion of output might yield higher revenues, although any effort to raise revenues by restricting output would require the close cooperation of competing producers, whether in Latin America, Asia, or elsewhere. As OPEC has demonstrated, producers' cartels tend to be extremely fragile structures and probably offer little hope for improving Africa's condition.

In the face of such grim projections, the question of what in fact is the proper development strategy for Africa has emerged as a topical issue of the 1980s. Debate centers on two highly significant documents which forthrightly address the question of Africa's economic future. Both documents were precipitated by the palpable deterioration beginning in Africa as the decade of the 1970s drew toward its conclusion.

The better-publicized of the two documents is the Berg Report, more properly known as *Accelerated Development in Sub-Saharan Africa*. It was prepared by the World Bank at the request of the African Ministers of Finance, who had requested that the World Bank take a close look at Africa with a view to determining why the continent's economy was experiencing such difficulty and what might be done to improve matters. The other document, which appeared in April, 1980, about 18 months earlier than the Berg Report, is the *Lagos Plan of Action for the Economic Development of Africa 1980–2000* (LPA). The LPA was approved and signed by heads of state of the fifty African nations. It was prepared by the Organization of African Unity (OAU) and the Economic Commission for Africa (ECA) at the request of the African Planning Ministers. Although the LPA received little attention outside of Africa at the time of its publication, the appearance of the Berg Report sparked a surge of interest in the LPA, for with both documents enjoying such prestigious sponsorship, comparisons were inevitable.

The thrust of the Berg Report was that Africa was experiencing a serious decline in its output and exports and that its other problems flowed from this. The decline was attributed to a number of improper government policies which were being pursued. Foremost among these were agricultural marketing and pricing practices, exchange rate policies, deficit spending, and excessive government involvement in the production and distribution process. The report set forth a number of recommended policy changes and urged donor countries to double their aid so as to enable Africans to introduce the necessary policy changes without subjecting their economies to an unbearable stress level. Aid was to be made conditional upon recipient compliance with the recommendations. Underlying the recommendations was the unspoken assumption that Africa's fortunes could be reversed by more efficiently pursuing its present development strategy rather than by choosing a new strategy.

The Lagos Plan, on the other hand, had come to the conclusion that the strategy itself was at fault. It recommended rejection of the existing strategy of externally-oriented, or export-led, development whereby Africa principally mines and grows items which it does not consume and ships them abroad to exchange them for the things it wants. It characterized this as a no-win strategy which left Africa dependent on the outside world to buy its products and pay a fair price for them. The terms of trade appear to move inexorably against the African nations, and the long-term outlook for many of Africa's commodity and mineral exports is not promising.

In place of export-led development, the Lagos Plan proposed self-reliance, or internally-oriented development, whereby Africa would stress producing goods for internal consumption rather than for export. This implies a modification in African consumption patterns and lifestyles as well as in production. Because of the small size of many African countries, it implies a substantial amount of sub-regional cooperation. It implies replacing narrow nationalism with a continental, or Pan-Africanist outlook. And because it will still require vast amounts of imported technology and expertise, it implies a need for a continued export effort to earn the foreign exchange necessary to implement the plan. Thus the basis for some harmonization of the Berg Report and the Lagos Plan is possible despite their differences in overall strategy.

Although there have been no official voices raised against the LPA, neither has there been any significant official support for it from non-African quarters. In all likelihood, the LPA has caused some uneasiness in the Western democracies; weakening of the linkage between Africa and the West which the LPA implies can be construed as a threat to Western security in both the political and the economic sense. It challenges the Western vision of the global economy, in which Africa is to be the storehouse of national resources necessary for maintaining the West's industrial power and leadership—hegemony, if you will. "Interdependence" is the currently fashionable term for this global relationship, encompassing the intricate panoply of connections which now link the many countries of the developed and the developing world: trade, finance, debt, travel, environmental concerns, nuclear threat, and so on.

That Africans should want to opt out of this system is apparently unimaginable to many Western leaders and helps to account for the lack of response to the LPA. However, interdependence has not paid off for the Africans, for it is an interdependence of unequals. For years the Third World has complained that the international trading, financial, and monetary system was biased against developing countries and has requested that developed countries join them in a north-south dialogue which could lead to the structuring of a New International Economic Order, more just and more fair to the Third World. The United States turned a deaf ear to such pleas, and as the Africans watched their economies deteriorate and their indebtedness to the West grow, they concluded that insulating themselves offered the most promising alternative.

The United States, like most other industrialized countries, has taken no official position regarding the Lagos Plan. Indeed, inasmuch as the document has the unanimous endorsement of the African nations, it is politically awkward to express opposition to it although deficiencies within the document itself have been criticized. Rather, we have largely ignored the document while we have simultaneously rushed to embrace the Berg Report—rendering to it the ultimate homage of emulation. American officials have not only repeatedly articulated the Berg Report's analysis and policy prescriptions for Africa, but the Reagan administration has modeled its new Economic Policy Initiative very closely on the Berg Report's recommendations. The requirement that governments seeking financial aid first agree to institute policy changes desired by the donor has been a traditional feature of IMF (International Monetary Fund) loans and has created considerable hostility for that agency both in Africa and in Latin America, where IMF-imposed austerity has led to rioting and social unrest. The Berg Report recommended the extension of such conditionality to some World Bank loans. The EPI extends it to American bilateral aid and implies that all donors should apply conditionality to their future aid,[8] a proposal which is already being referred to as the New Colonialism.

The polarization which is emerging, then, is that industrialized nations, under United States leadership, appear to be seeking expanded control over Africa while the Africans are seeking a means to reduce the linkage between themselves and their erstwhile benefactors. Because both groups need the other, it seems clear that a new *modus vivendi* must be worked out. Because its economy is so much stronger than those of the European Economic Community members, the United States could play the leadership role in developing this new *modus vivendi* but it would require more sustained attention and a greater sensitivity to Africa's myriad problems than we have demonstrated thus far.

What is called for, above all, is a willingness to listen to what Africans are saying to us and our acceptance of the possibility that they may know a bit more about their economies than we do. It also requires that we accept the reality that international economic relations are dynamic, not static. For 25 years the United States poured vast sums of money into South Korea and Taiwan in order to build strong economies to suit our political scenario. Now that those economies are beginning to flood our market with better-quality and lower-priced goods than we can produce ourselves, we take steps to keep their goods from coming in. Our banks lent large sums to Latin America and to Africa. These borrowers can repay us only if they can sell their goods here, but we balk because our economy is depressed and unemployment is high.

We cannot have it both ways. If we assist in its development, certainly Africa will become more competitive, more independent—and will probably create some problems for us because of this independence. But if we do not help, it will find its own way, perhaps with the assistance of powers we consider hostile. Africa's dependency is not a permanent feature of international economic affairs, nor is American hegemony. Our policy should be keyed not to prevent change, but to facilitate it. The best way to serve long-run American interests is to assist Africa to break its dependency on others, including ourselves, and to enable it to develop itself as an independent power center in world affairs. As long as we encourage Africa to remain divided, shoring up a few allies of the moment but failing to address the continent in a holistic fashion, we will be helping to perpetuate instability.

Most of Africa has been independent for a quarter of a century now. It is wiser, and in some ways sadder than it was in 1960. It faces economic problems of such magnitude that a total collapse of existing governmental and administrative structures is a real possibility in some areas. The continent is plagued with more than its share of ineffective leaders. In short, it presents an overwhelming challenge to American statesmanship. It is a challenge we should strive diligently to meet.

NOTE

The black American factor in American Africa policy does not fall within the topic of this paper; consequently no attempt is made to address it here. It is a topic which merits attention, however. Just as some American Jews appear to have especially strong feelings about Israel, so, too, many black Americans have especially strong feelings regarding Africa and generally display a greater sensitivity for African problems than do non-black Americans. This group is a resource which can be enlisted to assist government to fashion and implement appropriate policies in Africa. By the same token, the black American community constitutes a powerful obstacle in the provision of any United States troop support for South African whites should Washington ever be tempted to move in that direction. Some black Americans have even suggested that, should overt racial warfare break out in South Africa, any American attempt to provide support for the whites could easily spark parallel disruption here in the United States.

REFERENCES

1. George Shultz, "The U.S. and Africa in the 1980s," *Current Policy*, No. 549 (February 1984), U.S. Department of State, Bureau of Public Affairs.

2. Chester Crocker, "Regional Strategy for Southern Africa," *Current Policy*, No. 308 (August 1981), U.S. Department of State, Bureau of Public Affairs.

3. Shultz, "The U.S. and Africa."

4. The figures on aid are from *The 1984 Annual Report of the Chairman of the Development Coordination Committee, Statistical Annex 2*, U.S. State Department.

5. The data on minerals are from *Mineral Commodity Summary, 1981*, U.S. Bureau of Mines.

6. Harry F. Young, *Atlas of United States Foreign Relations*, U.S. Department of State, Bureau of Public Affairs, Washington, D.C., 1983.

7. World Bank, *Accelerated Development in Sub-Saharan Africa*, Washington, D.C., 1983.

8. "The Economic Policy Initiative for Sub-Saharan Africa," a background handout distributed at a press conference of Secretary of State Shultz, January 30, 1984, mimeo.

Commentary

Richard E. Feinberg

I presume that I was invited as an international economist to offer a comparative perspective. Let me start off perhaps by offending everyone here by suggesting that, from a global, strategic point of view, the relative importance of Africa as well as the potential threats that might emanate from Africa should not be overstated. Economically, Africa is of relatively little importance in terms of GNP figures, share of world trade, or share of world finance. It is a very small percentage, less than 5 percent or so. If we talk in power terms, traditional political terms, industrial plans and technology, organization, size of armies, air forces or whatever, Africa again, except Arab Africa, is very weak.

In order to justify Africa's being very important, I think one has to talk in humanitarian terms or perhaps cultural terms. This is not to say that Africa has no importance, but it is difficult to argue logically from a global point of view that Africa should be a top American priority. Let me also suggest that we ought not to exaggerate the potential threats from Africa. The Defense Department always puts out charts showing how the United States gets much of its raw materials from developing countries. In fact, commodity cartels are very hard to put together and very hard to keep together. Moreover, we have not seen any subsequent developments after OPEC despite numerous attempts. Most countries, particularly the poor ones, must sell their commodities to us on the global market regardless of their internal politics, regardless of their ideology. We see this in any number of cases. Regimes with all sorts of politics, from Iran to Libya to Marxist regimes, are selling their oil and other products just like any other country. I would also suggest that in those few cases where there might be a real concentration of commodities in one or two countries, stockpiling is the answer.

The fact is that the United States has very substantial stocks in most of the strategic raw materials. If you add together official Defense Department stocks and stocks held by private firms, there are, in most cases, one to two years' worth of stocks. Even if there were a temporary political disruption, we would have more than enough supplies. In terms of the shipping lanes, who exactly is going to interrupt them? The local power? The African countries lack the capability to do that. If we are talking about Soviet bases, the fact is that even African countries favorable to the Soviet Union have not generally given them real basing rights. What is more, the Soviets themselves hesitate to put substantial military assets into Africa because these would be highly exposed. In the event that we really wanted to take out any Soviet base we could do so, and the Soviets would be at a tremendous military disadvantage. The idea that shipping lanes would be disrupted somehow assumes that in fact we would be fighting a global war with the Soviet Union, a long conventional war. Most military analysts believe that a prolonged, global, conventional war with the Soviet Union is very unlikely, and that in fact if there were to be such a war, it would rapidly either escalate into a nuclear conflict or would be negotiated.

Let me also raise a question as to whether or not high-level attention is really good for Africa. In conferences dealing with Latin America, specialists inevitably complain that nobody cares about Latin America. Regional specialists typically feel that it would be great if the National Security Council expended more energy on their area. Yet, today when high-level attention is focused on Latin America, most Latin Americanists are unhappy with United States policy toward their region. The reason for this is that when there is sustained United States government attention in any area of the world, the regionalists lose influence in making policy. The Assistant Secretary for African Affairs will not be the one who makes policy once Africa becomes a high priority. It is the Secretary of State, the National Security Council—people who tend not to know very much about the region—who make policy. These people have other concerns—global concerns other than Africa. When they bring issues before any given president, he and the White House staff have domestic political concerns. So, high-level sustained attention is not always good. It may work in your favor, but often it will not. The other side of the coin is that if you want to get more aid resources, high-level attention can be good. But, as Dr. Browne points out, the distribution of those aid resources may not be what one wants. Therefore, I caution you on the value of high-level attention.

Let me now address the question of economics. First, on the cause of the crisis: Dr. Browne and I recently heard a talk by Chester Crocker in which he put great emphasis on the internal errors made by the African countries as the cause of the economic crisis. Clearly, governments anywhere around the world, whether one is talking about Washington or Buenos Aires or Nairobi, could have done better in dealing with the difficult international economic environment of recent years. But, at the same time, I think it is absolutely wrong, and ideological, to suggest that poor domestic management has been the prime or only cause of the crisis. Clearly, the international environment has tremendously disfavored African development over the last three or four years. This includes terms of trade, interest rates, declining markets for their exports: All of these factors have had a tremendously negative impact on Africa. This was true, regardless of the African governments' own internal policies. We should not blame only the Africans. There is enough blame to be spread around. The international economy has had a lot to do with the current crisis in Africa.

Given the international environment (this is improving somewhat, though not dramatically, for most African countries) what sort of development strategies might be appropriate for different countries in Africa? Today, throughout the Third World there is a general rethinking of development strategies. There is a certain disillusionment with those strategies that have been attempted up to now, even with pure free–market strategies. We have seen the collapse of the Chicago model in Chile, for example, and there are problems in the Kenyan economy. On the other hand, we also see a lot of criticism of statism and the various problems that that model has involved. In sum, there are criticisms of economies that are completely open, and criticisms of economies that are closed. What is the answer? There is a great deal of ferment right now among people who worry about these issues. We do not yet have a final answer; perhaps we never will. I would suggest that there is a certain convergence in the thinking between those who traditionally advocate the more interventionist and statist import substitution strategies on the one hand, and those who advocate market strategies or export-oriented strategies on the other.

The convergence which we see comes down to several factors: First, I think there is a widespread critique of excessive statism. The view is that there is not enough management capability to run the bureaucracies effectively; there are problems of corruption; and the problem of governments' setting all prices results in problems of resource allocation. One always heard those criticisms from the right, but you now hear them on the left as well (from President Machel in Mozambique and from others). At the same time, though, most people, but not all, would suggest that the state is still important, that there is a role for government. One cannot claim that only a free market and the involvement of the private sector are important in development, especially in the less developed countries of Africa. The market does not function perfectly: There are market failures that need to be corrected by governments. For example, the private sector often cannot put together enough capital to undertake the large investments that are necessary to build the roads, to put in infrastructure, and to build ports. The government has to do all that. Moreover, in the areas of education and health, there is an important role for government.

As far as industrial policy issues are concerned, the industrial countries such as Britain, the United States, and Germany, which talk free market, all have industrial policies in which the government intervenes in many ways to affect the private market, and to influence investment in both industry and agriculture. (The United States government has a very large scale program in agriculture. For example, these days the agricultural sector receives subsidies of $20 billion or more per year.) Clearly, governments have a role to play in deciding which industries are to receive more capital, which deserve subsidies, and so on. Finally, I would argue that government has a role to play in the area of income distribution. There are equity concerns, and there are basic human needs concerns, which cannot be left purely to the market. If you leave matters solely to the market, it would mean that whoever starts off with the endowments "starts wealthy and stays wealthy." The government needs to intervene in the distribution of income that would result from a pure market process. Also, I think it's recognized that in almost all African countries, the private sector is only incipient and relatively weak. To talk about the private sector's sponsoring development is to create something out of practically nothing overnight. From a long-term point of view, fifty years or so, the private sector may gradually grow and become strong. But at this point, if you dismantle the state there is nothing that can take its place. And, although there is an incipient private sector in African countries, that private sector needs help even in creating itself. That help inevitably will have to come from the government.

I am led to the conclusion, though not an unhappy one, that for Africa what we are really talking about is some sort of mixed economy—on the one hand, reduction of government activity in some areas where it has been inefficient; and on the other, strengthening of the private sector. There is still an important role for government. And this is true in the international trade sector as well. Many industries, agriculture or manufacturing, are going to need some protection—at least over the medium term—if they are ever going to make progress. There is the need for some short-term protective measures. This is true even in the United States. It is what the Europeans all do, as do the Japanese. Africa must do it also.

What is the United States' role? How can we help? First, I would start off by saying the African states must help themselves. The United States cannot make African development happen. We should not overestimate our capacity for positive influence in

Africa. Having said that, there are some things that we can do. What the Reagan administration continually repeats (and it is logically correct, although narrow in focus) is that encouraging growth in the industrial countries is the single largest contribution that the United States can make to African development. Strong economic growth here should at least have some positive impact in terms of trade in export markets. If we can improve the mix of our fiscal and monetary policies, that could bring down interest rates and would have some positive effect on the debt problem in Africa. With respect to trade, Browne talks about GSP in his paper. There is talk about graduation and concern that a lot of the benefits of GSP have gone to the upper-income countries, such as Mexico, Brazil, and South Korea. The administration believes that we actually do suffer from preferences to such countries when the idea is that the poorer countries, including sub-Saharan Africa, should benefit more from GSP. My Latin American friends, of course, are all opposed to graduation, but I think it would potentially be of benefit for Africa, at least in the longer run.

There is also a lot of talk about a north/south traderound in which there would be negotiations between the north and the south to open up some markets. There are potential benefits for Africa there, that is, if trade textiles policies were liberalized. In his paper Browne talks about the United States government's role in tariff escalation. We raise tariff levels on finished goods, as more value added is put onto the goods. That is, of course, detrimental to processing and manufacturing development in Africa. To reduce that escalation would also be a big help. Browne also mentioned Export-Import Bank credits, and the possibility of OPIC insurance for American firms. The problem is that both EXIM and OPIC do not want to put too much into Africa because they see risk there. These are both government institutions that are financially self-supporting. I personally think that both those institutions should get some directives from the Treasury Department on behalf of the White House which would tell them that they should be willing to take a little more risk than would a private firm. After all, this is why they are public institutions, ultimately backed by the United States government.

Let me just mention two other elements. There is considerable discussion about policy dialogue now. U.S. AID and the World Bank have been dialoguing with governments receiving aid about alterations in their macroeconomic policies. There is even a growing "culture of conditionality" in Washington. This partly grows out of the frustration that many people feel about what happened in Africa over the last few years. I think it is reasonable that when we provide help (we do provide money) we do provide certain advice. The sort that I would suggest would be to indicate the likely impact of certain alternatives, and to lay out alternative macropolicies to governments, indicating the impact in terms of growth and also in terms of equity. But I get nervous when "policy dialogue" really becomes dictation, even when one can easily understand the natural tendency of donors to do so. We think we know best; we feel we have leverage: We are putting up the money, so why should we not determine just what the money is used for? I think that is a dangerous policy politically because it is only going to produce resentment over the long run, and we will not get people to do what we want anyway. They may sign on the dotted line for this month, but as soon as they can, they will go about doing what they really prefer to do. We should offer advice, but not dictation.

Finally, my last words: Dr. Browne mentioned multilateralism, the World Bank, and the African Development Fund. As far as the Reagan administration is concerned, not only in Africa, but particularly in Africa, because of its attitude toward IDA, it has preferred bilateral as opposed to multilateral aid. At the same time the administration talks about the importance of donor coordination. I personally think the exaggerated emphasis on bilateral aid is a mistake. It is a mistake politically because of the sensitivity which occurs whenever we enter into policy dialogues at the bilateral level. Those sensitivities will be more acute, and we are all better off going multilateral. And, frankly, the World Bank has a much better staff than U.S. AID, particularly on macro isues. At the project level mode in some sectors, the World Bank also has more expertise. Therefore, I think we are pushing that expertise aside when we think U.S. AID can go in and dialogue by itself. The other advantage of multilateralism, of course, is credit leverage. We put in 25 percent only, leaving the Europeans and others to provide the remaining 75 percent. You do not get that same sort of "bang for your buck" if you go alone, bilaterally.

There are a number of things that we can do to assist African development, but I would repeat again that ultimately African development will depend on what Africans can do for themselves.

Robert Browne: Having thus encountered specifics of the United States effort in Africa, it is now useful to view the overall direction in which Africa is moving, and how our policies relate to that. I just want to talk a bit about what the issues are, because we want response to that also.

The swirling debate on Africa at the moment is around the two documents with which most of you are familiar. One is the World Bank's effort to look at what is wrong with Africa. This was initiated by the African Ministers of Finance (who are in fact governors at the World Bank) in late 1979 or early 1980. They were meeting with some of the other governors and staff of the World Bank and asked the World Bank to do a study on Africa, and see why Africa was going backward economically. The product of that study was called *Accelerated Development in Sub-Saharan Africa,* popularly known as the Berg Report, after the principal investigator, Dr. Elliott Berg, an American.

Shortly before this (one might almost say at the same time but it might be of some significance that it preceded it) the African ministers' planning was focused around the two African institutions, the Economic Commission for Africa and the Organization for African Unity. These were also taking a very careful in-depth look at the African economic situation and were sensing that things seemed to be getting worse rather than getting better. They worked out a plan for a special meeting of OAU in Lagos in April, 1980, and it has come to be known as the *Lagos Plan of Action for the Economic Development of Africa 1980-2000* (LPA). This plan was from an African perspective, on what Africans need to do and what the world needs to do. As Dr. Feinberg said, the Africans really have to do most of the work themselves. If the outside world can help, that would be wonderful. Sometimes the Africans feel that if the outside world just would not hinder them, that would also be a great help. These two documents, the Berg Report and the LPA, have now precipitated the debate which is *the* debate on Africa now.

It is true that the World Bank documents said in several places, including in the cover letter from President Clousen submitting the document to the public, that the Berg Report, or the World Bank report, builds upon the LPA which preceded it. The Africans do not see it that way. They really see basic contradictions between what the World Bank is saying and what the Africans themselves have produced. There are two controversies: One is the question of blame for African economic problems, and Dr. Feinberg touched on this (this is not the most important debate as I see it, but it is a big debate). What the World Bank essentially said was that, while there are a host of causes for Africa's economic deterioration, some of them external (that is, the causes over which Africa has no control), the most important are the internal causes which the Africans could have changed.

In the talk to which Dr. Feinberg alludes, in Crocker's view, the overwhelming evidence was that the Africans are responsible for their own plight, primarily because they followed incorrect policies. Of course, he made a bow to the external factors—the OPEC price increases, the drought, high interest rates, the recession in the industrialized countries, etc. However, Crocker insisted that these are all peripheral, and even in the face of all these external problems, Africa could have done better if it had followed correct policies.

It is from that kind of thinking that we got what Dr. Feinberg referred to as the increased emphasis on conditionality. That is to say, future aid by the World Bank, and to a confusing extent by the United States (the United States in trying to get other countries to do the same thing), will be made on conditions far more severe than in the past. This of course is not a new idea. The IMF has always (except in the case of first loans) had conditions attached to loans. These conditions have precipitated all sorts of problems in many countries, and there is great objection to them. Generally in Africa there is probably acceptance that, in many cases, the conditions may be necessary. The objection is not primarily to the existence of conditions, but to the IMF framework for imposing these conditions. This is much too stringent; the IMF wants things to change overnight and things just cannot be done that quickly. IMF—imposed austerity is the reason for riots, for governments' being overthrown, and so forth.

Because of the World Bank report, Structural Assistance Loans were launched. Instead of being project loans, these are loans for general budgetary support, for technical support, and for projects. But there are conditions. You get this money if you do this, you devalue that, or make a policy change as need be. The World Bank started this on a small scale, and now the United States is apparently moving bilaterally in that direction with a new economic policy initiative along those lines. There is growing resistance in Africa to this. Africans view this as a violation of their sovereignty, and they resist basic policy changes in how they operate their governments dictated from elsewhere. I would assume this would be the principal objection, but then there is the fact that the policies of outsiders are often wrong. I think it is a very great danger for the United States, or for any country, to put itself out on such a limb because if things do go wrong, the finger is pointed at the country that imposed the policy.

It is true that the IMF has been imposing conditions for some time, and the IMF gets a lot of flack. But that is IMF's flack. The IMF can absorb controversy because it is an enormous organization involved with 137 countries. When you attack the organization, you are attacking an entity. It is not very probable, but if a single country ruins another country's economy through erroneous policy impositions, then the blame is very easily placed. So I think conditionality is very dangerous ground. It is not because conditions are necessarily wrong, but that they are much better imposed by a group rather than on a one-on-one basis. There in a nutshell is one of the big questions: Where does the blame lie for African economic conditions, and to the extent that one accepts the World Bank and the United States positions, that the blame lies with the Africans, how far do we go in forcing them to change?

The other big question is the difference between the Berg Report and the LPA in terms of development strategy. What the Berg Report essentially does is to assume that the strategy was fine, and just goes into great detail as to how Africa can pursue that strategy more effectively. In contrast, the LPA argues that while Africa's present economic strategy preserves the independent states, it also leaves them dependent upon others. Therefore they must pioneer a new, self-reliant, internally-led development.

Let me not overstate it: The assumption is that the Africans are going to need foreign exchange so they will still export. Then they will say they will continue to export some tea and coffee since land is being used for that already. But it is a question of emphasis. Instead of expanding upon this approach, instead of building their economic development around exports, they should build their economic development around growing the things they need. The number-one need is food, of course, since self-sufficiency has become very important to the Africans. They see themselves becoming increasingly dependent upon food aid, with the unwelcome humanitarian and other subtle implications. But the Africans also feel that this is the only way they are going to be in control of their economy. The implication, of course, is that most of the African countries recognize that they are much too slow in developing internally on their own. Countries of one and two million, and ten and twelve million, are held not very viable economically for development. Therefore, the main theme running through the LPA is a self-reliant type of strategy, and that there must be sub-regional integration. Stress is being put on things like the preferential trade area in East Africa. This will be the beginnings of development, but not on a country-by-country basis.

All of this is good in theory, but of course it is very difficult to do when you've got fifty independent systems with very different perspectives. It is remarkable that all fifty African heads of state even signed the document, and one wonders if they really understood the full implications of it when they signed. The progress toward implementation has not been spectacular; nevertheless on some levels there is a great deal of interest in it. For example, I was in Tunisia in May at the twentieth anniversary celebration of the African Development Bank. It is the largest, virtually the only, African funding and development agency that exists. Now with the entry of the non-African countries into the African Development Bank, there are assets of about $6 billion. Although it is not a lot, the Bank is not an insignificant institution in the development of Africa, and since it is run by Africans, presumably it will be giving some directional leadership. At this twentieth anniversary the Africans took the opportunity to look at what the Bank had done for the first twenty years, and wanted to present a proposed program for the next twenty years. I was asked by the African Development Bank to come to comment on their proposal.

The theme running through the ADB plan for the next twenty years was definitely built on the Lagos Plan of Action: "We must lean toward a more self-reliant posture, we must trade with ourselves primarily rather than the outside; we must reduce our dependence upon the outside; we must develop sub-regionally, with a view by the end of the century to having an all-African common market." I think the time frame is probably fine, for the year 2000 is going to be here before we know it. But in any case, the African Development Bank is going to put increasingly large portions of its resources into projects which are supportive of the Lagos developmental thrust. I think the United States economic position toward Africa should be to fund those projects that are supportive of that African perspective rather than taking a contrary position.

DISCUSSION

The main points discussed in Dr. Browne's paper were: the nature of the linkage between United States aid to African countries and our military concerns there; the inability of American business to profit from United States support to multilateral institutions serving the continent; the issue of relatively little American private interest in Africa; the question of conditionality as it affects African development strategy; and the need to examine the Africa-sponsored Lagos Plan of Action.

One view was that while there was a positive relationship between United States strategic concerns and the level of aid given to specific countries, the case should not be overstated. Moreover, there was demurral regarding the suggestion that much of United States aid to African countries is military aid in disguise. It was held that much of United States aid is highly interchangeable, and that the ESF portion is about 40 percent of all aid, and may be rising. Moreover, the "ESF need not be confined to just non-project assistance. And to the extent that there are resources in a country, aid officials can peg these to the development strategy that country is pursuing. Therefore, to some degree, aid funds are interchangeable in terms of the uses they are put to for development purposes."

There was a general sentiment that American businesses were not profiting as much as were the Europeans from the amount of aid the United States gave to multilateral agencies concerned with Africa. One explanation was that in many cases American companies were not as interested in business as were the Europeans. The nature of the bureaucratic process in getting contracts from such agencies as the World Bank or African Development Bank was held to frustrate American companies. These companies were allegedly often ill-equipped linguistically, culturally, and technically to do business in Africa. The historical ties that European countries have to their former African colonies were also mentioned.

Cited as an increasing impediment to American businesses' obtaining an adequate percentage of the procurement, was the attitude of United States administrations to the business sector. It was judged paradoxical that with all the emphasis the administration gave to private enterprise, the equally negative attitude it had to the role of government in the economy prevented firms from counting on United States diplomats to intercede for them in many countries. This was said to smack too much of government control, statism, or worse. One discussant noted that:

> The French government has done more than assist French firms in setting up business in Africa. President Mitterrand, for example, thought nothing of getting on an airplane and going to help a French firm to close a deal. We are coming from a very different perspective ... and I think that our system does not permit us to do as those of us who are dealing closely with the private sector, would very much like to see us do.

37

It was suggested that American businesses profited so little because many American firms found contracts in African countries too small to be attractive, especially in view of the cost of setting up expensive offices to run them. One response was that while Americans may view contracts of even $10 million as too small, the Africans viewed them as very large. Another suggestion, and one which elicited much positive comment, was that American firms could well cooperate to establish regional offices to aggregate and manage any projects they may procure. The notion that American businesses may use foreign and smaller firms as proxies to do business in Africa was not well received. The political risks were considered too great for such a venture.

There was a great deal of comment about the issue of conditionality raised by both the presenter and the commentator. In response to the feeling that the United States was using colonial-type clout to further its own economic philosophy in African societies, it was emphasized that the use of multilateral agencies could preclude this from taking place. Attention was also called to the efforts of African states to control their own economies by limiting the percentage of expatriate investment. Decrying conditionality, one discussant felt that the African states often had to expend a great deal of their resources in developing high potential areas where the long-term economic benefit looks promising but where private enterprise failed to invest because of the emphasis on short-term profits. On the other hand, it was argued that much of the non-ideological support in favor of private sector and conditionality policies was simply to provide people with equal choice to do what they want to do rather than force people to do what governments wanted them to do.

Underscoring this argument about conditionality was the assertion that there was a need for "a policy framework that provides more choice to people and enables them to exercise their choices and to use their energies to sustain development." This notion was said to be running through much of the debate about what should be United States strategies regarding Africa in the 1980s. The speaker felt that the debate is about "a very critical situation" in which the World Bank (the Berg Report) had one idea and the Africans another one (the LPA). The clash here was between statism and private enterprise. Some people argued that the African states needed to control the "heights" of their economies because infrastructural development was costly and unprofitable; others felt that statism has not worked in Africa, and that private enterprise should be given a chance.

CHAPTER 2

UNITED STATES MILITARY AND STRATEGIC INTERESTS IN AFRICA

William J. Foltz

INTRODUCTION

The title of this paper is a sad sign of the times in which we live. Throughout almost all of United States history, America's military and strategic interests in Africa would scarcely have merited a paragraph in anything other than an ambitious naval officer's dream book. The significant exceptions were two brief periods: World War II, when North Africa became a theater of war and other parts of the continent harbored allied lines of communication and supply, and the early days of the cold war, when the United States operated Strategic Air Command bases in Morocco and Libya as instruments of a primitive phase of post-war containment policy. Only in the last decade, however, has the African continent acquired what has all appearance of a permanent and significant place in the military and stategic interests of the United States.

This paper will argue that such an increase in Africa's military and strategic significance to the United States is not a transient phenomenon, nor one conjured up by the perfervid imagination of born-again cold warriors. Rather, it stems from major changes in the United States' position in world affairs, including its relations with its major allies, from related changes in the position of the Soviet Union, from changes in military technology that are not easily controlled, and not least, from political and military changes in Africa itself and in neighboring areas. None of these changes will be easily reversed, though their consequences can be managed in widely differing ways. It seems likely, then, that papers with titles like this one will be part of academic symposia for many years to come.

INTERESTS: MILITARY, STRATEGIC, AND OTHER

The concept of "interest," particularly the interest of a complex collectivity like a nation, requires some preliminary clarification. "National interest," despite its brief vogue in the 1950s as a respectable analytic tool, has become more the stuff of campaign rhetoric or bureaucratic and special pleading than of dispassionate analysis. Yet policy analysis finds it hard to proceed without reference to the idea that even so large, disparate, and contentious a collectivity as the United States has in some sense relatively enduring and stable interests of a structural nature, interests that transcend, though do not supplant, the interests of the individuals making up the collectivity. These interests are expressed primarily through the governmental system, but reflect the desires and needs of broader economic and social structures, those that nourish—and employ—the government. Assuring these interests means assuring the prosperity and perpetuation of these broader structures, as well as assuring that United States citizens will retain a large measure of autonomous control over their eventual transformation.

Inevitably, conflicts—or, as some might prefer, contradictions—occur over what national interests are, or should be, once one descends from the most general realm of abstractions to the more difficult realm of policy. Everyone opposes destroying people's lives, but may differ on whether one gives priority to the life of a fetus or to that of a pregnant thirteen-year-old. Everyone favors full employment, but will disagree over the price to be paid for it—increased inflation? lower wages? a resurgence of labor union power? Similarly, everyone wants peace, but perhaps not at the price of losing a protected market or a valued ally, or even a cherished weapons system. The daunting task of government is to reconcile or amalgamate these contradictions as well as it can and to be sure that the mode of reconciliation or amalgamation does not produce policies that lead to the nation's collapse. Invevitably, at the policy level, one nation's interests risk conflicting with another's. Again, it is principally government's task to be sure that as far as possible those amalgamated interests prevail in the international arena when they come into conflict with other nations' interests, but without paying a price unacceptable in terms of other collective interests.

A nation's military and strategic interests do not exist by themselves; they interact with all national interests and are de- signed to serve that larger whole. Military and strategic interests are, thus, instrumental, not intrinsic interests. When one says that the United States has a "military interest" somewhere, one says, in effect, that the United States needs to be able to deploy military instruments, to deter an opponent's deploying them, or otherwise achieve a favorable balance of force, in order that certain policy goals that reflect national interests may be at- tained. One is "interested" in employing military instruments to support foreign policies, to defend and extend material and polit- ical interests abroad, and ultimately to "ensure domestic tran- quility." When the deployment of military instruments does not serve these goals, or it disrupts the domestic tranquility that it ought to favor, one cannot speak sensibly of military interests except as something apart from the interests of the nation as a whole. Our subject here is United States military and strategic interests, not the interest of the United States military, and at times those will differ.

National interest is a key phrase from the lexicon of *real- politik.* It consorts uneasily with the language of values and opinions, and with the inevitable reality of particularist bureau- cratic politics, yet these realms are closely intertwined. The more diffuse and public the foreign policy-making process, the more policy makers must take into account the values, opinions, and needs of significant groups. Somewhat greater latitude may be available to policymakers dealing with regions like Africa, which have low salience for public opinion, and are usually at the margin of leaders' concerns.[1] Nevertheless, policymakers should be aware of two particular complications. The first principally affects the policy-making community. Since most top leaders know little about the details of African affairs they tend to interpret them in familiar terms and to accentuate their connection with global affairs and American values. Zbigniew Brzezinski's phrase, "SALT lies buried in the sands of the Ogaden," is a fairly recent example.[2] The second complication concerns public opinion more generally. The tendency to see Africa through the lenses of familiar concerns means that events involving South Africa will inevitably be viewed in analogy with America's own racial relations. Military and strategic activities involving South Africa must to some degree take account of possible repercussions on this touchiest aspect of America's own domestic tranquility.

One further warning is in order. Serious policy analysis must resist the temptation to use a discussion of national interests to talk about what one wants the United States to be—the carrier of a great revolutionary tradition, beacon of Christian civilization, defender of individual liberty, or whatever—rather than the complex and imperfect nation it is. Doing so may produce soul-satisfying rhetoric, but it provides a poor basis for serious policy analysis.

THE UNITED STATES AS A WORLD POWER

A nation's interests, except in the most general sense, are not immutable. They change, if slowly, as domestic structures and values change; they change also with changes in the position of a nation within the world system, or—as the Soviets would phrase it—with the global correlation of forces. The United States' position in the world has altered over the last generation, and that change has implications for its military and strategic interests in Africa.

The United States emerged from World War II as the western world's hegemonic power, indeed as the only country with global economic and military reach. This reach did not betoken untrammeled control, but it did leave the United States as the only power able to contend seriously for advantage anywhere outside of Eastern Europe and China. In the hyperbolic terms of the time, 1945 inaugurated the era of the *pax americana,* or what Henry Luce was pleased to call "The American Century."

Pushed both by force of circumstance and by shrewd calculation of American interest, the United States began a process of internationalizing its own economy and building a set of international institutions that gave American decision-makers potentially decisive leverage over a wide range of decisions in Western nations. These nations and their overseas dependencies were drawn into an international regime based on open economies and comparatively free trade.[3] United States military preeminence provided both subtle pressure and a protective umbrella under which the Western nations, and eventually Japan, entered an American-centered world capitalist economy.

Similar forces of circumstance and calculation of interest led the United States to pressure its Western allies to divest themselves of their colonies. This, of course, was a continuation of long-standing American attitudes toward empire, rooted in laudable idealism. Franklin Roosevelt's insistence on such a course provided the occasion for the most serious disagreements with Churchill—and of course DeGaulle—during World War II.[4] After the war, United States pressure combined with European weakness made the outcome inevitable. Although cynical observers were quick to point out that countries with the biggest fleets and most efficient industries were always in favor of open markets and opposed to formal empire (as the British had been a century earlier), American motivations were as concerned with political and strategic factors as with economic. This was particularly the case in Africa where American commercial and investment interest was minimal. Nationalism in what came to be

47

called the Third World was seen as a force that could, if accommodated, be turned to Western advantage but that risked being subverted by Communism if opposed. United States support for Libyan independence in 1951 under a conservative king was an early example of this approach which yielded the strategic benefit of access to a major Strategic Air Command base.[5] Such undoubted anti-Soviet hawks as Secretary of State John Foster Dulles and then Vice President Richard Nixon were explicit in their advocacy of "preventive" independence, as, of course, was John Kennedy.[6]

United States support for African independence in the 1950s and 1960s did not mean that Washington—or Wall Street— sought to supplant Western Europe's dominant position. As Britain had a century earlier, it sought a shift from informal to formal empire, in which influence exercised through economic power and cooperative local elites replaced direct control. The United States became heavily involved in Africa only where Europeans defaulted (as in the Congo) or were not relevant (as in Ethiopia and Liberia) and readily yielded when the Europeans raised the stakes (Gabon in 1963 and, in a strategic mistake, Guinea in 1958). This "liberal" American policy toward African nationalism reflected the accurate judgment of policymakers that the combination of Western military reach and Soviet inability to project effective power removed at least sub-Saharan Africa from concern over major military confrontations. Confronting the "Soviet menace" in Africa was primarily a task for the State Department and the Central Intelligence Agency, not the Department of Defense. This did not mean that the Department of Defense was totally uninterested in Africa, merely that it did not expect to face direct Soviet challenge there.

The great exception to European acquiescence in African independence was Portugal. Under the mercantilist conservatism of Dr. Salazar, Portugal was only marginally integrated into the Americanocentric international economic order. The liberal vision of joint prosperity through open markets was of little avail against Salazar's sixteenth-century dream. Furthermore, Portugal insisted on American and NATO tolerance for its colonial policies as the price for providing major strategic assets to the West, most notably the Azores base whose lease had to be renegotiated at frequent intervals. Faced with a clear choice between a globally important military asset and a consistent political strategy toward African nationalism, the United States chose the former in the 1950s and 1960s—and paid the price in the 1970s and 1980s.[7]

"The American Century" barely lasted out Henry Luce's generation. By the mid-1970s, American economic dominance was challenged by Japan and Western Europe, and the post-World War II economic order was besieged by pressures from Third World oil producers and newly industrializing countries (NICs). America's share of world production, which had stood at 50 percent in 1950, had sunk to 21 percent by the end of the 1970s. The days of easy command were over; new approaches to foreign policy had to be learned. As Henry Kissinger has phrased it:

> For the first time, the United States was in the position that it had to conduct a foreign policy as most other nations in history: as one country among many, unable either to dominate the world or escape from it; forced to seek by persuasion, accommodation, negotiation what it could no longer achieve by unilateral fiat; obliged to learn the traditional techniques of balancing incentives and penalties; required to be steady, reliable, sensitive to marginal shifts in the balance of power and aware of the interconnections between events.[8]

American military hegemony outside the immediate Soviet sphere ended as well. The defeat in Vietnam was the most spectacular symbol of its demise, but furious debates over the Vietnam War have tended to obscure some of the underlying trends of global power relations that continue to affect United States military and strategic interests.[9] Some of these trends were directly linked to United States economic interests as well. By the early 1970s, balance of payment problems provided a serious constraint on America's ability to maintain foreign bases and deploy American forces abroad.[10] This in turn provided a major impetus to the search for "responsible regional powers" who could be relied on to preserve Western interests in their own corners of the globe.

In the purely military sphere, significant shifts took place as well in the bipolar correlation of forces between the United States and the Soviet Union. In the 1970s the Soviet Union for the first time achieved functional parity in strategic nuclear weapons with the United States. Thanks in large part to accelerated Soviet expenditures on strategic systems while the United States spent its money on the Vietnam War and on recovering from its after-effects, mutually assured destruction was now a reality. American strategists had to be aware that the equivalent of a Cuban missile crisis in the 1970s would entail vastly greater risks for the United States.

At least as important in its political effects, for the first time in its history the Soviet Union acquired the ability to project effective military expeditionary forces far from its borders. This was not a casual development; three factors were involved: First was Admiral Sergei Gorshkov's success in changing historic Soviet military doctrine to encompass the building of a "bluewater" navy—to replace the one lost by the tsar in the Straits of Tsushima. Although very small by comparison with the United States bluewater forces, it accorded the Soviet Union its first possibility of a worldwide naval presence.[11] Second was substantial expenditure on long-range airlift capacity and on careful cultivation of relations with strategically located Third World states for refueling, transit facilities, and overflight rights. Third was the partly fortuitous conjunction of interests between the Soviet Union and Cuba which provided the former with a source of effective military manpower with greater political acceptability in the Third World than Soviet forces would enjoy.[12]

It is the Soviet Union's new ability to project conventional military force that has had the greatest impact on United States military and strategic thinking about most of Africa. To appreciate the change, one need only contrast the Congo crises of the early 1960s with the events in Angola in 1975–1976 and Ethiopia in 1977. In the 1960s the Soviet Union was simply unable to support Lumumbist and Gizengist forces with weapons and troops to match the aid the United States was directly or indirectly providing the central government. By contrast, in 1977 the

Soviet Union was able to deliver a major expeditionary force and $1 billion worth of military equipment in a matter of weeks.

Soviet intervention in Angola provides the most telling illustration of how modest an effort is required, once a basic force projection capability is achieved, to undermine military hegemony in peripheral areas of the globe. What was important was not that the Soviet Union could deliver overwhelming military force to the region, nor that the American public and Congress were traumatized by the Vietnam misadventure, but that it could deliver a significant enough expeditionary force that opposition by the heretofore hegemonic power would have entailed a major decision and some risk of a serious military confrontation that could be lost if not substantially escalated. The development of such an expeditionary intervention capacity entails crossing a threshold; it produces a qualitative change in relationships toward functional parity in peripheral areas of the globe like sub-Saharan Africa. It is not a change that can be countered by one side's adding to its quantity of arms, certainly not to its stock of strategic weapons in a mad world. Much more sophisticated strategies, political and economic as well as military, are required.

A painfully close historical parallel is provided by the early expansion of the German navy in the late nineteenth century. This permitted expeditionary landings and eventual conquest, notably of South West Africa and Tanganyika, in direct contravention of the interests of the then-declining hegemony, Great Britain. Then, as in the 1970s, the dominant naval power possessed the absolute power to expel the interloper, but once the German forces were established their ouster would have entailed major military confrontations, with potentially catastrophic consequences for great power relations elsewhere.[13] In the 1980s, as a century ago, Africa provides a challenge to the ability of the great powers to adjust their mutual relations to changing times and often illusive opportunities.

AFRICA'S ROLES IN GREAT POWER STRATEGIES

Throughout modern history, Africa has played five interconnected roles in the calculations of the great powers of the era.[14] These roles are rooted in the continent's geographic position and in its peoples' historic military weakness in comparison to the strength of outsiders. Which of the roles has been most prominent at a particular moment has depended on the interests, actions, and relationships of the outside powers, on the state of military technology, and on the actions of Africans themselves.

1. *Obstacle*: Viewed from Western Europe or the eastern Americas, Africa is a geographic obstacle whose bulk lies heavily athwart direct sea lanes of access to Asia. Viewed from Moscow or the Middle Eastern states, Africa historically has been a useful buffer, providing them protection from Western flanking attacks and leverage over European trade with the East. Western efforts to find ways around the obstacle spurred the development of maritime technology and led to the first European settlements on the African coast.

2. *Sea Lanes*: Obstacles can be circumnavigated, and coastal settlements do not long remain passive way stations. Shore installations can threaten or protect passage along established sea lanes of communication, particularly at such obvious "choke points" as the eastern and western ends of the Mediterranean and the Cape of Good Hope. The scramble to divide up Africa in the 1880s had its origins in European perceptions of the "strategic imperatives" of control over vital coastal areas and their hinterlands, so as to protect trade routes heading elsewhere. Rivalries between African political systems and internal competition for control over them provided opportunities for outside powers to establish

suzerainty at comparatively little cost.[15] Closer to our own time, in World War II Western control over Africa played an important role in supporting military operations in the Middle East and South Asia as air routes supplemented sea routes in strategic importance.

3. *Launching Pad*: For the dominant sea power of any age, denying the use of a littoral to an enemy is more important than acquiring the land itself (though acquisition will appear to be the surest means of denial, if also the most expensive). For those who would attack, however, acquisition of coastal installations is essential, particularly if the attacker does not enjoy untrammeled maritime ascendancy. The Allied powers used North Africa as a launching pad for the invasion of Italy and southern France in World War II. Acting on the geopolitical theories of Mackinder and Spykman, the United States set up SAC bases in the North African rimland as part of early cold war containment efforts against the Soviet Union.[16] These installations eventually fell victim to the forces of African nationalism and technological change. The former greatly increased the cost of maintaining the installations; the latter diminished their value in comparison to newer technologies.

4. *Strategic Resources*: Since the fifteenth century, concerns of wider global strategy have provided the principal rationale for great power involvement in Africa. Once established on the ground, however, they have tried to derive secondary benefit from occupation by exploiting African resources of strategic interest to the metropole. West African gold and then Africans themselves were the first strategic resources. Although minerals began to be exported from southern Africa in the 1870s, it was not until the Belgian Congo's uranium helped fuel the Manhattan Project that African mineral production became a crucial resource for Western warmaking potential.[17] Since then, rapid technological development and the increased integration of the world

economy have increased the importance of several African minerals, most of them lying from Zaire's Copper Belt south to the Cape, and of African petroleum found in North Africa and all along the continent's western coast.

5. *Surrogate Terrain*: Much research has shown that in planning their African ventures, great power statesmen have paid more attention to their rivalries with other great powers than to the realities of the African continent itself. Thus Africa came to play a role as surrogate terrain where powers could play out these rivalries at less cost to themselves (if not to the Africans) than they could at home or in more economically valuable parts of the world. Africa provided a symbolic scorecoard for tallying national prowess, useful for intimidating rivals abroad and political opposition at home. Whether the case involved the Netherlands of the Dutch East India Company, the France of Charles X, the Germany of Wilhelm II, or the Italy of Mussolini, the symbolism of an African presence has provided the paramount motive for newer and weaker powers who sought external acceptance, for unsteady governments who sought popular support, and for colonial and maritime lobbyists who sought to advance to the front ranks at home.

The reigning hegemonic powers, Portugal in the fifteenth century, Britain in the nineteenth, and again France in the twentieth, have responded not so much to the symbolic challenge (though that was not without its effects) as to perturbations in low-cost informal arrangements on the African continent and to the possibility that other powers' actions in Africa would threaten vital interests elsewhere. Direct confrontations between major powers in Africa produced little more than pocket dramas at the time, but they helped destroy the informal rules of the international game and contributed to the breakdown of world peace in 1914, and again in 1939.[18] What appeared at the time to be the rational pursuit of great power national interest produced results disastrous for those interests. Today as in the past, decision-makers have a responsibility to separate symbolic advantages from real ones; more than ever they have an interest in not getting so embroiled that fights over symbolic advantage in peripheral areas escalate into wider wars with real consequences.

MODERN TIMES: TECHNOLOGICAL CHANGES AND AFRICAN CONFLICTS

The foregoing historical excursus should provide a broader perspective for consideration of United States military and strategic interests in today's Africa than is usually derived from the now-standard "bean counting" of mineral exports from South Africa, Cuban troops in Angola and Ethiopia, and Soviet trawlers in the Indian Ocean. It suggests at least that Soviet-American confrontation in and around Africa is not the startlingly new occurrence it may seem at first blush. Rather, it repeats a historic pattern of a rising military power challenging the informal empire of a declining hegemony with global economic interests, very few of them in Africa itself. Although the general pattern is familiar, now as before, the way it is played out and the strategic roles allocated to various parts of Africa reflect not only the structured relationship between the great powers, but the specific opportunities and constraints offered by the state of military technology at the time, political conditions within Africa, and ultimately the ability of policymakers to see beyond immediate events and pressures to longer-run interests.

Changes in military technology have, in recent years, had a major impact on Africa's relevance to military strategy. The enormous increase in the level of firepower concentrated in a single weapons platform—a ship or an airplane—has greatly reduced the size of navies and air forces in terms of discrete units or systems. Along with this, greatly enhanced speed and ranges of aircraft and ships have changed the relationship of military requirements to geographic location. Together, these factors have sharply reduced quantitative requirements for traditional base facilities overseas.[19] A huge forward base like Wheelus Field in Libya—however convenient the military might find it—no longer has the value it had in 1951. Compared to the "hop, skip, and jump" stops across the Caribbean, the South Atlantic, and Africa to fly supplies to Egypt in World War II, C-5 and C-141 transports fly from Delaware to Cairo without stop, and B-52s in Operation Bright Star flew non-stop practice bombing runs from South Dakota to Egypt and back. Indeed:

> One recent Rand report on overflights and use of overhead air-space indicated that with retention of just two small island bases—Ascension and Diego Garcia—in conjunction with adequate air refueling assets, the United States could conduct significant logistical operations almost anywhere on the globe.[20]

This would represent, of course, an extreme case, but it does point up that rather than a proliferation of integrated military bases, what the United States—or any global power—needs is friendly access, refueling, and overflight arrangements with well-placed ports and airfields. An excellent example has been quiet United States support for expanding civilian airport and harbor facilities in Dakar over many years—facilities the British greatly appreciated when Dakar became a carefully unpublicized staging ground for operations in the Falklands.

If quantitative basing requirements have been diminished by technological change, the need for numerous small electronic facilities for intelligence gathering, satellite tracking, missile telemetry, radiation sensing, communications, etc., has greatly increased.[21] As the United States military pays more attention to command, control, communications, and intelligence functions (C^3I), the need to place such facilities in and around Africa will increase further—at least until a new technological generation places all of them silently in orbit. Such land-based operations, in the interim, can all be made small, inconspicuous, and civilian in appearance.

A final significant technological change is America's increased reliance on submarine-based ballistic missiles as the only secure leg of the strategic triad, together with the increased range of these missiles and their platforms. This has meant that the waters around Africa have replaced the continent itself as a strategic launching pad. This change particularly concerns the Indian Ocean, the complex bottom formations and overlapping thermal layers of which make it a prime area in which to hide sub-marines.[22] Missile range has now increased to the point that virtually all of the water off Africa's eastern coast, down to Durban, is potentially usable by American strategic weapons systems. Such systems require no immediate land-based support; rather, they function most securely in the absence of Soviet land-based detection and interdiction systems.

African military weakness and internal conflict have histor-ically provided opportunities—or at least a permissive environ-ment—for outside powers to pursue their military and strategic purposes on the continent. In some cases these opportunities have appeared too good to pass up; those who have counseled restraint have been silenced by what has appeared to be a cost-less change for unilateral advantage in great power rivalry. The world political environment, of course, has changed radically; the days of military conquest by outsiders have gone, and formal empire is too unprofitable to bring them back. Fragile though it has always been, the Organization of African Unity (OAU) sys-tem, with its norms of territorial integrity and African solutions to African problems, has reduced opportunities and raised the political costs of unsolicited outside military intervention. These norms by and large have prevailed, maintained a high degree of stability in inter-state relations, and thereby served United States strategic interests well.

It is no secret that the OAU has fallen on hard times, and that the order it championed and incarnated has been cracked, if not broken.[23] To a considerable degree, this has been a result of the growth of military capabilities of the African states. African expenditure on weaponry—until very recently—has doubled every five years, and since the distribution of this expenditure has been highly uneven, it has introduced significant military imbalances on the continent.[24] Most important, some African armies have crossed the threshold of fire-power and logistic capabilities which make them a serious threat to their neighbors. With the (ultimately successful) Somali invasion of Ethiopia in 1977 and the militarily successful Tanzanian invasion of Uganda two years later, in effect some African armies were revealed as capable of overthrowing governments that were not their own. The military imbalances are clearest between the Mediterranean African states and those in and on the other side of the Sahara. It is this imbalance, more than any Arab-African cultural tensions, that has disrupted the OAU order.

The concern on the part of many African regimes for security against outside attack has led to greater arms imports, to increased dependence on arms suppliers, and in a few cases to willingness to yield political and military advantage to outside protectors. Overall, this has advantaged the Soviet Union more than the West. Though unable to compete effectively in investment, trade, or economic aid, and lacking long-standing ties on the continent, the Soviet Union is a competitive producer of military hardware and an aggressive and flexible salesman. It has used arms agreements as a means to acquire political influence and in a few cases, the first being Somalia, to acquire access to military facilities for its own forces. Since 1970 the Soviet Union has been far and away the premier supplier of arms to Africa.[25]

The problem posed by destabilizing arms transfers to Africa is not easily soluble. Overall, arms transfers to Africa are best explained by demand or "pull" factors, rather than supply or "push" factors. African states are arming because their leaders want them to arm, not because wily salesmen are shoving arms down their throats.[26]Unilaterally-imposed arms embargoes or sales limitations are not likely to be effective (or, if systematic, easily tolerated by African states). Even if by some miracle the United States and the Soviet Union were to abstain from supplying arms, the number of alternative suppliers—France, China, Brazil, North Korea, Israel, South Africa, Vietnam, Singapore, to name a few—would make a comprehensive embargo meaningless. The familiar problem of imbalances would soon create overwhelming pressures on the great powers to go back into business.

What difference does this make for American interests? While hard evidence is scanty, what there is seems to point to the conclusion that, by itself, arms supply dependence does not yield supplier nations any deep or long-lasting influence over African governments.[27] The abilities of Africans, as clients, to manipulate outside patrons and defect when a better offer comes along are well developed. The Americans should have learned this in Ethiopia (and perhaps in Morocco), and the Soviets have been treated no better by Somalia, Egypt, and Sudan. Recent work suggests that the level of Soviet political influence even in Ethiopia may be surprisingly limited.[28]

Arms dependence on the Soviet Union by itself, then, should not be a major military or strategic concern for the United States, nor should the United States seek to impose exclusive-supplier relationships on African states. What should be of concern are those situations in which the Soviets acquire actual basing rights, or access to major facilities for their own forces. With one exception—Somalia from 1970 to 1977—the Soviets have acquired such rights only when the African country involved has been *both* dependent for its arms on the Soviet Union *and* under serious attack from forces closely identified with the West. Ethiopia and Angola are the present examples, but perhaps the most telling case was that of Guinea. Sekou Toure granted the Soviets facilities to support submarine and air surveillance patrols in exchange for Soviet protection against Portuguese incursions from Guinea-Bissau. When the war ended next door, and the Soviet West African squadron no longer served Toure's purposes, he began his rapprochement with the West and curtailed Soviet operations.

The evidence from Africa—and from most of the rest of the Third World—points to the conclusion that almost all governments view foreign bases, particulary superpower bases, as political liabilities. They are potentially socially disruptive and provide a fine rallying point for domestic opposition groups. African governments will accept them only when they perceive their security or economic needs as requiring them to pay the political price. Since the Soviets seem unable to offer significant economic inducements, the United States may have a surprisingly great strategic interest in assuring the security of those African states most closely linked to the Soviet Union.

MILITARY AND STRATEGIC INTERESTS AND WHAT TO DO ABOUT THEM

Historically, the most dramatic military use of African territory has been as a launching pad. In classical strategic terms, in launching an attack on enemy territory, the African land mass itself is no longer relevant in any direct and significant way. Nevertheless, northeastern Africa has been allocated a major analogous role as staging area for the Rapid Deployment Force (RDF). Consistent with historic precedent, the RDF is designed to protect major economic interests outside of Africa itself—in this case in the Middle East. The staging areas include ports, airfields, supply dumps, recreation and repair facilities, and communications installations. These are located in Africa—principally Mombasa, Nairobi, and Nanyuki in Kenya; and Berbera in Somalia—for political, not military, reasons. (Mombasa is 2,500 miles from the Persian Gulf.) The political reasons, of course, are the realistic fears that a major United States military presence in the Middle East itself would destabilize already shaky Arab regimes in oil-rich countries. Only Sultan Qaboos of Muscat and Oman has taken the risk of allowing the United States to use facilities on the Arabian peninsula.

The very existence of the RDF is a response to changing political factors that led the Carter administration, enthusiastically seconded by its successor, to conclude after the Shah's overthrow that surrogate powers could no longer be relied on to protect American interests. As one Reagan administration official put it, "We have learned the painful lesson that in many global contingencies—in the Middle East, South Asia and elsewhere—there will be no viable substitutes for U.S. power projection forces."[29] Given the larger premises of United States interests and the political realities of the Middle East, this is not an unreasonable judgment.

But Africa has political realities as well, and military and strategic policies must take them into account. The United States has a considerable interest in assuring that the RDF's presence in northeastern Africa does not have a destabilizing effect, that it not exacerbate regional tensions or destroy the political base of the host governments. Considerable discretion is advisable, and the record of American dealings with Somalia and Kenya on these matters is, on balance, quite impressive. In Somalia the United States has imposed very strict limitations on the quantity and type of military equipment it has delivered to ensure that these did not pose a threat to Ethiopian control of the Ogaden. This enforced Somali restraint certainly played a role in the January, 1984, decision to reduce substantially the Cuban military presence in Ethiopia. In Kenya, despite a few unfortunate incidents during ships' liberty in Mombasa, the United States military presence has been kept low key. Significantly, there were no mutterings about any sort of role during the abortive 1982 coup attempt. It will be a major challenge to maintain such a low-key role as the RDF buildup continues, particularly since political tensions are running high in Kenya.

The most immediate problem in northeastern Afria is Sudan, where the United States has communications and logistic facilities. There an increasingly erratic government threatened by civil war has been busy circulating stories of a Libyan menace to produce a major United States military and economic commitment. The Sudan would not seem a place where the United States would want to commit its prestige for reasons of minor military convenience.

Sea lane protection continues to be a strategic concern involving Africa. An enormous amount has been written on the need to protect the route from the Persian Gulf around the Cape of Good Hope, along which a major portion of the West's oil is transported.[30] Virtually all serious analyses—including those of the United States Navy—conclude that along the ten thousand miles of this route, the only effective choke points are the Straits of Hormuz and the entry points to European harbors—all reachable by home-based Soviet air forces. United States military bases on African soil would be close to useless, or worse. Maintaining a sea lane in the open ocean is not like maintaining an interstate highway. The latter requires regular attention of men and machinery, the former is best-maintained by their absence. A major base is likely to attract forces from the other side, not keep them away.

Recent Red Sea mining demonstrates the special vulnerabilities of constricted waterways, and also an appropriate response. The response was as much civil as military; it was international and multilateral under the formal control of the riverain power. It thus did not polarize the situation into one that could call forth an ideological or other *jihad* against American military action.

This logic applies with particular force to the recurrent temptation to establish some type of formal military cooperation with the Republic of South Africa. Whatever initial attractions such an arrangement might have, they would quickly prove militarily as well as politically counterproductive. The one thing that could seriously threaten the southern African portion of the Cape Route would be a major Soviet military base in Angola or, especially, in Mozambique. The threat that governments in the region would find implicit in any close South African-United States military cooperation could be the one thing that would convince at least one of those governments that their only recourse was to invite a Soviet military presence on a massive scale. And the temptation might prove too great for calmer views to prevail in the Kremlin. Discretion in any military dealings with South Africa is well advised.

Discretion ought also to be the watchword for setting up those adjuncts of strategy, communications and monitoring facilities and overflight and refuelling rights. These are best assured through quiet diplomacy and economic incentives, with a strict minimum of public notice. The last thing the United States should want is to show the flag or even a uniform. The quiet friendship and appreciation of mutual advantage by a local government are better guarantees of continued access than a high-visibility treaty that becomes a political issue. Political protection is likely to be enhanced where operation of facilities is multilateralized—or even, like the port of Djibouti, kept essentially under an ally's control—so the symbolism of superpower presence is attenuated.

From Shaba and Gabon south to the "geological scandal" of South Africa, Africa remains a supplier of important minerals for civilian and military production. There is no doubt that minerals produced in this vast area are important to the American and other Western economies, and that a few of them—cobalt, chromium, manganese, platinum, and vanadium—are especially valuable for modern technologies. Questions remain, however, as to how strategic these minerals are and what ought to be done to assure their supply.

A reasonable definition of a strategic commodity is one whose steady supply would be essential for continuing military operations, or so vital for industrial production and so unsubstitutable that its interdiction would be crippling, and so concentrated in source that interdiction would be feasible. According to these criteria, one must agree with the National Security Council's 1967 judgment (in "National Security Study Memorandum 39") that no "vital security interests" are at stake in southern Africa.[31] Technical innovation, recycling, and substitutability make price and adjustment time the principal issues, rather than deprivation of an essential component. And prudent stockpile management can sharply reduce price and adjustment difficulties.[32]

The most farfetched worry is the specter of Soviet control over southern Africa which, together with the Soviet Union's own production of these minerals, would give the Kremlin a stranglehold over Western economies. Quite aside from the fact that the United States would have ample other reasons to oppose systematic Soviet control over so great an area, this "resource war" strategy would require a very high degree of control by the Soviet Union—at least as high as that over, say, Bulgaria and higher than that over Rumania. Since such a strategy would deprive local populations and governments of virtually their entire export economy, it would be ruinously expensive. Finally, there is not even a glimmer of such a policy option in Soviet thought. Indeed, Soviet policy in recent years has encouraged greater participation by African countries of "socialist orientation" in world capitalist markets.[33]

The core issue here is economic, not military. Above all, what is required from a capitalist power like the United States is a policy of prudent management that seeks to maximize the prospects for orderly production and marketing of resources in a competitive world market. This logically should emphasize United States interest in political stability throughout southern Africa, the redundancy and competitiveness of suppliers, and the extension and protection of production and transport infrastructure. Actual ownership of mineral assets is not a significant issue, nor, of course, is the distribution of melanin in the epidermis of individuals controlling local governments. Virtually all major American corporations active in southern Africa would agree on these points.

One must be at least mildly surprised at how the Reagan administration has ignored or overridden prudent capitalist principles by failing to put substantial pressures on the Republic of South Africa to curtail its sponsorship of guerrilla movements actively disrupting major mineral evacuation routes throughout the region, including the Beira and Benguela railroads. Presumably, the Reagan administration has decided also that southern African minerals are not a significant or at least immediate strategic problem.

While the administration is doubtless correct that the West can afford temporary disruption, a longer-range policy should stress two factors: First is the rehabilitation, protection, and—in the case of transportation—prudent duplication of resource-connected infrastructure throughout southern Africa. Eliminating cross-border attacks by guerrilla and regular military forces and investing in regional infrastructure networks seem highly desirable. Second, it is clearly in the interest of the United States to conduct its policies in the area without so closely allying with an objectionable South African regime that those black African leaders who for their own reasons want to cooperate with the United States find it politically dangerous to do so. Such policies may not have immediate vital and strategic impact, but over the long run they are the only prudent way to proceed.

Finally, we come to the use of Africa as a surrogate terrain, as a place for symbolic struggle where military means may be efficiently employed to attain broader political goals. While the ability to project military force is always a useful adjunct to political strategy, it is difficult to see how direct United States military action would provide the tool of choice in Africa. Political and diplomatic means—for example, United States participation in midwifing Zimbabwe's independence—appear to be much more effective in producing political change that undercuts Soviet influence. One could envisage on the African continent the existence of a political symbol whose protection with military force might be in the United States' interest. Such a case might be an African regime so competent and so profoundly Western in its economic orientation that its overthrow would be an embarrassing loss for the United States. Alas, no candidates come to mind. A weaker but perhaps valid case could be made that America's historic association with Liberia is important enough that the latter's public association with the socialist camp would be a significant symbolic defeat. Mere consideration of the case indicates how far one has to push the meaning of strategic interest to contemplate military intervention.

A different sort of case could be made that Africa provides a terrain in which the United States should be prepared to assert its military muscle to show that even lesser clients and interests should not be trifled with. The least one can say is that each such case should be very carefully thought through, with particular concern to the long-run obligations implicitly incurred. As Kissinger was quoted as saying, early in this paper, the United States must be "aware of the interconnections between events." This applies not only to the global arena but to the message conveyed to other African states as well.

One must conclude that by and large Africa does not provide a propitious terrain for the United States' military pursuit of symbolic advantage. Victories are evanescent and unlikely to stir widespread enthusiasm at home. The Soviet stakes in Africa are too small to provide major advantage and it would be excessively costly to root out those stakes militarily. Military competition is the only form of competition in Africa in which the Soviets can operate on a more or less even basis with the United States, and that is unlikely to change. The United States does have military and strategic interests on the African continent; it is more likely these will be assured by political and economic action than it is that military action will secure its much larger political and economic interests.

As a global economic power, albeit one whose comparative weight is declining, the United States has a very conservative interest in stability in peripheral areas of the world. Sources of instability in Africa are multiple; most are internal, but outside interference by the West as well as the East has contributed greatly to the problem. Prudent long-run policy interests would be well served by building Africa's own collective ability to stabilize regional relations. This ought to be more than a pious hope; it ought to be a permanent policy guideline counseling restraint and balanced dealings on the continent.[34]

This paper, as was its charge, has addressed exclusively American military and strategic interests. The warning against seeking symbolic victories in Africa can be made with equal force to the Soviet Union. The attractions of carving out a symbolic place in the African sun have proven evanescent and ultimately very costly for previous bumptious, rising world powers. Reinforcing some semblance of the OAU order should be ultimately as much in Soviet military and strategic interest as in that of the United States. It ought not be beyond the skill of prudent statesmen on both sides to arrive at and implement such an understanding.

NOTES

1. William J. Foltz, *Elite Opinion on United States Policy toward Africa* (New York: Council on Foreign Relations, 1979); James E. Baker, J. Daniel O'Flaherty, and John de St. Jorre, *Public Opinion Poll on American Attitudes toward South Africa* (New York: Carnegie Endowment for International Peace, 1979).

2. Zbigniew Brzezinski, *Power and Principle* (New York: Farrar, Straus & Giroux, 1983), 189.

3. Robert O. Keohane, *After Hegemony: Cooperation and Discord in the World Political Economy* (Princeton: Princeton University Press, 1984); Robert Gilpin, *U.S. Power and the Multinational Corporation* (New York: Basic Books, 1975).

4. W. Roger Louis, *Imperialism at Bay 1941–45* (New York: Oxford University Press, 1977).

5. Adrian Pelt, *Libyan Independence and the United Nations* (New Haven: Yale Press, 1970).

6. Christopher Coker, "The Western Alliance and Africa 1949–81," *African Affairs* 81, 324 (July, 1982), 319–335; Arthur M. Schlesinger, Jr., *A Thousand Days: John F. Kennedy in the White House* (Boston: Houghton Mifflin, 1965), 551.

7. Schlesinger, 562–63, 582–83.

8. Henry Kissinger, "American Global Concerns and Africa," (Paper presented to the South African Institute of International Affairs, Johannesburg: September 6, 1982).

9. For an extreme reaction that proceeds on the premise that what is most needed is the repeated demonstration of American "will," see Alexander M. Haig, Jr., *Caveat: Realism, Reagan and Foreign Policy* (New York: MacMillan, 1984).

10. Robert Gilpin, *U.S. Power, and the Multinational Corporation.* (New York: Basic Books, 1975), 152.

11. Sergei G. Gorshkov, *Red Star Rising at Sea* (Annapolis: U.S. Naval Institute, 1974).

12. William M. LeoGrande, *Cuba's Policy in Africa, 1959 – 1980* (Berkeley: University of California Institute of International Studies, 1980).

13. I have discussed this in "Africa in Great Power Strategy," Chapter I of William J. Foltz and Henry S. Bienen, eds., *Arms and the African: Military Influences on African International Relations* (New Haven: Yale Press, 1985); see also Deryck M. Schrender, *The Scramble for Southern Africa, 1877 – 1895* (New York: Cambridge University Press, 1980).

14. The following discussion is adapted from "Africa in Great Power Strategy."

15. See the classic argument of Ronald Robinson and John Gallagher with Alice Denny, *Africa and the Victorians: The Climax of Imperialism in the Dark Continent* (New York: St. Martin's Press, 1961).

16. William H. Lewis, "How a Defense Planner Looks at Africa" in Helen Kitchen, ed., *Africa: From Mystery to Maze* (Lexington, MA: Lexington Books, 1976), 278.

17. Gregg Herken, *The Winning Weapon: The Atomic Bomb in The Cold War 1945 – 1950* (New York: Vantage Books, 1982), 102 – 105.

18. See Geoffrey Barraclough, *From Agadir to Armageddon: Anatomy of a Crisis* (London: Weidenfeld and Nicholson, 1983); and A.J. Barker, *The Civilizing Mission: A History of the Italo-Ethiopian War of 1935 – 1936* (New York: Dial Press, 1968) for discussions of two African preludes to wider conflict.

19. Robert E. Harkavy, "Military Bases in the Third World" in W. Scott Thompson, ed., *The Third World: Premises of U.S. Policy* (San Francisco: ICS Press, 1983), 175 – 200.

20. Ibid., 182. The study in question is P. M. Dadant, "Shrinking International Airspace as a Problem for Future Air Movements — A Briefing," Report R-2178-AF (Santa Monica: Rand Corp., 1978).

21. Ibid., 183 – 85.

22. See Larry Bowman, "The Indian Ocean: U.S. Military and Strategic Perspectives" (Paper presented at meetings of African Studies

Association, November 5, 1982) for a good review of these issues.

23. See the discussions in Yassin El-Ayouty and I. William Zartman, eds., *The OAU after Twenty Years* (New York: Praeger, 1984).

24. William J. Foltz, "The Militarization of Africa: Trends and Policy Problems," chapter VII in Foltz and Bienen, op. cit.

25. Louis George Sarris, "Soviet Military Policy and Arms Activity in Sub-Saharan Africa," Chapter II in Foltz and Bienen, op. cit.

26. Joseph P. Smaldone, "U.S. Arms Transfers and Security-Assistance Programs in Africa: A Review and Policy Perspective" in Bruce E. Arlinghaus, ed., *Arms for Africa: Military Assistance and Foreign Policy in the Developing World* (Lexington, MA: Lexington Books, 1982), 202–212.

27. David J. Sylvan, *Arms Transfers and the Logic of Political Efficacy,* Military Issues Research Memorandum ACN 78041 (July 1978), U.S. Army War College, Carlisle Barracks, PA.

28. I am grateful to Robert D. Grey of Grinnell College for a look at his work in progress on "The Soviet Union and African Political Autonomy."

29. Fred Charles Ikle, "The Strategic Principles of the Reagan Administration," *Strategic Review* 11, 4 (Fall 1983), 15.

30. For careful reviews of the evidence see the analyses of Larry W. Bowman, "The Strategic Importance of South Africa to the United States," *African Affairs 81, 323 (April 1982), 159*–191; and Robert S. Jaster, *Southern Africa in Conflict: Implications for U.S. Policies in the 1980's* (Washington, D.C.: American Enterprise Institute, 1982).

31. Mohamed A. El-Khawas and Barry Cohen, eds., *The Kissinger Study of Southern Africa: National Security Study Memorandum 39* (Westport: Lawrence Hill, 1976), 89.

32. H. E. Goeller and A. M. Weinberg, "The Age of Substitutability," *Science* 191 (1976); William J. Broad "Resource Wars: The Lure of South Africa," *Science* 210 (December 5, 1980); Bruce Russett, "Dimensions of Resource Dependence: Some Elements of Rigor in Concept and Policy Analysis," *International Organization* 38, 3 (Summer 1984), 481–499.

33. For an excellent analysis of Soviet views, see Elizabeth Kridl Valkinier, *The Soviet Union and the Third World: An Economic Bind* (New York: Praeger, 1983).

34. For a similar argument, see Helen Kitchen, *U.S. Interests in Africa,* The Washington Papers/98, Vol. XI (New York: Praeger, 1983), 71–80.

Commentary

Morton A. Kaplan

Professor Foltz has presented a splendid account of the role of Africa in the world, the history of American involvement in the area, and the strategic importance of Africa in terms of American interests. The areas in which I would take issue with him are perhaps minor. Professor Foltz accepts the conclusion of a recent Rand report that Ascension and Diego Garcia Islands "in conjunction with adequate air refueling assets, [would permit] the United States [to] conduct significant logistic operations almost anywhere on the globe." He then adds: "This would represent, of course, an extreme case, but it does point up that rather than a proliferation of integrated military bases, what the United States—or any global power—needs is friendly access, refueling and overflight arrangements with well-placed ports and air fields."

I am willing to concede that in certain minor affairs this conclusion may follow. Bases, however, are very important, although they may be so politically counterproductive as to be contraindicated. I seriously doubt that "friendly access, refueling, and overflight arrangements" would permit the United States to do much more than to show the flag in the Middle East against any Soviet operation. The concentrated shipments from near supply depots that basing permits would be absent. Thus, the facilities of which Professor Foltz writes might permit the United States to provide marginal resupplies to Israel in a Middle Eastern war or to provide marginal assistance to a beleaguered government fighting an internal uprising. In the absence of a local ally with considerable staying power, the military capability of the United States to influence political changes in Africa is quite small except when the popular and institutional base that supports the government or a revolutionary group is minimal. For instance, I believe that it would be relatively easy to support a revolution in Ghana.

The victory of the Marxists in Angola could have been prevented. Here, however, it would have been continued South African intervention, assisted by the United States, rather than American intervention alone, that would have produced this result. Contrary to what Professor Foltz suggests, I do not believe that the Cuban and Soviet presence was a significant deterrent to United States intervention. It was the United States Senate that prevented the effective intervention that otherwise would have occurred.

However, unlike Professor Foltz, I see very clear American interests in not opposing the destabilizing tactics of the Republic of South Africa in Angola, for instance, although I do agree that it would be a serious mistake for us to cooperate with the Republic in its activities. For both moral reasons and domestic political reasons, the United States must keep a certain distance from the government of South Africa until there are clear indications that South African blacks are brought into its political process in a dignified manner. However, because of its control of the Cape route, because it possesses the only significant industrial economy in Africa, and because it possesses or dominates much of the mineral wealth of the continent, the Republic is an extremely important asset and a potential ally. Moreover, even if African states under Marxist regimes do have an interest in selling minerals to the West, gross instability in the south of Africa could threaten the reliability of supplies; and the Republic is a major barrier to such instability. If its neighbor states continue to be radicalized and if the Republic cannot use its military to force them into neutralization, its ability to play its role in the region could be threatened.

Although one might argue that what happens in the rest of Africa is peripheral to the course that the Republic takes with respect to its domestic arrangements, the political process is always affected, and often importantly, at the margin. A regime compromise in Angola, following a sustained and a relatively successful guerrilla war by UNITA (Union for the Total Independence of Angola), and the prevention in southwest Africa of the types of political change now apparently occurring in Zimbabwe, would reduce some of the barriers to political change in South Africa, although obviously these would not occur speedily in any event. The chief advisers to the prime minister in South Africa had been holding out hope that Prime Minister Mugabe would be a moderate with whom compromise was possible. They also had great respect for his intelligence. His recent moves toward a one-party state and a socialist economy are likely to make even moderate South African leaders wary of trusting black leaders to build stable, pluralistic states that are capable of development. The popular response will surely be much more negative.

Furthermore, the failure by South Africa to move forward with the process of internal political change would present the United States with embarrassing and even possibly dangerous alternatives. Although it is likely that South Africa would be able to suppress internal violence of a level that would threaten the supply of vital minerals and raw materials to Europe—which is much more dependent on these sources than is the United States and the health of which is vital to the United States—the excesses that might occur in producing the requisite degree of order might make it difficult for the United States to oppose either Security Council resolutions or indirect but significant Soviet intervention in the affairs of the Republic. This may occur in any event—for it is unlikely that South Africa can move fast enough in terms of internal reform to save its moderate black leadership—but it is more likely to occur if the Republic confronts an even more unfavorable environment.

Although there is no immediate problem in resource- and mineral-rich Zaire, for the corrupt and inefficient regime of that country appears to have developed a decentralized system of sharing the "swag" that inhibits effective rebellion, one suspects that eventually the regime will face internal difficulties. In that event the United States may be so closely identified with the present regime that it is unable to influence the process of change. One wonders whether there may not be something to be said for a process of slow but gradual disentanglement of the United States from the embrace of the current regime.

On the whole I agree with Professor Foltz's advice against the United States' becoming either too involved with particular regimes on the African continent or too opposed to them. Most of them have little importance for us. Even were Nigeria to embargo oil to the United States, it must sell it somewhere; and there are many alternative suppliers.

Except in the situation confronting South Africa, disinterested and rather remote friendship is the best posture for the United States. Until the African states can produce effective governments and firmly developing economies — and outside assistance is not the major problem here — they can be of little help to the United States and can do only minimal damage to other states. Moreover, until they bring their own affairs into order, there is little that others can do to help them. A strong argument can be made for benign neglect.

Although there may be exceptions, the United States should not allow itself to become involved in the internecine conflicts of the African states. And it must not be misled by the rhetoric of African politics to pursue unwise policies, as it did when it bought "Soviet" (but really Rhodesian) chrome, thereby merely paying the USSR as a middleman, while the African states were heavily involved in trade with South Africa. Every black political leader in South Africa to whom I have spoken regards disinvestment, if effective, as a barrier to both political change in South Africa and the welfare of South African blacks. Moreover, most of them believe that disinvestment would be ineffective and would merely shift investment opportunities from the United States to Europeans or Asians. An enhanced Sullivan code, on the other hand, would likely be of benefit. And I am sorry that the politics of the black caucus in the United States Congress made it impossible to separate productive from counterproductive pressure, thus reducing the influence the United States might otherwise have had on change in South Africa.

DISCUSSION

There was a sharp debate about the suggestion that the United States' policy toward Africa should be guided by the sole desire to prevent Soviet domination of the periphery. The opposing point was that it would be a mistake for the United States to view South Africa as a strategic ally at this moment, given the conflicting political situation there. There was also the assertion that many moderate Afrikaners felt that the United States should not consider a military alliance with their country if it wants changes there.

Another point made was that given the importance of South Africa, the United States should attempt to help to facilitate a political solution there before the area becomes a military problem. This policy would entail thinking about what type of political system we would like to see in South Africa. Whether the Afrikaners would accept the principle of "one man, one vote" was discussed at length. Some participants felt that this solution was the only one consistent with American democratic traditions, and therefore was important to our long-term economic and strategic interests. Other participants doubted that Afrikaners would accept this principle and noted that the Africans were not pushing the issue.

Concern was expressed that when the blacks do come to power, the major ethnic groups in the country such as the Zulu might advocate bringing related peoples in the neighboring states under South African control. This would lead to black imperialism, which in the opinion of some participants might lead to more political problems in the region.

There was a great deal of debate as to whether the United States could persuade South Africa to deal with Sam Nujoma, given the fear of Afrikaners that a radical SWAPO-dominated country could spell disaster for them. A number of discussants were not sure that the United States could or should try to deal with this issue. There was the suggestion that neither South Africa nor the United States should fear that radical states could develop in the region, because most states there were highly dependent upon the Republic economically. It was also suggested that the United States would welcome what some analysts view as the "bourgeoisification" of blacks in all the regions of southern Africa. One discussant felt that Reagan's economic policy in the United States could have revolutionary implications for South Africa. With the decline in the price of gold, South Africa's economy is being badly hurt, and this can precipitate changes there.

Fear was expressed that the United States was taking a short-sighted approach to problems in the Horn of Africa. The opinion was voiced that there were grounds for believing that there could be a rapprochement between the Marxist government there and the United States. This being the case, it was suggested that the Ethiopians should be assured that the United States would favor the breakup of their country by supporting separationist guerrillas.

CHAPTER 3

UNITED STATES RESPONSE TO INTER-AFRICAN REGIONAL PROBLEMS AND PROSPECTS

FOREIGN POLICY IN A TURBULENT AGE

William H. Lewis

Since the early 1950s, when the processes of decolonization were coming into full tide, successive American presidents have felt compelled to address a central issue of our times: how to maintain order and stability in an increasingly disorderly world. The cumulative answers provided have been more numerous than the sum of the challenges presented. On occasion rhetoric has sufficed; on other occasions the dispensation of material resources has proved sufficient to meet crises. Only rarely have the armed forces of the United States been called upon to redress regional imbalances, to support moderate regimes, or to turn aside the expansion of Communist influence in unstable Third World areas. Vietnam, with its associated trauma, proved the exception; we have been spared the spectacle of direct military intervention in Africa.

Over the past three decades strategies fashioned to deal with turbulence in the Third World have followed no fixed pattern. Trial and error have produced an abundance of errors, revealing flawed strategies. During the Carter presidency the preferred approach emphasized diplomacy to resolve local disputes, as well as to accommodate American interests to the forces of revolutionary change arising in the Third World. East-West rivalries were to be muted, and arms control was to serve as the primary vehicle for reducing international tensions. This approach was placed at risk, however, by the Khomeini revolution in Iran, the injection of 20,000 Cuban troops into the Ethiopian-Somali conflict, and the Soviet invasion of Afghanistan in December, 1979.

Despite its adoption of a more aggressive stance, the Reagan administration confronts comparable disappointments today. In Africa armed conflict is common coin, and efforts to dissuade Qadaffi and others from intervention in the affairs of neighboring states have not proved productive. Wars of liberation abound—in Ethiopia, in Namibia, and in the western Sahara—and the continent is beset by far-reaching economic and political difficulties that may be beyond the ken of any one nation to ameliorate.

As a nation increasingly inclined in recent years to engage in self-evaluation, we have directed much of our frustration and ire at the incumbent in the Oval Office. Flawed strategies are held to be the product of flawed individuals. Only on rare occasions have the more introspective among us concluded that international order and stability are beyond our national capacity to achieve, and that we must accept certain realities:

- That turbulence and disorder are likely to be the norm rather than the exception in the Third World.

- That the United States has neither the resources nor the need to address the overwhelming majority of Third World "crisis situations." Indeed, if anything, the community of nations has a greater capacity to generate conflicts than the United States possesses to resolve them.

- That so-called "surrogates" and "allies" will pursue interests that, not infrequently, will be found at variance with the objectives and interests of the United States and the Soviet Union. The prudent policymaker, therefore, cannot assume that relationships with Third World leaders are immutably fixed. Constant changes in alliances and coalitions are likely to prove the rule in the years immediately ahead.

These maxims have particular relevance for the American policymaker and practitioner concerned with African affairs. With the end of Mr. Reagan's first term and with his re-election, a period of policy review is clearly in prospect. Various "experts" and specialists can be expected to proffer advice, some solicited and some not. The issues identified and analyzed will cover a broad spectrum—ranging from the economic infirmities besetting many African nations to the vagaries of African and Arab politics in various subregions of the African continent. The prescriptions presented will cover an equally broad spectrum reflecting the assessments and preferred action programs of globalists and regionalists, maximalists and minimalists, those favoring a *realpolitik* approach and others who endorse what might best be characterized as an *idealpolitik* emphasis. All too often, what will be lacking in these presentations is a sense of history—an appreciation of past American policies in Africa, strategies adopted, and reasons for change in American strategy.

THE FIVE PHASES OF AMERICAN POLICY

A commonly encountered postulate on the part of policy experts is the notion that Africa has not loomed large in the perspective of American policy architects. Each new administration is invited to discover the continent in all of its complexities and contradictions. A vast arena of diverse cultural and ethnic groupings, Africa is often presented as a panorama of contrasting exotic communities and bizarre leadership groups. A consensus has evolved around the notion of an "awakening giant," confronted with a multitude of disorders and instabilities that defy the American imagination. This somewhat pathological school of analysis invites the notion of a continent awaiting central direction and foreign policy control. In reality, American specialists have a wealth of experience and knowledge about the continent that goes well beyond superficial, essentially touristic impressions. Our policies have been the product of lengthy contact with the area and of substantial familiarity with forces operating in its several subregions. In this context it is instructive to examine and understand the several phases through which our policies have evolved.

FIRST PHASE—1949-60: Modern-day American involvement with Africa dates from the landing of American forces in Morocco and Algeria during World War II. The November, 1942, intervention produced a major Allied victory that forced the withdrawal of German and Italian military units from the northern portion of Africa. The region subsequently served as the launch point for the Allied invasion of Sicily, Italy, and southern France. North Africa's strategic importance was not to decline with the defeat of Germany and Italy, however. The emergence of East-West rivalries at the end of the war and the formation of NATO in 1949 led to a resurgence of military interest in North Africa.

This interest was the product of a "defense in depth" strategy by NATO which viewed North Africa as a geostrategic anchor or, more precisely, a means to achieve military ends. The strategy was predicated on a perception of the vast superiority of Soviet military formations; embryonic Western European conventional forces were believed weak and incapable of effective defense against them. (In 1950 the bulk of American combat forces were deployed in Korea; the American atomic arsenal was limited both in numbers and in delivery capabilities.) NATO strategists believed that, in the event of hostilities, they could not hope to defend the narrow waist of Western Europe; therefore, North Africa must serve as a refuge from which American and other NATO forces might be mobilized for reinsertion into Europe when Soviet numerical advantages had been offset. What was required under the defense-in-depth strategy was the creation of a number of lodgments and military installations to receive NATO forces, as well as air and naval bases from which to launch strikes against Soviet forces on the European continent and in the Mediterranean basin.

Consonant with this approach, the United States negotiated the Caffrey-Bidault agreement of December, 1950, which permitted the United States to construct four Strategic Air Command bases in the French protectorate zone of Morocco, a naval air station at Port Lyautey (present-day Kenitra), and a communications intelligence complex at Bouknadel. The government of Morocco was not consulted; France, as the protectorate power, enjoyed full responsibility for the management of Morocco's foreign relations. Elsewhere, the United States negotiated for access rights to Wheelus Air Base near Tripoli, Libya, after that country achieved its independence under United Nations auspices in December, 1951; in Eritrea, a former Italian colony federated with Ethiopia in September, 1952, the United States opened a major intelligence collection station that monitored communications in the Middle East. Great Britain and France supported the strategy by improving their base facilities in the Suez Canal zone, el-Adem (Libya), Bizerte, Mer-el-Kebir, Casablanca, and a dozen other locales throughout North Africa.

Military necessity clearly overrode political considerations in American foreign policy for the region during much of the decade of the 1950s. American diplomats with expertise in the region were increasingly distressed by the high priority assigned to military "requirements," often at the expense of ties with emergent nationalist forces. During this period, the United States receded from support for the principle of self-determination when the question of Moroccan and Tunisian independence arose in the United Nations. No word of protest emanated from Washington when Habib Bourguiba, leader of the Neo-Destour Party of Tunisia, was arrested and imprisoned by French authorities in 1951; nor did the State Department offer objection when Sultan Sidi Mohammed Ben Youssef, leader of the Moroccan nationalist movement, was deposed by French protectorate authorities in August, 1953, and trundled into exile. The official American record during the early stages of the Algerian struggle for independence also leaves little room for national pride. All opportunity to serve as a broker between local nationalists and colonial authority was subordinated to overriding security interests.

SECOND PHASE—1960-69: Political changes in Africa ultimately compelled an adjustment in policy. A floodtide of independence was beginning to sweep the continent, beginning with Libya in 1951 and running through the northern reaches of the continent. Morocco and Tunisia severed their colonial moorings in 1956; in West Africa Ghana followed in 1957, Guinea in 1958. Meantime, the Algerian struggle for independence had brought down the French Republic, and the rise of President Charles de Gaulle spelled the end of the French colonial presence in Africa, beginning in 1960.

Cognizant of revolutionary changes in progress, the State Department established a Bureau of African Affairs in 1958 and two years later determined that American embassies should be established in each of the newly independent African nations.

The arrival of the Kennedy administration in January, 1961, marked a turning point in American attitudes and policies in Africa. One of the first senior State Department appointments announced by President Kennedy was that of Assistant Secretary for Africa—the former governor of Michigan, G. Mennen Williams. Williams immediately brought on board a coterie of able assistants, many with extensive experience in Africa. Together they fashioned a strategy of economic assistance that was to serve as a bellwether for other programs to aid lessdeveloped countries. Their's was an effort intended to demonstrate the advantages of close association with the United States. It involved a major increase in resource transfers and training to five carefully selected African nations—Zaire, Nigeria, Tanzania, Ethiopia, and Tunisia. Williams and company intended to demonstrate in all five that American "know-how" would lead these countries to assured stages of economic "take-off" and self-sustained growth.

In this second phase, the emphasis on military facilities began to dissipate. Military technology, together with nationalist forces on the continent, diminished the importance of the area in terms of the defense-in-depth strategy that had been embraced a decade earlier. Nevertheless, the continent was viewed as an important arena in the context of East-West rivalry. Zaire became a focal point for this rivalry; the overthrow of President Lumumba emerged as a major goal of the Kennedy administration. With respect to the "white redoubt" regimes of southern Africa, the Kennedy administration faced a policy dilemma of the first order. Politically opposed to the perpetuation of white minority rule which redounded to the disadvantage of the black African majority, the President was also called upon to deal with certain other strategic realities. Key among these was the imperative of meeting American security commitments in the Middle East. Early in the Kennedy presidency, the Oval Office received a memorandum from the Chairman of the Joint Chiefs of Staff, observing that access to the Portuguese base in the Azores was critical in terms of landing troops and military materiel in the event of a future crisis in the Middle East. The *quid pro quo* for such access would have to be to grant military assistance for the armed forces of Portugal. While such materiel was not be used in Portugal's African provinces, it would release other money for prosecution of the war against African liberation movements, notably in Angola and Mozambique. Confronted by these imperatives, President Kennedy endorsed the Joint Chiefs' proposal to increase the level of military aid to the armed forces of Portugal. This decision ultimately outraged the majority of African leaders in the nations bordering on the white redoubt region and severely diminished American credibility in southern Africa for more than a decade.

THIRD PHASE—1970-76: The African continent suffered a severe regression during the initial years of the Nixon administration for reasons that have been adumbrated by various scholars, including the redoubtable Henry Kissinger. Part of the explanation can be found in the *realpolitik* views adopted by the President and his national security advisor. These views placed high priority on detentist accommodation with the Soviet Union, while seeking to ensure a global balance favorable to the interests of the United States. A corollary was the search for emerging regional powers in the Third World that shared American objectives. Thus, in the case of the Middle East, the British announcement of a British military recessional "east of Suez" because of financial stringencies led the Nixon administration to identify Iran as a key potential role player in the Persian Gulf. The consequence was a perceptible rise in American arms transfers to the Shah's regime. In the Asian arena the People's Republic of

China was similarly identified; the hallmark of the Nixon-Kissinger approach was to seek rapprochement with Peking, as symbolized in the Shanghai communiqué of 1972.

Africa presented a difficult challenge. The Nigerian civil war had produced shock waves throughout the continent. It was the largest black African nation possessing rich economic potential, and most Westerners found its bloody conflict a portent of future instabilities in the area. In addition, by the end of the 1960s, a plethora of military coups had swept away the first post-colonial generation of African leaders. Finally, the economic performance of many of the new states—faced with rising population, diminished agricultural resources, and adverse balance-of-payments—left little room for optimism.

Under the rubric of National Security Study Memorandum 39, the American foreign policy community conducted a series of special studies, in which specialists foresaw continuing instabilities in the region between the Sahara and the Limpopo River. To the south, in the white redoubt belt, however, the specialists forecasted unshakable white domination throughout the coming decade, despite the emergence of increasingly effective liberation forces in Angola, Mozambique, and Rhodesia. The result of this exercise was the decision taken by President Nixon to tilt American policy in favor of the white redoubt area, and to adopt a posture of benign neglect with respect to the remainder of the sub-Saharan region.

For approximately five years, the Nixon-Kissinger strategy remained the touchstone of official American relations with Africa. By late 1974, a series of events compelled then-Secretary of State Kissinger to recast his approach. The Portuguese effort to retain control over its African possessions had collapsed, along with the demise of the Salazar regime in Lisbon. Elsewhere in the white redoubt, the regime of Prime Minister Ian Smith in Rhodesia was hard-pressed as a result of the mounting military prowess of African liberation forces led by Joshua Nkomo and Robert Mugabe. The Republic of South Africa, increasingly regarded as a pariah in the world community as a result of its apartheid policies, felt itself beleaguered in Namibia as well. There, the South West Africa Peoples Organization, under the leadership of Sam Nujoma, was launching guerrilla attacks that threatened Pretoria's hold over the former United Nations Trust Territory.

Rather than withdraw, Kissinger determined that bold new initiatives were required to stem the tide of instability and what he perceived to be a mounting challenge to American influence in southern and central Africa. One must remember that Kissinger, at that critical juncture, was going through a Spenglerian phase induced by the collapse of his détente strategy toward the Soviet Union; the specter of "Eurocommunism" in Spain, Portugal, and Italy; and the Turkish invasion of Cyprus. At the same time President Nixon's fall from grace in the United States, together with spreading domestic dissent on foreign policy, was viewed by Kissinger as a grave threat to continued American leadership in the world community. He also believed that the Soviet Union had determined that it could challenge American policy in Africa by gaining a presence in Angola, where post-independence civil war had erupted among three factions. The Soviet Union was perceived as favoring the MPLA under the direction of Augostinho Neto. Kissinger decided on a covert campaign of support for opposition groups led by Holden Roberto and Jonas Savimbi, in collaboration with the Republic of South Africa.

The effort ended inconclusively on the battlefield, and American intervention terminated summarily through Congress's enactment of the Clark Amendment to the 1976 Foreign Assistance Appropriations Act, which proscribed covert military or paramilitary involvement in the civil war. Nettled by this congressional action, Kissinger directed his considerable talents toward the Rhodesian problem, succeeding in persuading principal parties to the conflict to participate in a roundtable conference, sponsored by the British, in Geneva. The conference never came about, and the American national elections of November, 1976, produced a change of administration and denial of further opportunity for Kissinger to bring his powers of persuasion to bear on the Rhodesian problem.

FOURTH PHASE—1977-80: The arrival of the Carter administration was singular in terms of American relations with Africa. American policy under Kissinger was held in low esteem by many black African leaders, who resented the tilt in favor of white rule, as well as the decline in official American economic assistance to their economies. They tended, on the whole, to greet the new administration and its much-publicized espousal of human rights policy with reserve, if not outright skepticism. The United States had little credibility in its professed claim of sympathetic interest in internal African problems. Too many American promises had not been honored. Moreover, American leadership in the world community had declined prodigiously for a variety of reasons, ranging from involvement in Southeast Asian wars to the resignation of President Nixon under unfortunate circumstances.

President Carter was personally aware of these sentiments and, in the initial stages of his stewardship, accorded the African continent high priority in the foreign policy realm. He personally selected senior officials for the United Nations delegation—most notably a close friend, Andrew Young, to head the American contingent—and the State Department to deal with African issues. Few new nostrums were offered for Africa during the first several months of the Carter presidency. Instead, to establish a greater degree of credibility for American diplomacy, Ambassador Young and other senior officials were dispatched to the region to lay a foundation for broader personal contact with African leaders. To offset past impressions of American neglect, Washington's approach was to define, and then identify with, the black African viewpoint on the continent's many vexing problems. To accomplish this goal involved expansion of the traditional narrow base of personal contacts by building ties with Nigeria, Guinea, Tanzania, Somalia, Mozambique, and Angola, where previous relations had ranged from cool to icy.

South Africa and Namibia became a litmus test for the new administration. Ambassador Young and his colleagues made clear at African conferences that the United States regarded the racist policies of Pretoria as anathema, since apartheid embodied the worst forms of human rights abuse. Hence, President Carter would shift toward a confrontationist posture with South Africa; at the same time, he took the lead in organizing a contact group under United Nations auspices to negotiate with South Africa its withdrawal from Namibia and the earliest possible transition of that territory to independence. The other members of the group included Great Britain, France, West Germany, and Canada.

As for the remainder of the African continent, Secretary of State Cyrus Vance spelled out American policies in a speech before the 58th Annual Meeting of the United States Jaycees on June 20, 1978. The basic ingredients were outlined as follows:

- Stronger United States commitment to social justice and economic development in Africa

- Further efforts to resolve African disputes peacefully

- Greater respect for African nationalism

- Further support for legitimate African defense needs

- Greater respect for human rights, which strengthen the fabric of African nations

Vance was at great pains to point out that foreign intervention to resolve African disputes should be eschewed. The United States had also taken the lead in attempting to secure Soviet acquiescence in a regime of restraint regarding arms transfers to Africa. President Carter had announced a policy of self-denial and had entered into discussions with the Soviet Union, called the Conventional Arms Transfers (CAT) talks. At the same time, Washington had invited the Soviet Union to join with the United States in providing economic and humanitarian assistance to Africa.

By mid-1978, the Carter administration had become distressed over the inclination of the Soviet Union and Cuba to intervene in African disputes through "arms diplomacy." Contending that the forces of African national independence should be supported and that disputes should be resolved through peaceful means, the Carter administration expressed growing worries about the presence of more than 40,000 Cuban troops in Angola (inserted in mid-1975) and in Ethiopia (inserted early in 1978 to thwart the movement of Somali forces into the Ogaden Province of Ethiopia). According to the secretary of state, Africa should not be considered an arena for East-West competition. Rather, Washington and Moscow should rely on the African imperative for independence as the primary source of strength in coping with local disorders and instabilities.

Eighteen months later, serious misgivings were developing in the Carter administration about the feasibility and relevance of its initial approach to Africa. The Shaba crises of 1977 and 1978, in which the copper-rich province of Zaire was invaded from neighboring Angola, were viewed as a Cuban-inspired adventure, turned back largely as a result of military actions on the part of Morocco, France, and Belgium. In the instance of the Ethiopian-Somali war that erupted in 1977, Moscow responded with a massive airlift of emergency arms to hard-pressed Ethiopian forces, on the magnitude of $1.5 billion. These arms, together with the Cuban military intervention, finally turned back the Somali contingents that had seized control of more than 90 percent of the Ogaden. Soviet arms, funneled through Libya and Algeria, were also becoming an important factor in the ongoing war that had erupted between Morocco and Saharan elements over control of the western Sahara. By late 1979, the Conventional Arms Transfers talks with the Soviet Union had collapsed, and, quite obviously, Moscow intended to increase its arms supplies to selected African nations. At the same time, efforts to contain the policy adventures of Qadaffi were proving fruitless, with the Libyan chieftain widening his efforts to destabilize regimes in Sudan, Chad, and elsewhere.

Events in southwest Asia finally compelled the Carter administration to set aside its *idealpolitik* approach. The overthrow of the Shah of Iran, the taking of diplomatic hostages in Tehran, the fulminations of the Ayatollah Khomeini, and the December, 1979, Soviet invasion of Afghanistan demanded an effective American response. In his January, 1980, State of the Union address, President Carter declared the Persian Gulf vital to American national interests and, consonant with this declaration, announced that an American Rapid Deployment Force would be formed to protect these interests.

The implications of this altered stance for Africa were far-reaching. Almost overnight, the United States government embarked on a frantic search to secure access, overflight, and other military rights in northern Africa for the Rapid Deployment Force. In short order, facilities agreements were concluded with Egypt, Sudan, Somalia, and Kenya, and advance parties of American engineers were dispatched to conduct site surveys. Concomitantly, Washington promised significant increases in military equipment and economic aid as *quid pro quo* for access rights. In the case of the western Sahara war, President Carter approved an about-face in Americans arms supply policy to Morocco permitting the forces of King Hassan to employ weapons in the defense of the western Sahara. When the Qadaffi regime helped to organize and to orchestrate a raid by Tunisian dissidents in the Gafsa area of Tunisia, the Carter administration promised to supply military materiel to meet any future threats. These changes in policy represented a considered judgment by the President. Washington could no longer afford to remain passive while its traditional friends and allies were overthrown. The lesson of Iran had been learned in the national security committees of the American government.

The implications of the American resolution were significant for the northern third of Africa. Much as during the early stages of the cold war, the region began to be viewed as an important geostrategic area—on this occasion, however, not for the defense of Western Europe, but to protect American interests in the Middle East. Northern Africa would serve as a geographic means to achieve military ends. In the process, the United States would address any challenges posed by the Soviet Union and its surrogates—such as Libya and Ethiopia—through whatever measures might seem appropriate. If such a stance meant the polarization of the area into two contending factions, the United States was prepared to help its friends and allies to defend themselves. This approach flew in the face of the public appeals by senior African leaders for the two superpowers to avoid involving themselves in African disputes or making the continent a cockpit for cold war rivalries. Lieutenant General Olusegun Obasanjo, the Nigerian chief of state, cautioned both sides during the 1978 Organization of African Unity (OAU) summit meeting in the following terms:

In the context of foreign intervention in Africa, there are three parties involved. These are the Soviets and other socialist countries, the Western powers, and we the Africans. If the interests of Africa are to be safeguarded, there are certain considerations which each of the parties should bear in mind. To the Soviets and their friends, I should like to say that, having been invited to Africa in order to assist in the liberation struggle and the consolidation of national independence, they should not overstay their welcome. Africa is not about to throw off one colonial yoke for another. Rather, they should hasten the political, economic, and military capabilities of their African friends to stand on their own.

The Nigerian leader offered the following advice to the West:

To the Western powers, I say that they should act in such a way that we are not led to believe they have different concepts of independence and sovereignty for Africa and for Europe. A new Berlin-type conference is not the appropriate response to the kind thrown up by the recent Kolwezi episode [in Zaire]. Paratroop drops in the twentieth century are no more acceptable to us than the gunboats of the last century were to our ancestors. Convening conferences in Europe and America to decide the fate of Africa raises too many ugly specters which should be best forgotten, both in our and the Europeans' interests.

Obasanjo called upon his African peers to reject military or political alliances fashioned and "teleguided" from Washington, Moscow, or Western Europe. The primary priority, he remonstrated, was for African leaders to grapple with the "cruel dilemmas" that confronted their nations—national integration, effective management of slender resources, and improvement of the material conditions of Africa's more than 500 million people.

FIFTH PHASE—1981-PRESENT: The arrival of the Reagan administration signaled several new departures in American policy. Forged in the crucible of perceived East-West rivalries, most

American policy makers now tended to view African problems in a global context. This demanded significant departures from the Carter period, in that Washington should be prepared to employ all of the instruments at its disposal—including military force—to cope with threats to American friends and allies in Africa. At the same time, the United States would have to fashion programs to help cope with the decline of African economies.

For purposes of analysis and evaluation, the Reagan administration initiatives may be organized along subregional and functional lines. Geographically, the continent was divided into: (1) the northern third, where geostrategic factors were paramount; (2) the middle third, where commercial considerations were overriding; and (3) the southern third, where Assistant Secretary of State Chester A. Crocker fashioned a conceptual design that was anointed as a policy of "constructive engagement."

Like its predecessor, the Reagan administration has evolved through two distinct stages in its approach to North Africa. Continuous throughout has been a view of East-West relations as the decisive factor in shaping the "global balance of power." By this term the Reagan administration means that Soviet attempts to secure a position of global hegemony are the principal challenges confronting the United States and its allies in the 1980s. The willingness of the Soviet Union to attract and support surrogate forces in the Third World, which seek to destabilize unfriendly governments closely associated with the West as well as to assist liberation and terrorist movements, is implied. The imperative for the United States is to frustrate these efforts by providing essential military equipment and, if required, visible evidence of American support by projecting military power into regions where Soviet proxies are threatening the security and stability of their neighbors.

In phase one (1981-82), the Reagan administration moved into a confrontationist posture in North Africa. Almost immediately, Washington (1) denounced the Qadaffi regime in Libya and launched efforts to challenge its annexation claims in Chad and in the Gulf of Sidra; (2) fashioned a special political-military relationship with King Hassan of Morocco for the avowed purpose of "stopping the spread of radical forces in North Africa"; (3) increased American military assistance to selected countries, notably Morocco, Tunisia, Egypt, Sudan, and Somalia, in an effort to buttress their self-defense capabilities; and (4) kept at arm's length the government of Algeria, despite the latter's clearly expressed desire to improve relations with the United States.

The American rebuff to the government of President Chedly ben Jedid proved puzzling in view of the constructive role that it had played in securing the release of American diplomatic hostages in Tehran early in 1981, as well as the significant trade ties that existed between Algeria and the United States. Algiers was particularly troubled by the visit of former Secretary of State Alexander Haig to Morocco in mid-1982, a visit that produced agreement for American access to Moroccan military facilities, by pledges of increased United States arms transfers, and by the announcement that a joint Moroccan-American Military Committee would be established. These developments provoked an unfavorable reaction in Algiers. As I have noted elsewhere:

> What dismayed Algerian policymakers in the reportage of the Haig visit and subsequent developments was the disregard for the intricacies and historic roots of North African political relationships ... the rigidly East-West interpretation placed on the Saharan war (by Washington), and the slighting of Algeria's posture and sensitivities demonstrated by the singlemindedness with which Washington has pressed for stepped-up military collaboration with Rabat.[1]

The timing of the agreement proved disturbing to the Organization of African Unity which was engaged in sensitive diplomatic efforts to broker a negotiated settlement to the western Saharan war. Shortly after the Haig visit, OAU efforts aborted, largely because of reported "lack of flexibility" on the part of the Moroccan government.

Elsewhere in North Africa, the confrontationist posture of the United States was yielding even more dramatic results. In August, 1981, over the objection of the Libyan government, which had laid claim to the Gulf as part of its inland sea, elements of the United States Sixth Fleet embarked on naval exercises in the Gulf of Sidra. This led to the downing of two Libyan aircraft. In the superheated atmosphere that followed, the Qadaffi regime excoriated the United States, threatened retaliatory action, entered into a defense alliance with Ethiopia and the People's Democratic Republic of South Yemen, augmented its purchases of military equipment from the Soviet Union, and intensified efforts to topple Egypt's Anwar Sadat and Sudan's Jafar Nimieri. The assassination of President Sadat in October, 1981, sent shock waves throughout North Africa and so alarmed the Reagan administration that it dispatched AWACS aircraft to Egypt, accelerated the schedule for Rapid Deployment Force maneuvers in Egypt, and directed elements of the Sixth Fleet to the coastal area adjoining the Libyan-Egyptian border. Several weeks later, intelligence reports indicated that a Libyan-financed hit squad had been dispatched to the United States to attack senior government officials, which set off alarm signals in Washington itself.

The latest byproduct of the confrontationist posture has been somewhat less than reassuring. In 1983 the Qadaffi regime widened its efforts to topple the Nimieri government; in February, 1983, fears of a coup led to the reintroduction of American AWACS in Khartoum; Libyan force deployments in northern and central Chad have been augmented in an effort to overthrow the government of Hissen Habre. Concomitantly, Qadaffi's allies, Ethiopia and Yemen, have supported his actions in Sudan and, over the past two years, in Somalia. For its part, the United States has been powerless to forestall these actions and has confined itself to attempts to isolate Qadaffi in the OAU, and to embargo oil trade with Libya, calling as well on American companies to withdraw personnel assigned to Libya. The latter effort has proved unsuccessful—Libya continues to derive substantial American revenue through the international "spot market," and more than 600 American specialists remain in Libya on contract hire.

Phase two in the Reagan administration approach to North Africa opened in mid-1983, when efforts to force a retreat of Libyan forces from Chad proved fruitless. Once again, American air units were deployed to Sudan and a naval force was stationed off the Libyan coast. In addition, emergency supplies of military equipment were rushed to Ndjamena. Nevertheless, Qadaffi proved intractable. Libyan forces, in concert with elements supporting Goukkduni Weddei, continued their attack on Chadian positions. Startled and frustrated by this display of resolution, the Reagan administration turned to Paris in August, 1983, imploring the Mitterrand government to intervene with its armed forces since "Chad remains an African nation within the French sphere of influence." The French government reluctantly complied but, in the interim, has sought to distance itself from the anti-Qadaffi confrontationist strategy of Washington, preferring instead to pursue, initially at least, a diplomatic path to settlement of the dispute.

Probably of greater weight in the quiet shift in Reagan administration approach have been recent efforts on the part of Morocco, Algeria, Tunisia, and Libya to establish a basis for normalization of relations. Beginning early in 1983, King Hassan and President ben Jedid met at the border town of Oujda and announced that their countries would seek to resolve their differences amicably; steps have been taken to reestablish commercial and diplomatic relations between the two countries. These efforts have been emulated by Tunisia and Libya, which have concluded several agreements involving enlargement of commercial ties and the welcoming of thousands of Tunisian workers into Libya, where employment opportunities are ample. In mid-1983, to the surprise of many observers, King Hassan met with Qadaffi in Rabat, and both leaders have indicated willingness to compromise their differences. Thus, reconciliation appears to be in the air in North Africa—a prospect that, if realized, requires a reexamination of some of the basic premises of United States policies in the region. Of course, efforts at normalization and reconciliation have been tried in the past and have failed. Nevertheless, these undertakings, while in progress, afford the United States breathing room to reevaluate past strategies and to explore future policy options. Should the opportunity be seized, the Reagan administration will have to address several critical problems that loom close on the horizon.

By any objective standard, the recent American performance in North Africa has failed to yield significant gains for the United States or for nations in the region that share a community of interests with the United States. The politics of polarization—or confrontation—has merely added to local tensions without clear advantage accruing to any of the adversaries. In the process the United States has lost both a measure of freedom in the policy choices available to it and an opportunity to serve as "honest broker" in local disputes. In the first instance, American options have been narrowed through the process of alliance formation upon which Washington has embarked since 1980. (An effective alliance requires a common set of policies and objectives on the part of its members, and frequent consultation concerning military and diplomatic initiatives contemplated by individual members—conditions that are notably absent in the instance of the United States and its North African friends.) In addition, by aligning itself with particular adversarial groups, the United States has disqualified itself as an arbiter in unfolding conflict situations.

In the middle third of Africa, growing commercial ties have produced an essentially constructive relationship with various African states. During the oil embargo of 1973, Nigeria became the first and is now the second-largest foreign supplier of oil to the United States. Gabon, Liberia, the Ivory Coast, and Kenya are today important trading partners with the United States, and private American investment in the region has grown over the past several years. However, the middle belt of Africa suffers a number of economic frailties, as pointed out by Assistant Secretary of State for African Affairs Chester A. Crocker in an address before the Council on Foreign Relations on October 5, 1983:

> The adverse economic impact of the 1973 and 1979 oil price increases, record high debt servicing costs, galloping inflation rates, and slowed economic expansion due to the recession in the West, have brought many African states to the verge of bankruptcy. Development programs must be scaled down and major internal structural reforms will have to be carried out to weather this crisis. The recent meeting of the international Monetary Fund and World Bank focused on these grim issues and could offer no easy outs, no quick fixes.

The Assistant Secretary was not overstating the case. Two-thirds of the countries designated by the United Nations as being least developed are located in Africa. Over the past decade their difficulties have multiplied as a result of local conflicts, massive droughts, population growth, and declining output. There is in Africa today a permanent food crisis. The Reagan administration has sought to meet the region's needs through a multipronged strategy involving not only emergency supplies of food but a well-conceived program intended to improve local capabilities to increase long-term production of foodstuffs. This has come in the form of a five-year program intended to provide incentives in the area. The magnitude of the program, which is receiving congressional scrutiny at present, is to be on the order of $500 million and, if implemented, should assist African governments to alter existing policies and restructure their own domestic agricultural programs.

In southern Africa, the Reagan administration has diverged somewhat from the policies of the Carter period. With respect to Namibia, it has carried on a negotiating process with the Republic of South Africa to move that territory to independence. The negotiations, first launched in 1977, have been conducted under the auspices of the United Nations, with the United States heading a five-nation Contact Group which includes Great Britain, France, West Germany, and Canada. While progress has been registered, the South African government has demanded, as a precondition for its final agreement, that all Cuban combat troops be withdrawn from neighboring Angola. The United States has supported South Africa in its demands. Thus, should the negotiations falter and ultimately fail due to South African recalcitrance, the United States could earn a substantial measure of African opprobrium and censure.

The Reagan administration has also made a significant tactical shift in its approach to South Africa and its internal policy of apartheid. Unlike President Carter, who adopted a posture of direct confrontation, Reagan and his foreign policy advisers prefer an approach involving constructive engagement. Assistant Secretary Crocker outlined the attributes of this approach in an article published in *Foreign Affairs* prior to his appointment:

> [A] useful building block is ... understanding that European-American collaboration and mutual respect are the only valid

basis for any future undertakings directed toward South Africa — on this or other issues. Similarly, we should continue the readiness under recent U.S. administrations to bring our policies out into the open and to meet publicly with Africa's top leadership when circumstances warrant it. Constructive engagement is consistent with neither the clandestine embrace nor the polecat treatment.[2]

The results of the constructive engagement strategy are inconclusive at this stage. Namibia is not yet independent, nor has South Africa made far-reaching changes in its approach to black-white relationships. However, the time of testing for United States policies will be a lengthy one during which early judgments are likely to prove hazardous at best. What is clear at this juncture, however, is that the Reagan administration's posture is confrontational with some regimes in Africa (Libya and Ethiopia) for geostrategic reasons, and accommodationist with South Africa for the same reasons. This two-track approach requires diplomatic skill and dexterity to achieve positive results in terms of our national objectives.

The United States appears to have come full cycle over the past three decades. Once again, the African continent is at the center of globalist planning and our political-military needs. Whether our hopes and expectations are well-grounded will be determined in the critical period immediately before us.

POLICY GUIDELINES FOR THE FUTURE

The majority of independent African nations suffer from a disturbing number, and a complex mix, of disabilities. Key among them are competing regional and ethnic loyalties, tensions between traditionalists and so-called modernizers, weak bureaucratic structures, and thin administrative networks. These disabilities were reflected in frequent eruptions of violence, civil war, and secessionism. At one point in mid-1982, armed hostilities claimed the western Sahara, Chad, Eritrea, the Ogaden Province of Ethiopia, Uganda, Namibia, and Angola; episodic outbursts claimed other regions and nations with disturbing frequency.

The African continent, as a result, has attracted foreign intervention in various forms, including commando raids and filibustering expeditions by European mercenaries, the injection of Cuban combat troops into Angola and Ethiopia, and the use of French "intervention forces," among others, to protect allies and friendly regimes throughout French-speaking Africa. The continued presence of Cuban forces has produced some uneasiness among African leaders and, in the instance of the governments of Angola and Ethiopia, a realization that Soviet and Cuban military assistance is not an unmixed blessing. Moreover, in southern Africa their support for the MPLA regime at Luanda has resulted in a widening of hostilities and military burdens without compensating involvement in the negotiations dealing with the future status of Namibia in progress among Pretoria, Luanda, and the United Nations contact group led by the United States.

With Reagan's victory in November, 1984, a fresh examination of American policies with respect to Africa appears to be warranted. The size of his popular mandate for a second term might well lead him to conclude that his previous approach has been justified by events of the past four years. A more prudent approach would be to examine where we have been, what has been achieved, and the reasons for policy failures that have materialized.

In evaluating American interests in Africa, it may be useful to address a broad range of questions:

- Should the United States view Africa as a separate, clearly identifiable geographic area or as part of a Third World spectrum in which American interests will be strengthened or weakened depending on how this country responds to deepening African economic crises?

- Does the United States have significant political-military interests in Africa? How do these interests relate to our concerns in adjacent geographic areas?

- Should the United States seek to buttress African military capabilities to meet threats posed by Soviet surrogates? To meet peacekeeping requirements? In short, what arms supply policies would be appropriate for the period immediately ahead?

- What should be the American response to Soviet intervention in local African problems?

South Africa undoubtedly will remain one of the most important factors in any consideration African leaders accord future American policy. Our current posture of restraint has fueled African suspicion regarding American purposes and objectives. An increase in tensions over the next several years, ultimately resulting in outright conflict, may prove the final test by which American policies are judged. While South Africa's virtual defenestration by African and Asian nations from various international organizations may be an ill-considered approach, the United States, for its part, has failed to produce a viable policy alternative. Moreover, from the African perspective, violence and revolution have yielded promising results in the Portuguese territories and, most recently, in Zimbabwe. Should this path be pursued in South Africa, however, the consequences are likely to be more than destabilizing. In due course the United States might well be confronted with a critical choice—to intervene with military force (at African-Asian urging) or to support South Africa's white supremacy regime. Neither alternative would prove acceptable to us, but the lesson to be learned is that an active policy in support of black African aspirations carries with it certain moral and material imperatives that may prove unpalatable.

As our reassessment of American policy begins, we need to sort through the welter of opposing views, positions, and premises in an effort to develop a coherent starting point for United States policy and overall strategy. Set forth below are a series of principles that Chester Crocker and I initially formulated for an article that appeared in *Foreign Policy* during the third-quarter term of the Carter administration. They are presented here for comment and evaluation by specialists in United States foreign policy and strategic planning, as well as by African scholars and officials concerned with America's unfolding role in the decade immediately ahead.

We start from the position that new premises are needed. First, it should be possible for Washington to agree that African turmoil is based simultaneously on African, Soviet, and Western origins. The public dialogue needs to move beyond the simplistic polarities of East-West and black-white conflict. A corollary of this more nuanced line of reasoning is that no neat distinctions can be drawn between African goals and interests, which are "good" and compatible with ours, and Soviet ones, which are not. It is no longer possible to generalize about the "African viewpoint," and Washington should stop using the fictitious concept of African unity to deter itself from doing things it considers to be in its own interest.

Second, African problems and United States-African interests warrant a greater share of American foreign policy resources than they are getting (and have ever gotten before). Real resources in this context mean both intangible political commitment, including commitment to fight hard for budget requests in Congress, and concrete financial and military assets. If private enterprise is, indeed, a potent instrument for advancing American interests, the time has come to conceive means of backing its role in Africa—jointly with others if possible, separately if necessary. To a skeptical Congress and public, Washington must speak more candidly about the effects of continuing our limited and largely verbal activism. By saying "no" to governments that face real problems and which have been traditionally thought of as friendly or at least neutral, we simply invite a further decline in African stability and future Soviet-Cuban adventures. This, in turn, will erode such basic United States interests as the survival of moderate governments, increased African mineral output and Western access to it, accommodation in southern Africa, and a greater degree of balance and restraint in superpower behavior on the continent.

Third, Washington should cease defining, as some officials do, all forms of outside involvement as legitimate or illegitimate. We live in a competitive world, and so does Africa. Some pronouncements seem to imply that Moscow and Havana have a right to work actively against United States and Western interests, a right which is somehow strengthened further if we actively oppose them. This trivializes foreign policy and raises serious questions in Africa and beyond about our purposes.

Fourth, Washington should articulate publicly and candidly its basis for political relationships in Africa. Westerners may have a lower tolerance than others for being openly associated with the barbarity and authoritarianism of some Third World governments. What one should be able to expect is a greater American responsiveness to requests for tangible aid from some of Africa's more decent and more important governments. The criteria for assistance should include: an African government's past and current attitude on issues of both regional and global importance to the United States; its posture on foreign investment and nationalization; its current and potential contribution to regional or international peacekeeping; and an estimate of its likely durability as a governing group in light of the challenges it may face. Additional criteria would focus on the inherent attributes of an African state (rather than its government), including its size, resources, and location in relation to key conflict areas or transport routes.

The mix of criteria to be applied can only be decided on a case-by-case basis. Moreover, greater effort should be made to recognize and support the compatible African efforts of our European allies and our Arab and Chinese friends. France's role in the Horn (at Djibouti), the Maghreb, Zaire, and the Saharan belt of states from Mauritania to Chad remains of pivotal importance to regional stability; we cannot afford the luxury of rhetorical posturing against this still-viable legacy of a former era. On the basis of such premises, it should be possible to identify four major areas of United States policy focus in Africa: (1) containing the damage to American interests in the Horn/Red Sea region by firm support of the Sudanese and Kenyans (as well as neighboring Arab friends across the water); (2) joint Western effort to assure the territorial integrity of Zaire; (3) resolution of the Namibia conflict which does not place Cuban troops on the Orange River and does not require South African troops on the Zambezi and the Cunene; and (4) the curtailment of the spread of radical Arab influence across the Sahara to the porous and weak states on its southern periphery.

Two things should be said about this seemingly ambitious agenda. First, it cannot be done by Washington alone; nor would it need to be. What is needed is active and substantive American participation, sustained by the regular involvement of the highest levels of the administration. Second, it does not require assistance on the scale of the Marshall Plan or the dispatch to Africa of American troops or advisors. The level of tangible resources required to bolster United States interests more effectively could probably be acquired by doubling our bilateral development assistance programs (if designed more flexibly) and tripling government spending on security supporting assistance and military sales. Africa would continue to receive but a fraction of our worldwide aid resources, but it would be a sharply increased fraction and therefore, a far more credible one. The biggest change would occur in our thinking, not our spending.

Would it work? The primary grounds for doubt are domestic. Congressional and public support are unlikely to develop so long as the administration is seen as insincere or confused in Africa. When it scares off domestic support for American activism by warning that direct military intervention would be needed to counter instability and Soviet adventurism, whose effects are defined as transient in any case, the administration guarantees the failure of even its own modest aid efforts. Absent is a forthright and comprehensible statement of the American interest in regional stability and economic access and a description of how United States policies contribute to those ends. If the executive branch made a serious effort, it should be possible to encourage a tolerable level of consensus behind commitments, which at most amount to a 5 to 10 percent increase in overall United States aid resources.

Recent events can serve as instructive guidelines for the future. In rethinking past strategies, the American policy establishment might take account of the following useful precepts:

- *Proportionality:* Exaggeration of problems and threats to American interests, as well as to those of its friends in the region, only diminishes our credibility and the degree of support we can expect to receive from friends and allies in the Middle East, Europe, and Africa.

- *Commensurability:* Differences in perception of existing problems lead inevitably to divergences of approach in problem-solving. These divergences are to be expected and should not be treated to the ambiguities of which diplomats are overly fond.

- *Relevance:* The projection of East-West rivalries into North Africa's endemic problems, or the treatment of these problems in eschatological cold war terms, diminishes the capacity of Washington to influence the decisions made by local governments in efforts to resolve their basic problems.

- *Unilateralism:* It is arrogant in the extreme to presume that the United States is the sole or most important external element capable of shaping the political and economic landscape of North Africa.

North Africa is of greater economic and political importance to the nations of Western Europe than to the United States. They share with Washington a desire to deny both Soviet access to military lodgments in the region, and a commanding Soviet presence in the commercial field. France, Spain, and Italy in particular have substantial stakes in maintaining close and harmonious ties with the region, and their views warrant close consideration by the Reagan administration, especially given their ability to help resolve some of North Africa's existing and anticipated problems.

REFERENCES

1. William H. Lewis, "Why Algeria Matters," *African Index,* March 1, 1982, 5.
2. Chester A. Crocker, "South Africa: Strategy for Change," *Foreign Affairs,* Winter 1981, 346.

Commentary

I. William Zartman

I enjoyed Dr. Lewis's paper very much, and I agree with most of it. It would be presumptuous of me to pick out things that were problems and add some good words of advice. I would certainly emphasize, though, the last point, that we have simply over-played Africa. We promised too much in many cases and we are put in the position of trying to think that we can change things—from African conditions north of the battle line to social/political relations south of the battle line. We cannot change things with the wave of a wand. I cannot disagree with Dr. Lewis because the paper takes an historical view of events that I think puts them in a very tidy order. I would like to pick out just a couple of points and give a view of Africa that is probably not too different from Dr. Lewis's but does differ in several details. This may give some focus to our discussion.

My view is that the place of Africa in the world is as part of the free world—a term that we don't use often enough. Unlike Asia and perhaps parts of the Middle East, and unlike other parts of the world, Africa was not essentially divided by the cold war. Though there are a couple of small exceptions, Africa is an area that has its major ties with the West—its economic ties; its values; its nationalistic movement, political goals, and aspirations. They are closely associated with Western history. I do not mean that Africa is an adjunct of the West; I mean it is part of a community that interacts together, rather than being simply off by itself, or torn between East and West. This means, it seems to me, that Africa is a responsibility of the richer or stronger countries of the West—the United States for example.

It is obvious too that Africa is a non-aligned part of the West. That is, it is not part of a security system in the same sense as some other parts of the Western world such as the North Atlantic. But we have often mixed up alignment and membership in the free world. These are overlapping, but not coincidental. My emphasis in pointing out this responsibility is that this situation bounces back on us. This is not an imposition on Africa; rather, it is something that gives us certain roles to play with respect to Africa. I would like to highlight three results which I think flow from this. To some extent, I agree, and to some extent I disagree, with what Dr. Lewis has pointed out.

The one specific disagreement I have (although I'm not sure we would disagree specifically in applied cases) is that we have a conflict resolution role in Africa. We should be useful where—but not everywhere—we can help African states resolve problems by which they are trapped. I think problems are very often like that. Whether we're talking about the human level or the state level, people get locked into situations which they create for themselves. Here, a helping hand is often quite useful and quite positive. I am not talking about policing. I am not talking about destabilization. I am talking about a useful presence.

There are three cases where we have played varying degrees of a role, from nothing to a great deal, and which we can cite as examples of various things we can do:

The first case is Chad. There we have not tried to play a conflict resolution role. I cite Chad because I think the role of France in this current development (certainly not the last development in regard to Chad) is a useful one. The role of France is exemplary and came in two forms. First of all, France entered in a military sense. (Let me remind everybody that in intervening in a military sense France helped check what I think can only be defined as aggression.) But France also brought in an item of give and take, an element of trade which they could finally bargain away against the other side (the Libyans) for a joint withdrawal of foreign forces. United States policy was to ask France to enter in the first place. There was a lot of misunderstanding that was very regrettable on both sides. We were doing similar things in trying to get our own way, but were getting in each other's way. But, instead of fulminating against the foreign presence in Chad, the French did something, and they definitely played a positive role there.

The second example is the western Sahara. Based on my recent visit, I have the impression that anybody who wants that area to be independent is only stirring up trouble. The basis of an independent viable country, visible in the landscape, is nil. (We can go into this assertion which I think may surprise some people—I hope not too many people. But that is not my point.) Nonetheless, we have a situation here in which a number of countries with which the United States has good relations are locked into a conflict from which they cannot get out. The latest turn of events, beginning with Qadaffi's visit last year, is certainly not the last turn of events in Morocco-Libya relations. It has moved the conflict to a situation that makes it very difficult to handle.

In the first half of 1983, there was a time when Morocco and Algeria were reaching out to touch each other. They felt they understood what each other was about. From there on things began to fall apart simply because the parties were not reading each other clearly. At each turn something unexpected happened, and each party said it had been double-crossed and so on. Each then tried to get even with the other. The fault lies with both Morocco and Algeria. The parties needed some help at that point. The problem was that the United States was not talking to Algeria. We were supporting Morocco in its conviction that it was right, as opposed to making sure that it could get support in the world. At a time when the parties needed help to communicate with each other, the United States was not there. We should have been.

The third example is Namibia. I think we have been trying very hard to play a positive role, and I would even have defended the way the Cuban linkage was brought up in the beginning.

Now I can do nothing but conclude that after four Reagan years, in addition to the four Carter years, nothing has been accomplished. A lot has happened, but no results have been achieved. Moreover, I have very great doubts about the intention of South Africa at this moment. To my mind, the simple key to understanding the situation is that South Africa has not made any decision because it has had no need to do so. Therefore it plays along, not in bad faith, but just keeping things alive, hoping that something else will come up. For our part, we keep on going.

If that is the name of the game, then it is important to bring about the need for a decision. I think we have the need to make some tactical points. Speaking facetiously, the best thing we could have done to get South Africa to make a decision in the third year of the Reagan administration was for that administration to declare that it was going to lose the elections. Now it is too late. I admit that may have been asking a lot. But that aside, there are other things that we can just throw on the table and argue over afterwards. One is that we do have a threat (it is not a sanction) to leave the process and let it rot. I think it is a threat that was used very effectively by Kissinger in very different circumstances in the Middle East in the shuttle negotiations. It is a threat that we have not even dared imagine, and I think we are at fault for that. And, since we now have gotten from the Angolans an offer that is a reasonable basis for discussion, small sticks such as withdrawal of some of the earlier carrots to South Africa can be useful to get that discussion going.

The second point related to our African policy is that, on the continent of Africa, we have a situation in which we have no allies and no enemies. In the global strategic picture I do not think that people should be viewed as the concerted enemies of the United States. If you want me to put it more specifically, Qadaffi is not worthy of our disdain. He is not enough of a dangerous influence in this world to merit all the opprobrium that we have heaped on him. This administration seems to like doing that kind of thing—to pick small people and beat them up. We did that in Grenada and we do it to Qadaffi. There is a certain appeal in that—I guess some cultural anthropologists would say that this appeals to an aspect of American character. But I think that this has been quite counterproductive and quite unworthy of us, to treat an African case in that manner. Please do not misunderstand me. I am not denying Qadaffi is doing outlandish things, or saying that he is a nice guy, or that we should try to sign a treaty with him.

On the other hand I am saying that I have grave doubts about the semi-alliance relationships that we have with a number of African states (Morocco, Somalia, Kenya), and with the leverage that the base agreements give them over us. That troubles me to some extent. I am not talking about good relations. I think we have a history of good relations with countries such as Morocco, Kenya, and others. But I am talking about the specific form of security relations that they have given us. In Dr. Lewis's paper there are some wise words about alliance relationships. But the quality and mutuality of an alliance relationship does not exist between the United States and African states to the extent that can help in the South African situation. I can understand the development of a policy which tries to dispel hostility between the United States and South Africa in order to create the fruitful basis for negotiation on Namibia. I cannot understand the lack of a clearer policy against earlier efforts of destabilization in Africa, and I cannot understand the rationalization that destabilization has led to good agreements, peaceful agreements, and so on. This is to forget that these were based upon bullying, and that is poor international practice.

The third example or element—let me say this outrageously, too—is that in relations with Africa, we are faced with a situation in which there is no Soviet threat, but a tremendous economic threat and, therefore, opportunity. The problem with Africa today (and so many people have said it for such a long time, but now it seems to be more striking than ever before) is that military security is not the problem, but an endemic insecurity in the nature of the societies, reinforced, on the one hand, by a previous Soviet threat and, on the other hand, by a present deepening economic crisis. That is where efforts need to go.

Let us take the Soviet threat, first of all. There is no denying that there are Soviet and Cuban troops in Africa. They are at present in Ethiopia and Angola. But as one looks at reasons why they came in, one sees justified but non-replicable situations. A genuine revolution, as in Ethiopia, recognizable as such in Communist terms, combined with an aggression and occupation of a third of the country by a neighbor, is just not likely to occur elsewhere. And it seems to me that, in this case, the occasion for the Soviet Union coming in was justified. It would have been nice if we could have done it instead, or done something to have kept it from happening, but it was one of those situations where there were few alternatives. Similarly, the possibility of a Marxist-Leninist movement coming to power after ten to fifteen years of struggle, as in Angola, and then needing outside help against the threat of being ousted before the state was set up, is not the kind of situation that is likely to recur. Perhaps some decades down the road this is an evolution that we might hope to avoid in South Africa itself. So the two occasions where the Soviet Union physically entered Africa are really non-replicable. While there is an understandable emphasis in trying to get the Soviet presence out, from an American point of view, I do not find it justified as an overriding fixation. It may be an important policy goal, but I think more important is the fact that the threat is not there in the form that is sometimes imagined or portrayed.

Maybe we need not say a lot about the economic problem. We have seen that options—African options, Western-suggested options, and ideological options—for all the economic recovery, or the economic rebuilding of Africa after independence, have all failed. I think that Africa finds itself internally in an economic mess and in such a situation that even the strongest have defected just to survive. What does this mean? We need to pay more specific attention to aid criteria. One can only argue for more aid while applauding what has been given. One needs imaginative solutions, but again I come back to this notion of responsibility. This does not mean that in two years we can make any African state agriculturally independent, or even try to. But it means that there has to be imaginative addressing of the problem in ways that one could use technology. (I think many of us political scientists are discovering all the intricacies of agriculture, and we drop our subject and leap to discussing farmers and talk about farming relationships as part of our domain.) One of the points that I find very striking in this connection is that after twenty, forty, sixty years of research in institutes of technology for African agriculture, there is not enough known about what is required for tropical agriculture, in terms of technology. This is an area of imaginative solutions that I think we can look into. Again, and the present administration is much concerned with this, this is not a time for adopting the New International Economic Order. That is a woolly affair, and much too big. But it is a time for paying greater attention to the multilateral agencies' aspect of this problem and bringing multilateral help to our overburdened bilateral efforts to give assistance to Africa.

DISCUSSION

The discussion revolved around the major points raised by William Lewis and those of the commentor, I. William Zartman. There was general agreement that the United States does not have the resources to tackle, alone, the problem of preventing turbulence and disorder in Africa. But there was not agreement about whether Africa could be said to be part of the West, because of historical or of sentimental ties and values. The issue of what it means for Africa to be non-aligned, but to have alliance-like relations with Western nations was debated. The role of the French in Chad, and the attempt of the United States to regard that role as important in dealing with the problem there, came in for a great deal of discussion. There were a number of questions about whether the United States should try to emulate France's approach to regional issues in Africa. France was praised for the subtlety of its policies, but also criticized for continuing what was viewed as a "colonial-type" relationship with its former colonies.

In contrast to the pragmatism of the French in dealing with both its friends and opponents in Africa, the United States' policy was viewed as often quite inflexible. We have a tendency to regard some African countries as friends and others as inveterate enemies. There was agreement that states normally have only permanent interests.

Apropos to the lack of flexibility of United States approach to African regional problems was a long debate about the Sahara.

There was some appreciation for the contention that a Saharan state would not be viable, but more critical was the feeling that the United States was not being as "clever" as the North Africans. The Africans were being subtle and self-seeking in a narrow sense while the United States was not. The criticism was that it looked as though the United States' embassies in North Africa were not talking to each other and this lack of coordination harmed our policy in the region. In rebuttal was the suggestion that perhaps the problem was not in the field, but in the State Department itself. There was disagreement about how much power United States ambassadors had in influencing policy which came out of Washington.

There was great concern about the possibility that the United States' policy in the southern Africa region was failing. This was attributed to the hesitation of the United States to lean on South Africa to take bold steps in the region, especially with respect to Namibia, on the threat of United States' leaving the region to stew in its own juice. The failure of the United States to encourage the Angolans to make an offer the South Africans could not refuse was also attributed to the lack of flexibility in our policy toward that region. What alarmed many of the discussants was the absence of African initiatives to solve the political problems in the region. This was viewed as the inability of the United States to have either strong friends or strong enemies among the Africans. The latter was not viewed as totally negative, but the hope was expressed that the United States could pay more attention to the efforts of Africans in southern Africa to create viable regional economic institutions.

Finally, there was some debate about the ability of research institutes of all types to understand the nature of Africa's economic impasse, especially its agricultural system, and to recommend adequate technology to help. Also suggested was that the failure of the United States to help create viable economic approaches to helping Africa, such as the Korry Report (c. 1968) occurred because we did not have the techniques to deal with the problem. The hope was expressed that the United States would add its own bilateral aid to helping the multilateral approaches now attracting the attention of many African countries.

CHAPTER 4

UNITED STATES POLICY TOWARD POLITICAL AND SOCIAL CONFLICT IN AFRICA

Robert I. Rotberg

Of all the obvious violent conflicts of contemporary Africa—the struggle for Chad, the battle for the soul of Ethiopia and its hinterland, the civil war in Uganda, the civil war in the Sudan, and the long-running competition in the western Sahara—none is more consuming and more desperately in need of a new United States policy than the enormously bitter, globalized, and reputedly cataclysmic conflict between white supremacy and majority black aspirations in southern Africa.

Included within the parameters of this confrontation are the struggles for supremacy in Angola and Mozambique, the contentious but less encompassing battles in Lesotho and Swaziland, the much more muted but still dangerous array in Zimbabwe, the war for Namibia, and the central conflict in South Africa. It is this last antagonism around which the others revolve, and to which they all, and much else in the southern half of Africa, relate. Each has been fueled by the heat of the core conflict; each continues to attract the attention of the United States (as well as of the Soviet Union) and the West as potential sources of global rivalry as well as regional instability. Overriding each situation, and at the very nucleus of the South African dilemma itself, is the perpetuation of the fundamental inequality—and the consequent tensions—that stem from apartheid and the maldistribution of power.

The conflict in South and southern Africa is different in character from those elsewhere in Africa. Elsewhere black elites, sometimes supported by external forces, vie for power, access to power, and autonomy (escape from power). But the South African struggle, and thus the surrounding and related battles, is for respect, dignity, participation, privilege, human rights, and civil liberty, as well as access to and the wielding of power in its rawest form.

The making of United States policy respecting a struggle which has close analogies to our own ought to prove easy. But it has instead been enormously difficult, for South Africa, albeit white-ruled and afflicted with the cancer of apartheid, is a strong nation, rich in resources, locally dominant, Western in character and alignment, and historically an associate of the West. Moreover, the United States has long traded with and invested in South Africa. Despite the obvious injustice of apartheid, the United States has been both reluctant and unable to abandon ties and influence or to attack blindly without knowing what would follow. The United States wonders whether or not moral repugnance offers a solid and sustainable basis for the development of workable American policies. Furthermore, the precise location of United States self-interest has always been in question. So has efficacy: If the test of self-interest could be met, would the policy succeed in changing South Africa for the better—presumably making it more humane and just, and providing for the fuller participation in power of the majority?

The nature of the conflict in South Africa is wellknown, and little changed in essentials. South Africa is permanently at war. Its 22 million Africans are subordinated politically, economically, socially, educationally, medically, and in every other conceivable way to the 4.7 million whites who rule South Africa as they have ruled it since the seventeenth century. In addition the whites control the destinies of the 2.6 million Coloureds (persons of mixed white and black descent), and .8 million Asians who are regarded by the South African government as non-white and who fill out the demographic profile of the troubled country.

The war for South Africa has several aspects. Whites, recognizing the enormous disparity between their own and African numbers, fear the kind of shifts in power in their country which would diminish their own preeminence and/or transfer even a scintilla of prerogative to Africans. Thus whites, who have always controlled the governments of South Africa, refuse to give Africans a vote in the national political arena, limit African freedom of movement from the countryside to the town or among towns, make them carry and produce identity documents or passes, closely regulate where they can live, be educated, worship, how they can travel, and with whom they may cohabit. For the same reason the white government denies Africans citizenship in South Africa, and has created ten homelands where Africans supposedly may enjoy political and other privileges. The combination of laws which subjects Africans to white-determined rules is collectively called apartheid, or separation. Other nations oppress their own people, and discriminate against them in one or more ways, but South Africa is the only one which does so exclusively on the basis of color.

Coloureds and Asians are also subject to nearly all of the exactions of apartheid, with an important qualified exception. In 1984 the white government changed its form from one with a Westminster parliament and a ceremonial president to one headed by an executive president and with a legislature consisting of a tricameral parliament with one dominant house for whites and weaker houses for Coloureds and Asians. Coloureds and Asians now vote, but only for representatives to their own racial chambers. Africans still are denied the vote, except in the homelands and in some color-restricted cities.

The other side of the war is black resistance to white domination and subjection. There is sullen, passive rejection of whites, which occurs every day. There is public criticism of the government by a number of harassed but functional political groups like the United Democratic Front, the Azanian People's Organization (AZAPO), the Soweto Committee of Ten, the Forum, and so on. Within the white parliament, too, the Progressive Federal Party attacks the apartheid policies of the ruling National Party. But the major indigenous opponent of white rule is the long-banned African National Congress (ANC), a Soviet-backed guerrilla movement which infiltrates South Africa from outside and periodically sabotages government-owned or government-related installations. Since 1977 the number of incidents has multiplied 200-fold; many insurgents have been captured and tried. South Africa has increased its anti-guerrilla patrols, but the spate of attack on property, and occasionally on individuals, continues largely unabated.

The clash between white and black is for South Africa, but it is not yet a clash of culture (since both sides are Western), of religion (both are more or less Christian), or of ideology (despite the Marxist associations of the ANC). It is a fundamental, basic clash between peoples differentiated solely by color whose overriding grievance is the denial of their birthright and full participation in a country which is theirs, and their white rulers, who want to continue to retain their leading position (and their wealth, privileges, and way of life) in a country which is also theirs. Whites simply refuse to believe that the strong, rich country which they have run for so long (with African labor) can or will remain the same (for them) if Africans share or hold power. Thus prejudice is less the basis of the clash than is a fundamental rivalry for power, and for all that power means in the modern world.

The overriding issue which today separates Africans and whites is, in its starkest sense, political representation. Whites, especially those in government, are prepared now more than ever before to modify the exactions of apartheid in many ways, providing that their own power is in no way eroded. Africans, who welcome increased economic opportunity, the freedom for the first time to form and join trade unions, and a modest provision of social services, insist that they will never be appeased by less than the franchise, and thus at least a meaningful portion of basic political power. They want what they have always wanted—basic human rights in a country which was theirs before the whites came, and in which they were systematically deprived of privileges and power by the might of whites.

Originally a microcosm of the South African situation, Namibia now is a separate but synergistically related zone of conflict where the issues are stark, the solutions largely obvious and widely accepted, and success tantalizingly close at hand, but still (and despite claims to the contrary) beyond easy grasp. There are about 1.1 million indigenous Namibians, approximately 600,000 of whom are Ovambo living in the northernmost eighth of the country. The Kavango, also northerners, the Damara of the central region, and the Herero, also of the central region, number fewer than 100,000 each. The other indigenous peoples all have smaller populations: the Caprivi of the northeast corner, the Tswana and the San who straddle the eastern border with Botswana, the Nama and the Basters of the south, and the Coloureds of the urban center. Of the remaining 70,000 whites, most are Afrikaners, although up to 25,000 were originally German.

South Africa has controlled Namibia since 1915, when its soldiers ousted the Kaiser's Germany. After World War II, the government of South Africa refused to acknowledge that its authority there, which derived from a League of Nations' mandate, had become subordinate to the United Nations. Indeed, in the 1950s South Africa virtually incorporated Namibia. There was an obvious indigenous reaction, leading to the creation of a national political movement, the South West African People's Organization (SWAPO), in 1960. In 1966 SWAPO declared war on South Africa.

That war continues today, although in 1984 at a level less contentious than in the late 1970s. Despite the very disparate strengths of the opposing sides, it is a war which neither seems able or likely to win. SWAPO's guerrillas, now based in Angola, number as many as 5,000. Funded by the Soviet Union, and trained and guided by Soviet and Cuban advisors, they have in recent years infiltrated northern Namibia in small groups, attacked isolated farms and installations, and sabotaged facilities connected to South Africa. Although SWAPO draws most of its support from Ovamboland, and although many Ovambo work throughout Namibia, the guerrillas have rarely proved able to penetrate into the central or southern reaches of the country. Nor have they been able to escalate hostilities and embolden the masses of the countryside.

The 25,000 soldiers of South Africa who defend Namibia from bases in Ovamboland instead maintain the initiative. They have superiority in numbers and boast better training and logistical support. Their intelligence is more than adequate and, most of all, they have the air cover and air surveillance which SWAPO lacks. South Africa has been able to invade Angola with impunity, destroy SWAPO's forward bases, and use innumerable obstacles of distance and disclosure to destroy SWAPO's maneuverability and its attack capability. The Soviets have been unwilling or unable to give SWAPO armaments capable of combating the South Africans. They have also been incapable of preventing South African domination of all of southern Angola. Indeed, only Western diplomatic action can claim to have moderated, if to a limited degree, the extent of South Africa's Angolan outreach and interference.

If SWAPO cannot hope under present circumstances to oust South Africa from Namibia by force of arms, it can expect to win any election in Namibia which is internationally arranged, sponsored, monitored, and presumably free. South Africa has since 1975 been attempting to foster the creation of an indigenous client-type alternative to SWAPO. There are arithmetical grounds for such hope—the existence of an Ovambo majority worries many among their traditional rivals, who obviously need to combine with the whites if a new Namibia is to avoid an eventual rule by its most demographically powerful group. But SWAPO also draws support from all of the non-Ovambo elements in the country, and even from whites. It is regarded as the territory's only legitimate political entity, and all of the possible political substitutes—the Democratic Turnhalle Alliance, the Multiparty Conference, the South West African National Union (SWANU), and a host of smaller parties—have been backed only mildly by Namibians. None has emerged as a plausible or popular middle force. And none will, for the taint of South African backing spells illegitimacy.

Although there has been rough agreement since 1978 between South Africa, the West, the United Nations, and SWAPO concerning under what rules and how an election will be held, no internationally validated balloting which would bring SWAPO to power will be held in Namibia until either South Africa is comfortable with a SWAPO victory and what that result could mean for regional relations or South Africa feels compelled to submit to Western pressure for a similar result. Although there are many reasons why South Africa should want to devolve power in

Namibia quickly, arguments for the retention of the territory have always appeared more powerful.

The war in Namibia is costing South Africa about $2 billion a year, roughly 9 percent of its total annual national budget. With the price of gold low, recessionary pressures continuing, inflation high, and a two-year-old drought an added burden, there are strong voices favoring an exodus from Namibia. Military arguments could also be made: South Africa's own borders provide undeniably easier frontiers to defend. Then, too, a departure from Namibia would demonstrate that the South African government of President Pieter W. Botha was truly bent on reform. South Africa's leaving Namibia would please the West and vindicate recent American policymakers.

But the war for Namibia continues with little sign that South Africa will soon vacate. It goes on despite South Africa's demonstrated ability to exert its will militarily in the region, despite the likelihood that South Africa's might and comparative economic weight could overawe any new government of a state as sparsely populated and economically weak as Namibia, and despite the fact that South Africa has no important financial, resource, or labor dependence upon Namibia.

Why? First, giving up Namibia could have adverse domestic political consequences for the National Party that rules South Africa, but such a result is more and more discounted. Second, a withdrawal of South African troops might bring a Soviet-backed enemy that much closer to the heartland of the white-run regime. But the capital of Marxist Mozambique has always been located geographically much nearer to Pretoria and Johannesburg than Windhoek, Namibia's capital. Anyway, South Africa has proved itself militarily more decisive in the local context than was the Soviet Union. Third, South Africa wants to stay until a credible non-SWAPO local group is ready to receive power. But that day will never come and nearly all influential South Africans now realize that no combination of local interests and persons can conceivably appeal to the ultimate electorate more successfully than SWAPO. Moreover, as much as SWAPO operates with Soviet funds and arms, it cannot be asserted that a SWAPO-run Namibia could evade white South Africa's clutches any more than could the committed leadership of Mozambique.

These are all reasons for delay. But they are balanced or matched by arguments for a positive response. Two additional analyses are vital, if not decisive, in tipping the balance in favor of the status quo. First, for four years the intermediate details as well as the overarching design of United States policy has rewarded South Africa, and thus limited its incentives to depart. Second, without the leverage which control over Namibia gives South Africa in its long standing tug of war with much of the remainder of the world, white rule would stand naked. Namibia is the prime bargaining counter for South Africa. So long as the United States and the West are engaged in the pursuit of Namibian independence, South Africa can afford to forestall Western attacks on apartheid itself, and on the central core of white power. Thus Namibia has diminished value for its own sake, but—particularly so long as Angola welcomes Cuban troops— enhanced worth for the long-run defense of white rule in South Africa.

A solution to the Namibian conflict is intimately related to and intertwined with the war in neighboring Angola. After Portugal relinquished control of its colony in 1975, three African groups competed for the right to succeed. Although the United States supported the Front for the National Liberation of Angola (FNLA), and to some extent backed the Union for the Total Independence of Angola (UNITA), Soviet and Cuban armed assistance to the Movement for the Popular Liberation of Angola (MPLA) proved decisive, especially after South Africa intervened on behalf of UNITA. Later the FNLA became moribund. UNITA, however, began working closely with South Africa and, by the late 1970s, posed a major threat to the MPLA's governance of the new country. In 1984, thanks to South Africa and to widespread support among southern Angolans, UNITA's military prowess threatened the hold of the MPLA government over at least three-fifths of Angola. Recently, UNITA raiders attacked installations in the distant Cabinda enclave, captured foreigners working at the northern diamond mines, attacked a port city, and continued to cut the main railway line with impunity. Only the presence of 25,000 Cuban troops, resident in Angola since 1975, and the guidance of Soviet and East European advisors, prevents an all-out battle for the whole of Angola.

The government of Angola believes itself militarily the equal of the forces of UNITA, but only with Cuban help. The United States has been urging Angola to send the Cubans home in exchange for American recognition and economic aid. The Reagan administration has argued that once the Cubans go, South Africa can be persuaded to leave Namibia. After South Africa pulls back, logistical and air support for UNITA will wither, and a negotiated compromise or political coalition will be possible. Otherwise, Washington has argued, both wars will continue indefinitely, Angola will remain weak, the Soviets and the Cubans will reap their recompense in raw materials and coffee, and the possibilities of domestic growth will remain severely limited.

The Cubans, who last fought the South Africans seriously in 1975, and who rarely engage UNITA, are officially Angola's bulwark as well as its albatross. Their presence provides a convenient excuse for South African intransigence over Namibia. The official United States acceptance of this position has also stymied the efforts of Washington to dampen or end hostilities in both countries. Indeed, American policy for the region is buried beneath the rubble of failed attempts simultaneously to satisfy South Africa over the Cubans and the MPLA government over UNITA/South Africa when every group (for SWAPO must also be included) naturally distrusts the intentions of the others. There are other obvious flaws, too, for a Namibian settlement, and even a South African withdrawal from Namibia, need not guarantee or mandate a South African disengagement from or disavowal of UNITA. Even if it did, without the Cubans the MPLA might well be too weak to hold the guerrillas of UNITA at bay. There are too many imponderables, and too much at stake, for well-meant entreaties to prevail simply on their merits.

In early 1984, there was a flurry of optimism when Mozambique, beleaguered by drought, ravaged by a cyclone, crippled by mismanagement, and severely harassed by a South African-promoted insurgency, signed a humbling peace and friendship treaty. Mozambique pledged to rid its terrain of the ANC, South Africa's prime guerrilla opponent. Despite Mozambique's friendship for the ANC and its abhorrence of apartheid, the former Portuguese colony was prepared to supplicate in order to obtain help. Most of all, South Africa promised Mozambique to cease supporting Renamo, or MNR, the insurgent group. By March, when the Nkomati Accord was signed, Renamo was active in nine-tenths of Mozambique, and had helped to cripple much of the poor country's economy. At about the same time, South Africa persuaded Angola to curb SWAPO in exchange for a withdrawal by South Africa from a 250-mile-long salient of territory which the whites had occupied (as part of their offensive against SWAPO) in 1981 and 1982.

Toward the end of 1984, optimism about South African intentions had faded. Renamo was still active in Mozambique. Economic targets remained vulnerable; the government of Mozambique had not yet begun to derive substantial benefits from its moral sacrifice at the beginning of the year. In Angola, claiming that the MPLA could not curb SWAPO, South Africa had been slow to return its troops to Namibia. In September white soldiers still were sovereign over a 25-mile-deep stretch of the southern section of the country. UNITA had stepped up its attacks on the MPLA-governed parts of Angola. Only in Zimbabwe had South Africa visibly moderated its backing for opponents of the nation's constituted government.

South Africa was supporting an underground movement opposed to the government of President Lebua Jonathan in Lesotho. Paradoxically, the Lesotho Liberation Army, its client, had a Marxist-oriented history. In Swaziland, South Africa had helped to install pliant Swazis in important positions in the transitional neo-monarchy that runs that former British protectorate. In exchange the Swazis moved forcibly against the ANC. Yet, even though South Africa has successfully overawed its smaller neighbors—Lesotho and Swaziland—has made Botswana wary, and has ended the use of Mozambique as an ANC sanctuary, guerrilla attacks on South Africa continued throughout 1984. The destabilization of southern Africa by overt and covert South African military action has thus proved effective—the neighbors have acknowledged their inherent frailties—without achieving either freedom from attack for South Africa or freedom from assault for Lesotho, Mozambique, or Angola.

In terms of the elimination of intraregional conflict—a United States policy objective—there were some positive accomplishments during 1984. With the end of South African assistance, however limited, to the Ndebele rebels in southwestern Zimbabwe, the incipient civil war there has largely been quelled. South Africa claims to have ceased its thoroughgoing involvement with Renamo. Botswana is peaceful. South Africa has not lately raided little Lesotho. Swaziland is calm, at least on the surface. South Africa has backed most of the way out of Angola. Most of all, certainly from the South African and probably from the official United States point of view, the influence of the Soviet Union in the region and on the conflicts of the region has been minimized, effectively by the Angolan-South African ceasefire and the signing of the Nkomati agreement between Mozambique and South Africa. The Soviet Union was shown to be powerless—a paper tiger, even if only temporarily—and unable to help Mozambique, Angola, or SWAPO in their times of need. If a patron cannot assist its clients in a crisis, of what value is patronage?

These recent accomplishments doubtless are contributions to the peaceful evolution of southern Africa. To that extent they can be said to serve the aims in Africa of United States foreign policy. But the fundamental conflicts remain. In South Africa the recent urban riots have testified to the meaninglessness of 1985's white-imposed notions of reform for Africans. A death toll of forty is but a fraction of the totals in the Soweto riots of 1978, but it is forty times greater than the deaths from incidents of urban unrest in the years since 1977. With a less particularized perspective, it is evident that the newly introduced South African constitution and its tricameral parliamentary configuration holds no particular relevance for Africans. Nor are the still-to-be-imposed new urban arrangements advantageous for Africans. With the tightening of controls on unions, the harassment of the UDF, the detention of black leaders, and the government's disavowal of any desire to improve their political position, Africans are as disenchanted as ever with the practical workings as well as the philosophical underpinnings of apartheid. As far as they are concerned, nothing fundamental has changed. There are increased economic opportunities and broader social possibilities—but more so for the black elites and the middle class than for most Africans. Conceivably Africans could derive some political benefit from the participation of Asians and Coloureds in the new parliament, but most Africans (and most liberal whites) doubt that those groups will be able to play a meaningful legislative role in a parliament that will still be dominated thoroughly by whites loyal to the National Party. (The recent low polls by Coloureds and Asians confirmed this disdain by blacks for the new, supposedly reformist, dispensation.)

The external aspect of this same conflict between black and white in South Africa still exists. Despite South Africa's successful assault on ANC basing privileges in Swaziland and Mozambique, and its equally skillful chilling of sanctuary possibilities for the ANC in Lesotho, Botswana, and Zimbabwe, guerrilla attacks show no diminution in quantity or quality. The ANC still survives to destroy fuel storage tanks, government offices in several cities, critical strategic facilities, and so on. Moreover, in the eyes of the mass of blacks, the imprisoned leaders of the ANC are more popular now than in the 1960s and 1970s. According to several different respected opinion polls, Nelson Mandela and Walter Sisulu, the aging, originally militant leaders of the ANC, are the overwhelming favorites of the inhabitants of the black cities and townships. Everything that the white government of South Africa has done to combat the ANC since 1976 has instead enhanced its status and given Mandela and Sisulu the glory of folk heroes.

Beyond South Africa's borders the positive accomplishments of recent months still leave smoldering wars in Angola, Namibia, and Mozambique. The scale of the conflict in Mozambique may lessen by the end of 1985, but the battles for the other two locales seemed certain to continue at their present levels, if not intensify, during late 1984 and 1985.

At the core of all these rivalries, even that of Angola, is the persistence of apartheid. Moreover, the only standing that the Soviets still have in the region is as an opponent of white domination. They lack credibility as a donor or investor, but they do give funds and arms to liberation movements. If the United States is concerned about the Soviet and Cuban threat to stability in southern Africa, and the links which such a threat must continue to have to larger, global antagonisms between East and West, then apartheid is the prime obstacle to a significant reduction in East-West tensions in much of Africa.

The strategic aims of United States policy, despite some tactical changes, are nearly the same as they were in late 1980, before the presidential election of that year. Very little of a positive nature was achieved during the next four years. Indeed, from critical South African perspectives, the years from 1980 to 1984 set the region and black interests in South Africa distinctly back. White South Africa is now more powerful locally and regionally than it was in 1980. Its might is unchallenged in a way which was unthinkable in 1980. Yet the economic and social conditions of its neighbors as well as the economic, social, and political conditions of its internal black majority are more miserable than they were in 1980. Economic mismanagement in the black countries, climatic misfortune, and the sad currents of world economic reverse have all played crucial roles in the neighborhood, but so have the economic and military assaults of South Africa. Within that country, too, the performance of indicators of black economic growth have been spotty. Certainly life in the homelands, where there is abundant malnutrition and overcrowding, is demonstrably poorer. So, too, is it in many cities and towns, where housing and other social services have been curtailed, squatters attacked, and the noose of apartheid tightened. Nor can apologists—not even Elliot Abrams, Assistant Secretary of State for Human Rights—show solid evidence of new political opportunities in South Africa for Africans. The crux of all debates is political participation, and in that fundamental aspect, as in so many other aspects of apartheid, nothing has changed since 1980. South Africa's apartheid remains a charge on the conscience as well as the self-interest of the West.

The Carter administration sought to curtail conflict in southern Africa and accelerate the abolition of apartheid by castigating and isolating South Africa. It fulminated in private and public. It threatened the imposition of unspecified sanctions. It shunned trade, embargoed commodities, minimized investments, and limited lending. Occasionally, it rewarded good efforts. It had a goal: progress toward full political participation by all South Africans regardless of color. It suggested a means: consultation and negotiation between blacks and whites—something along the lines of a constitutional congress. But it never demanded one man, one vote.

The Carter administration can claim several achievements. It compelled South Africa to reverse a long-held position and admit that Namibia was, in fact, an international responsibility and was not, *de facto* or *de jure*, a part of South Africa. It persuaded the South Africans to begin a process of negotiation over Namibia's future which, even if it still limps along, has already resulted in a series of agreements which could, someday, lead to an internationally validated establishment of independence.

Harder to demonstrate is the impact of the policies of the Carter administration on internal improvements in South Africa. The significant labor reforms which were begun then owe at least some debt to Western criticism. One perceptive South African commentator claims that there is no doubt "that the threat of sanctions, boycotts and disinvestment played a role in deciding Pretoria to give trade union rights to blacks."[1] Western carping also encouraged the discussions, however flawed in their ultimate execution, that led to the construction of a new parliament which now includes representatives of dark-pigmented people. Perhaps the Carter policies prevented more relocations and removals than there were, and the razing of more squatter camps.

Perhaps South Africa deferred the destabilization of its neighbors until President Carter lost the election of 1980. Or perhaps the timing of much of the military action against South Africa's neighbors reflected changes in official thinking and military tactics which were unconnected with the shift in American policy.

Whatever the etiology of South African resurgence in the 1980s, there is no doubt that in 1984 its armed forces were stronger and bolder than they were in 1980. None can dispute their willingness to attack and overawe their neighbors by one after another audacious raid. Indeed, in 1983-84, they faced down the Soviets, and won. Toward the end of the Carter years, South Africa did raid SWAPO bases in Angola. But the wholesale adoption of this tactic, and the occupation of large areas of territory occurred during the Reagan administration's watch. So did air attacks on Maputo and Maseru, the subversion of Swaziland, and the promotion of a wholly concocted insurgency movement in nearby Mozambique.

South Africa tried in the 1980s to give Swaziland large chunks of homeland South Africa. Near its internal homelands it relocated, removed, and shifted nearly a million Africans with impunity. It sharply reduced the numbers of persons banned, but continued to detain and interrogate Africans for long periods without charges or trials. South African critics of their government have claimed that human rights and civil liberties for blacks have deteriorated severely during the Reagan years. The policy of constructive engagement which was introduced with fanfare in 1981 as a break with the Carter administration's antagonism, has brought little discernible improvement to the daily life of blacks in South Africa. The main cruelties of the apartheid system—the forced removal of Africans from so-called white areas; the relentless inferiority of black education, health, and housing; and the security laws that give police virtually unlimited powers to enforce racial codes—all remain intact.[2] Outside of South Africa, Namibia is still held in thrall, and Angola is menaced by UNITA, Mozambique by Renamo, and Lesotho by the Liberation Army.

Constructive engagement was designed to do what it has not—to deliver Namibia, end globally-connected and South African-inspired conflict in the region, and start South Africa down the evolutionary road toward fuller political participation for all. Constructive engagement stresses friendship and relaxed dealings with white South Africa. As a result, and despite the Reagan administration's reiterated abhorrence of apartheid, American relations with South Africa since 1980 have been much more amicable than at any time since 1960. This closeness—even bonhomie and camaraderie—was intended to produce positive results.

Chester Crocker, Assistant Secretary of State for Africa, and the well-meaning architect of constructive engagement, summarized his personal approach in an interview with a South African magazine editor. He was asked how he perceived the relationship in 1984 between the United States and South Africa, "especially in view of past posturing." Crocker replied:

One develops personal familiarity with key decision-makers which pays dividends. We hope that we have achieved that with

South Africa and with other key countries in the region. It's a two way street—a matter of developing a track record. Undoubtedly one can over time do business more effectively when one knows the people at the table, where they are coming from, and how they tend to think and operate. We take the South African Government as an important and serious partner. We share certain goals. We see clearly where we don't agree. The past few years have been a learning process. I believe each government takes the other seriously—which has not always been the case.[3]

Crocker persistently rejects claims that white control of South Africa has been strengthened during his time in office. "The dynamic we see," he recently told *The Guardian,* "is one of growing debate, open discussion and ferment in the white community, but also among Coloureds and Asians." He said that the South African government "has decided to test its own power base" by broadening the nature of its parliamentary representation. He believed that the Nkomati Accord dealt "a body blow" to the illusion that armed struggle would solve South Africa's problems. The Nkomati agreement was important because it endorsed sovereignty for South Africa's neighbors as well as itself, and showed the importance of statehood and survival. It also presaged economic cooperation. On Namibia, Crocker blamed the Cubans for the failure to achieve independence. This was the rock on which constructive engagement had truly foundered. But Crocker explained: "There has to be something in it for everybody, including the party which controls Namibia today. There is no doubt in our minds that the South Africans would like to see a settlement in Namibia sooner than later."[4]

To engage South Africa constructively was less venal than naive. The South Africans, confident of the power of their Namibian hand, simply dangled the specter of cooperation before inexperienced game theorists who had foresworn sanctions (and therefore the employment of effective sticks). Crocker and his associates were left with carrots, each and all of which the South Africans were pleased to consume. The United States relaxed its commercial embargo, reaffirmed intelligence links, moderated public criticism at home and abroad, and affirmed closer relations in and with South Africa. But the biggest carrot of all was the Cuban issue. To have made the Cubans hostage for Namibia reversed the entire drift of negotiations, permitted South Africa to relax, and has delayed independence indefinitely. For no Angolan government could easily throw itself on the mercy of the West (and South Africa) when UNITA remained a clear and present danger.

Crocker and his associates may still think that they can square the unholy triangle, but to believe so is optimistic. The United States has made dozens of concessions. South Africa has been rewarded. But there has been no attempt at operant conditioning. South Africa has feared no little punishment. Indeed, the basic flaw in constructive engagement was, and is, its lack of an incentive structure. The concessions were made willy-nilly, in no hierarchical sequence which might have commanded South African attention, if not positive performances.

What next? It *is* in the self-interest of a United States government which wants to minimize conflict in southern Africa, negate the influence of the Soviet Union in that region, and encourage conditions there favorable to rising standards of living and broader political participation (not to mention justice, equity, and human rights), to devise a new policy which will achieve short- and long-term results without instantly forfeiting the ability to influence trends as they develop. We do want evolution rather than revolution to be South Africa's fate, providing that the evolution is progressive and that it commences soon and proceeds at a more than deliberate pace. We want South Africa to remain prosperous, but in shared hands. We want South Africa to continue producing its minerals and crops, and to play a greater and more responsible role in the politics and economics of Africa.

The test of a new policy will be its ability to concentrate the mind of official South Africa—to pull or push the oligarchical state to think anew about its real options in the world, in the region, and at home. By rewarding positive trends and withholding rewards or ensuring at least verbal unpleasantness for negative departures, South Africa could again begin to appreciate the real risks of acts and policies deplored by the West. Since 1980 South Africa has borne almost no cost, suffered no shame or obloquy, and (among whites at home) accelerated from strength to strength. There are sanctions which can be threatened, mostly in the field of communications and transport. If necessary, at minimal cost to the United States, those threats could be made real. Continued lending and investment could be subject to progress along defined paths, as Senator Paul Tsongas once proposed. Boycotts of various kinds are possible. But it is the aggregate of pressure that matters. It will prove influential only when the leaders of white South Africa count the cost too high and agree to sit down to talk with the true leaders of the black community. The point is not to strike out blindly at South Africa but to devise a carefully calibrated series of incentives which that country could reasonably be expected to seek and which would bring about the major policy shifts which black leaders in South Africa, many whites, and many foreigners, so patently desire.

In exchange for its continued friendship, the possibility of broadened trade relations and increased investments, the United States can expect the cessation of destabilization, a swift finalizing of the independence arrangements for Namibia, and a beginning to the long and arduous process of negotiating new internal political instructions and arrangements with representatives of the majority. It can encourage the gradual decay of apartheid and the slow but necessary integration of Africans into the fabric of what is now a powerful, privileged white society. These overdue utopian steps will be wrenching, painful, and will take time. The United States has a role not as an arbitrator, but as a catalyst and, if absolutely necessary, as a facilitator. Since any reorientation of policy, American or South African, will take time and patience, there are a few interim postures which ought to be struck by official Americans in South Africa, and by the United States with regard to the South African question more generally. We should search for the pressure points of the white society, and make it known that we *do* intend to push hard—but fairly—on those very spots. We ought to offer more vocal public and private criticism of South African misconceptions and missteps. Not for moral but for bargaining reasons we should have expressed our outrage at the attempt to give KaNgwane and Ingwavumaland to Swaziland. We missed an opportunity at Dreifontein, after Saul

Mkhize's death, to put white South Africa on the metaphorical rack. We can specify particular goals in the labor and industrial fields, quietly if necessary, but firmly. We can help find funds for black schooling. We need publicly to resume contacts with black opponents of the white government, affirmations of friendship which have subtly been permitted to wither during the Reagan years. We need to take black politics seriously, an omission of recent times. We can talk to the ANC, abroad. We can fruitfully employ the multinational contact group formula to give even more weight to any determined approach to South Africa.

Is this an efficacious formula? Certainly, at least in theory. Its flaw is its "Pollyannaish" quality. But its virtue is in stressing the obvious. Certainly a policy of carrots without sticks has been shown unworkable and foolish. A policy of sticks alone will achieve nothing. There is a middle way, but whether the vicissitudes of real time and real events will permit an incentive-based, hierarchically structured, simple psychological model to achieve results in the complex environment of white-dominated South Africa is more a hope than a promise. However, such a shift is imperative if our own foreign policy needs are to be achieved, and if progress is to be attempted in the modernizing of South Africa.

REFERENCES

1. Alister Sparks, *The Star Weekly,* July 30, 1984.

2. Glenn Frankel, "South Africa and the Black Homelands," *The Washington Post,* July 29, 1984.

3. Interview between Hugh Murray and Chester Crocker, "Crocker," *Leadership SA,* III, 2 (1984), 41.

4. Crocker, quoted in *The Guardian,* 1984.

DISCUSSION

United States response to political and social conflict in South Africa dominated the discussion. There was not much disagreement with the allegation that because of the administration's emphasis on southern Africa, it failed to develop a coherent foreign policy toward the rest of Africa. The criticism was voiced that, while normally a country's foreign policy toward a world region would encompass a coherent approach to trade, aid, the military, and educational and cultural problems there, the United States was reduced to dealing in an *ad hoc* manner with almost all African affairs outside of South Africa. The result, according to one discussant, was a vagueness which prevented most of the African states from knowing how to respond to United States initiatives. Most were convinced that somehow the United States posture toward South Africa and the Soviet Union would determine everything. Faced with this lack of coherence, many African states allegedly were forced into an unaligned position when a more coherent United States policy might have encouraged them to act otherwise.

The point was repeatedly made, and seldom challenged, that the administration's policy of constructive engagement did not live up to its original intention of encouraging South Africa to move towards a more just and effective way of dealing with its overwhelming black majority. Failure here was attributed to the reluctance of United States officials to exact a sufficient *quid pro quo* from South Africa, thereby stimulating change. One discussant remarked that instead of "using a carrot and a stick," the administration never even used a "twig." This allegedly left the South Africans free to exploit United States fears of Soviet penetration of the region and relentlessly to pursue its policy of apartheid.

There was rejection of the suggestion that the United States was not interested in ending apartheid. Instead, there was a comment that the administration's overcommitment to constructive engagement placed its practitioners in such a situation that they applauded even slight and cosmetic changes in the Republic. Again, the allegation that the United States was ignoring the ethical problems posed by overt racism and doing business with a "pigmentocracy" was countered with a statement that in foreign relations, power, rather than sentiment, was the operating principle. A further suggestion was made that policies such as constructive engagement, when applied to South Africa, would not work unless "calibrated" in such a manner so as to exact the greatest change possible in the behavior of the country to which they are applied.

The opinion that the United States does not have the economic leverage to induce South Africa to change its policy toward the blacks was challenged. The 17 percent investment of United States businesses in the Republic was deemed "not insignificant" since only West Germany and perhaps Great Britain did more business there. It was pointed out that tightening restrictions in those "gray" areas of United States-South African relations might bring that regime around. Examples cited were: United States prohibition of landing rights to South African airplanes at Houston; United States attempt to make the Sullivan principles mandatory for most businesses; and encouraging the boycott of krugerrands as a prelude to stiffer economic restrictions.

South Africa's lack of movement on Namibia was cited as further evidence of the failure of constructive engagement. It was alleged that linking the withdrawal of Cubans from Angola with pressure against the South Africans to release Namibia was a grave mistake. It was doubted that Angola would expel the Cubans unless convinced that it could deal effectively with UNITA. And since this was deemed questionable, the suggestion was that the MPLA would not agree to a Cuban departure. The result was, according to the speaker, that United States policy effectively permitted the South Africans to stand pat in Namibia. Another discussant suggested that the United States could have suggested to South Africa that it was quite easy to "Finlandize" Namibia (that is, to transform that state into a supple neighbor, if not a client state), even if Namibia received independence under the United Nations plan.

The influence of United States policy on South Africa's behavior toward the states in the eastern part of the region was scrutinized. It was charged that South Africa's pressure against Botswana had forced a normally anti-Communist state to consider overtures from the Soviet Union, thereby vitiating a major thrust of our global policy. And while South Africa was viewed as powerful enough to pressure Mozambique to sign the Nkomati Accord, thereby demonstrating to the other regional states that the Soviets could or would not help Marxist-Leninist converts, doubt was expressed that this development was a victory for the United States in the cold war. One discussant expressed deep confusion regarding the "contradiction" which led the administration to grant "non-lethal" aid to Mozambique to defend itself against the MNR.

Viewed as equally dangerous for the United States in southern Africa has been the alleged domination of Swaziland by South Africa. Concern was expressed that this development would exacerbate the succession issue there. Activities such as these did convince some discussants that in sum, constructive engagement has resulted in a stronger and more belligerent South Africa. It was felt that the United States should have been working to help South Africa become the type of country that could use its natural preeminence in the region as a source of regional strength rather than regional conflict.

United States neglect of events outside of South Africa was given as one of the reasons why the Libya-Morocco understanding may be detrimental to our policy in North Africa and toward Chad. It was suggested that perhaps the State Department could do little to prevent the impending instability in Morocco and Libya. One speaker suggested that United States policy had served to weaken Polisario, but that it was too soon to expect the cessation of conflict in that area. Another discussant declared that while the United States should have been pleased with France's role in Chad, the issue there is far from clear. It was doubted that the French would keep their promise to return to Chad if Qadaffi were to violate his mutual withdrawal treaty with them.

Several discussants felt that the United States kept open the possibility of reestablishing amicable relations with the Ethiopians by not taking the option of establishing a naval base at Berbera. The decision of the Ethiopian government to install a vanguard Marxist-Leninist Communist party was viewed by one observer as not really affecting the country. It was held that the decision of the United States to provide food for the starving Ethiopians even though opposed to their government indicated that in periods of crisis, American principles still held. The suggestion was made that by working with the West Germans and the Scandinavians, who were providing most famine relief in Ethiopia, the United States could effect a rapprochement with the government of Ethiopia.

CHAPTER 5

UNITED STATES FOREIGN POLICY TOWARD REFUGEES AND IMMIGRANTS IN AFRICA

Mabel M. Smythe

Give me your tired, your poor,
Your huddled masses yearning to breathe free,
The wretched refuse of your teeming shore.
Send these, the homeless, tempest-tost to me,
I lift my lamp beside the golden door!
—Emma Goldman

Emma Goldman's evocative lines have done their part to fix in the popular mind the image of the United States as a great and generous haven for the world's dispossessed. Although this perception enjoys widespread acceptance in the 1980s, there is simultaneously a much more complex reaction to the stranger at our gates. It follows a decade of dramatic experiences with the boat people of Indochina, with Mexican and Haitian migrants seeking a better life without attending to the legal niceties, with Biafran and Ethiopian students reluctant to return home—to name only a few components of the rich pastiche of our recent experiences with refugees and immigrants. Many of those groups arrived at a time when the American public was more openly than ever before reassessing "the melting pot" in favor of the "pluralistic society." A major issue in the reassessment was whether educational instruction ought to be provided in the immigrants' native languages or in the English of their adopted country. At the same time, after a period of liberalism in which it was not considered acceptable to be openly racist or anti-foreign, American unions were pointing to the labor market depression caused by the influx of desperate job-seekers, just as the oil crisis was slowing down the economy.

Most of this concern for labor competition did not have Africa in mind. The number of Africans seeking to immigrate did not compare with the waves of Europeans, Latin Americans, and Asians who sought asylum. The number grew at times—during the Biafran War, during the Ethiopian conflict when Haile Selassie was deposed, during the intensification of hostilities over Eritrea, and during periods of heightened nationalistic fervor in southern Africa. For a time, growing numbers of African students remained to work after completing their education, often with some tentativeness; the Organization for African Unity (OAU) made no secret of its unhappiness over the possibiilty that American universities would foster individual ambition when newly independent African states had such urgent need of their foreign-trained personnel to help with nation-building.

The United States was caught between its traditional commitment to individuals' rights to self-determination and its wish to cooperate with friendly African governments. Under the watchful eye of black Americans, there was an ever-present consciousness that racism might be a factor in our being less hospitable to black applicants for immigration than to others. American immigration procedures and practices were criticized by Africans as giving preference to the talented, the educated, the ones best able to contribute to African development. Yet the fact remains that at a time when the United States was increasingly restrictive in admitting aliens in general, Africans did not find admission easy.

Surprisingly, the mostly small and undramatic movement of African refugees and other immigrants to the United States has made an impact on this country. African economists at the World Bank, professors in American colleges and universities, and taxicab drivers in large American cities are increasingly visible. Many of them see their future as repatriation to the countries of their birth; but after five or ten years of living in a developed country where people speak their minds with little concern for the consequences, many of them are ill-equipped to return to homelands with vastly different cultural expectations, especially if they have wives and children accustomed to American life.

REFUGEES

The concern for African refugees became acute in the late 1970s, when hostilities between Ethiopia and Somalia and the Eritrean-Ethiopian conflict raised the African refugee total to three million. Moreover, fighting in the western Sahara, Chad, southern Africa, Uganda and other trouble spots continued to spew forth refugees. According to the International Conference for Assistance to Refugees in Africa (ICARA) literature, the number of African refugees rose to an estimated five million—half the world's refugee population. Ethiopia alone produced a million persons, 60 percent as large as the total outflow from Indochina.[1]

The United States' initial response to such an immense problem was to identify it as a humanitarian emergency, deserving of international burden-sharing. This was in keeping with our support of the role of the United Nations High Commissioner for Refugees (UNHCR), whose post was established early in the history of the United Nations when Jewish refugees from Hitler's Germany were the focus of world attention. First and foremost, those refugees seemed to need an international legal status which would protect them from exploitation and inhumane treatment. The issue of providing food and shelter for refugees came later; the role of UNHCR continues to change in response to the evolving refugee characteristics and needs. History has expanded that role, which is still growing and changing.

Then as now, the humanitarian role of providing disaster relief—food, shelter, and perhaps health care—for the refugees is obviously basic and easily justified. It is also politically popular, possibly because it puts donors in a position psychologically superior to that of the recipients of their largesse, who become objects of charity. Whatever the reason, the picture of a starving child is clearly believed by fundraisers to be more appealing to the American public than any number of adults in need of vocational training and self-reliance. Survival is for some reason persuasive to people who often show little understanding of the need for a quality of life worth living. This cluster of values may justify lifesaving emergency action without any consideration of how that life will serve its owner, family, and neighbors.

Specific to Africa, familiarity with the needs of the people suggests that saving the lives of refugees is useless and may even increase the misery of themselves and their neighbors unless they can be helped to achieve self-reliance and contribute to the economic life around them. Dependency demeans them and leaves them unable to regard themselves as productive members of society. At the same time, the focus on survival stems from the tendency of the public to respond without question when life is threatened; it also fits into the traditional image of the United States as protector of the dispossessed. We were not alone in our short-term humanitarianism emphasis; the UNHCR lacked a mandate to involve itself in such concerns as education and economic development, and the United Nations bureaucracy was not geared for the flexible rearrangement of responsibilities a more ambitious and longer-term approach would require.

Yet experience consistently has shown that the short-term approach is inadequate. Emergency camps, set up in haste to handle a crisis situation, have sometimes remained in active use, sheltering many of the same refugees after a decade or more. The problem has not gone away; and many of the causes show no sign of weakening, let alone disappearing. A growing awareness of the necessity for addressing the root causes and stopping or at least reducing the refugee flow began to raise the question as to whether the OAU had been right in opting to maintain existing colonial boundaries. Those arbitrary boundaries kept together traditional enemies, divided loyal ethnic groups among two or more national jurisdictions, and maintained the basis for border disputes which clearly had merit on both sides. The longer those borders remain, the vested interests with a stake in maintaining them will grow larger and more entrenched, and the wisdom of Solomon will be required to disentangle them. Addressing the root causes will not be an easy or a short-term task. It will require painstaking diplomacy and great statesmanship, neither of which is in abundant supply.[2] The United States identified the exploration of root causes as an urgent requirement for the Second International Conference on Assistance to Refugees in Africa (ICARA II).[3] There are currently heavy pressures within the OAU to reopen and deal with the question of boundaries and ethnic reunification.

Over the past five years, a more persuasive and immediate change has been developing in dealing with the issue of African refugees. There is an African tradition of hospitality which has ameliorated problems of refugees by providing them with a welcome, even when the host country has few resources to share. The world has had to recognize that many—in fact most— African "countries of asylum" (COA) are themselves in serious straits, unable to feed their own populations without outside help and in a precarious financial position due to severe indebtedness. Worse, few of them have been blessed with experienced and capable management, so their scarce resources may not be used with maximum effectiveness.

With the help of the United Nations Development Program, the World Bank, the International Monetary Fund, the African Development Bank and Fund, and other international agencies and donors, these countries are now actively planning for economic development and pursuing strategies arrived at in consultation with international planning specialists. However, when a neighboring crisis dumps in a nation's lap an indeterminate number of refugees (fleeing on foot without resources, needing immediate assistance with food, shelter and emergency health care), a nation's prepared strategy and development plan are at once rendered obsolete. Demographic data change—often significantly; food requirement estimates are no longer valid; refugee camp land can no longer be used for its targeted purpose, and the question of access to the camp area for delivery of food and other supplies changes infrastructure plans and budget. If, as everyone hopes, the refugees' stay is short, the COA is out of pocket. If the cause of the hostilities or other source of disturbance is prolonged and the emergency remains, the government of the COA generally resorts to a request for assistance from the UNHCR and perhaps other donors which, in any case, are supporters of UNHCR. It is therefore important to recognize that there is no surplus remaining from relief funds, and the net effect of dependent refugees on the economic well-being of the COA is negative at best.

If, on the other hand, refugees can become self-reliant or can be integrated into the economic development plans of the COA, it is possible for economic development questions to be addressed in the context of refugee care and support and for refugee arrangements to be integrated into the economic development strategy of the COA. Replication can be avoided, vocational training and other benefits can be shared by citizens and refugees alike, and the two populations can forge a means of working together constructively for positive goals while avoiding wasteful parallel facilities. The prospect of mutual benefit makes cooperation more likely than would competition. Best of all, mutual benefit promotes united efforts for the overall goal of economic development.

In the past six years private voluntary organizations (PVOs), academic researchers, United States government offices responsible for refugee matters, and United Nations agencies increasingly have become convinced that the strategy of caring for refugees within the context of economic development is valid and appropriate. It is vitally important that plans for development take into account the realities of the needs of all parties. Continued economic development requires both a clear understanding of the consequences of the refugee presence and such material remedies and resources as the relevant agencies and donor community can develop.

Refugees who cannot yet return home are generally better off if they are not required to move to distant countries, primarily because they are likely to have greater understanding of, and be more easily absorbed by, neighboring ethnic groups than by those who are relatively strange; it usually minimizes psychological adjustments and costs to resettle refugees in the country of first asylum if they cannot return home. Moreover, if conditions change so that they can return home, it is easier for them to do so if they have not traveled very far.

Except for the young, urban, education-oriented refugee who seeks a university scholarship, there is not a heavy demand to be resettled in developed countries. As has been pointed out above, the OAU has made it clear that it does not favor the prospect of a "brain drain" of the best-trained and ablest refugees to developed countries from which, once settled, they are unlikely to return to a less certain economic and political future in Africa. The wishes and perceived interests of such refugees, therefore, are in conflict with national development interests as viewed by those in power. The United States, geared philosophically to respond to individuals, has a budgetary interest in keeping the influx to a minimum, even if the relatively low priority given to Africa and the racial implications of such an inflow did not skew the response.

Refugees, like most of the African population, tend to come from rural backgrounds and are better prepared for placement in a similar community. The bulk of them do not seek distant opportunities and would not find it easy to make the adjustment to a new linguistic and cultural environment.

United States policy tends toward providing relief for those who have fled their countries to escape drought and the resulting hunger crisis. As in the case of other refugees, it supports UNHCR initiatives. These refugees are generally farmers or pastoral nomads. If, however, they have not crossed an international boundary in their flight, they are defined as displaced persons, rather than refugees, and are not within the mandate of UNHCR. The United States government maintains both Food for Peace and Disaster Relief offices within the Agency for International Development, and contributes to international emergency relief programs; however, it provides no special support for seekers of better economic opportunities.

Table 1.1
Budget Requests for African Refugees, 1983– 85

Fiscal Year	Amount
1983	$64,171,000
1984	53,800,000
1985	54,500,000

SOURCE: U.S. Department of State. FY 85 and Supplemental FY 85 Migration and Refugee Assistance Programs (Washington, D.C., 1984), 1256.

UNITED STATES POLICY TOWARD REFUGEES

As has been noted above, the United States government has long been associated with generosity toward humanitarian crises, such as the plight of African refugees. At ICARA I its pledge of $285,000 constituted more than half the funds raised worldwide. ICARA II was not a pledging conference, and any increases in budget inspired by this conference will require a supplemental request to Congress. There are, of course, provisions for supplemental budget requests for unforeseen needs, and Table 1.1 is taken from a recent submission to the Congress.

The declining budget for refugees accompanies a dwindling estimate in the number of refugees, now 2.063 million, compared with five million in 1981 (ICARA I).[4] The United Nations High Commissioner for Refugees offers a higher estimate: four million.[5] Reliable statistics are not easy to come by in the constantly changing world of refugee camps and unregistered city refugees, and those who provide them are seldom disinterested observers.

In addition to the decline in the estimated numbers of refugees, the figures reflect several changes in policy which are worth noting:

1. The Reagan administration has made clear its intention to shift some responsibility for refugee assistance from government to the private sector. In the words of Ambassador H. Eugene Douglas, United States Coordinator for Refugee Affairs:

We are committed to returning the principal responsibility for the resettlement of refugees to the private sector, albeit with adequate Federal assistance in the early stages.... [6]

2. The consolidated or per capita grant program will be used, again in the words of Ambassador Douglas:

... to provide states with much needed flexibility in their approaches to helping refugees obtain self-sufficiency and make them more accountable for the successes and failures of their management.... The status quo needs improvement and the best improvements come from the local level—not from Washington.

....The initiative is intended as a first step toward local solutions to the welfare dependency problem.

Congress is currently debating its initiative to bar refugee access from public cash assistance for the first 90 days they are in the country.... Though the Administration has several problems with the proposed legislation, I agree with the underlying premise that traditional sponsorship and other private initiatives must be revived....

The Administration's refugee team will continue to explore alternative programs for the delivery of services to refugees other than through the current federal and state welfare network....

We will also continue to encourage self-help initiatives by refugee community organizations specifically aimed at refugee small business development. [7]

3. A reduction in the expense of handling refugees can be realized through "emphasis on cost effectiveness and sound managerial practice," according to James N. Purcell, Jr., Director of the Bureau for Refugee Programs in the Department of State. His concern extends to the operation of UNHCR, which has not been noted for its efficiency. [8] At the same time, one might note that

some of the defects come from operating in circumstances dependent upon the cooperation of the COA and from shortcomings in quantity as well as quality of professional staff.

4. The UNHCR will be encouraged to expand its roster of donors and correct the attitude of some donor countries that the United States will take care of the problem, a belief that has had currency for some years. In the present administration, the coordinator has organized a group of countries offering asylum (Australia, Canada, Japan, and the United States) and which will meet with the UNHCR to discuss policy issues, in the hope of increasing the effectiveness of resettlement programs.

5. It has been decided to hold down resettlement of refugees and to bring pressure to bear on countries of origin to take back those who fled in the past. This, however, is a delicate issue, because for some time there has been a generally accepted principle that repatriation would not result from external pressure on the refugee, but must be voluntary. Ambassador Douglas suggests some awareness of this problem when he argues that "repatriation must be rehabilitated as a moral and practically worldwide refugee picture, even though it will face us all with difficult, at times even tragic, choices."[9] Those concerned for the safety and protection of refugees must ask to what extent this issue has been thought through and under what circumstances "tragic choices" may be made in the number of refugees resettled in the United States for reasons of budgetary savings or reduction. In a sense the drawing of boundaries to American humanitarianism by budget restriction is nothing new; it is the acceptance of tragic choices that makes us pause, since until now we could always assume that the budget or admissions quota would be adjusted in the case of personal tragedy.

If we consider overall the changes in policy, we note that philosophical commitment to humanitarian concern has given way to a businesslike preoccupation with efficiency, and refugees are subtly reminded not to be more troublesome than is absolutely necessary. There is a presumption that any who are resettled in the United States will be ready to "hit the ground running" and adjust quickly to a job situation, since they are not to have access to welfare or other such programs on arrival. Presumably, private sponsors will be asked to support them in the beginning, with federal assistance available in some cases.

Given this policy background, the notes of an observer at ICARA II are illuminating. She recalls that ICARA I grew out of the concern that the African countries which were offering asylum to millions of refugees might be suffering the loss of development opportunity as a consequence. ICARA I was intended to step up the burden-sharing and to attract development-oriented assistance to relieve some of the strain; $570 million in funding announced at that conference was in part made up of already-committed funds. By 1983 the funding was just about exhausted—and the end of the refugee flows was nowhere in sight. A second conference was proposed, but "the majority of donor countries, and the United States in particular, emphatically rejected the idea of ICARA II as a pledging conference." They wanted durable solutions, mainly the resettlement of the refugees in the African country of asylum, as well as serious attention to the root causes of refugee movements. Since, consequently, ICARA II did not result in pledging, the amount of assistance forthcoming for development-related refugee projects cannot be assessed. However, there was a clear concensus that the impact of refugees on economic development in the countries of asylum should be addressed, and quickly. That point of view is widely shared now throughout the bureaucracy in both the United States (and other donor countries) and the United Nations agencies, although it may have a lower priority at policy-making levels. In fact, Bradford Morse, Administrator of the United Nations Development Programme, said in his address to ICARA II:

[The General Assembly] mandated this Conference to consider the impact imposed on the national economies of the African countries concerned and to provide them with the assistance required to strengthen their social and economic infrastructure so as to enable them to cope with the burden of dealing with large numbers of refugees and returnees.

The General Assembly has recognized that in order to help refugees move from their present condition ... into full participation in the development process, it is necessary to build up the physical, social and economic infrastructures in the countries of settlement. This can ... be done [only] by linking refugee settlements to the rest of the country with roads and other communication facilities; by enhancing their education and training; by strengthening facilities for health, sanitation and clean water; and above all, by providing the increased support that will increase the refugees' productive capability, whether it be in agriculture, fisheries, forestry or in other human endeavours. It is crucial that all development projects to assist countries of settlement benefit not only refugees and returnees, but also nationals in neighbouring communities.[10]

Chester A. Crocker, Assistant Secretary of State for African Affairs, recognized the penultimate principle when he reported in January, 1984, that a "significant approach has been our $1.5 million training and education program for southern African refugees aimed at making them self-sufficient and alleviating the burden they represent to host countries."[11]

Those who speak for the refugee programs in the Department of State seem so far to have put less emphasis on the benefits of integrating refugee programs into the economic development of the countries of asylum, despite two statements in a new publication of the Department of State, produced for ICARA II:

Experts have discussed the link between refugees and development for years. The message of ICARA II is that the time has come for the international community to act, to find solutions.

....The infrastructural burdens that large numbers of refugees place on African countries of asylum did not emerge overnight. Nor will they be disposed of easily or quickly. They should be addressed as long-term needs that will require long-term solutions. The United States has taken a leading role in adopting this approach and is committed to it for the future.[12]

There is persuasive logic in coordinating economic development and refugee programs. Refugees and unskilled local populations require vocational and literacy training; both are dependent on roads and communications which are in short supply. Why not develop training programs for them together, reachable by roads placed where they can be accessible to both? Why not plan camps or resettlement areas where local citizens can also benefit from the communications or schools being provided? Why can they not share health clinics and dispensaries, water systems, and electrical power sources? Since many of these benefits come only when the density of local population justifies the expense, why not combine populations to speed progress? Even if the stage of rapid progress has not yet been reached, the potential for greater cost of coordinated programs undoubtedly inhibits some planners who recognize that developing refugee self-reliance costs more per year than merely providing them with the bare essentials for survival. However, it is cheaper in the long run to make them self-supporting citizens than to support them as dependents for years. We are penny-wise and pound-foolish if we save money by continuing to maintain refugee camps indefinitely, as is happening all too often. To foster the will to be a self-reliant, contributing citizen of whatever country becomes one's home is to provide the maximum chance of survival.

AFRICAN IMMIGRATION

The black population of the United States is an "old" population, descended chiefly from the slave population brought from Africa before the slave trade was outlawed. Very little immigration since the Civil War has affected it.[13] Geographic distance and cultural and political ties to former metropolitan powers are obvious reasons why the United States would be unlikely to attract large numbers of contemporary African immigrants. It is difficult to assess African reaction to such factors as the American reputa-

Table 1.2
Immigration into the United States, 1820–1981

Last residence	1820	1820–1981	1981
All countries	8,385	50,252,552	596,600
Africa	1	172,281	15,029

SOURCE: U.S. Department of Justice, Immigration and Naturalization Service, 1981 Statistical Yearbook of the Immigration and Naturalization Service, Washington, D.C., 2–4.

tion for race discrimination or the sense of obligation to their own ethnic group or nation.

African immigration, recorded as a total of one in 1820 (see Table 1.2), increased very gradually over the years. In 1981 all immigration from the African continent amounted to 15,029. Over the 162 years between 1820 and 1981, inclusive, it totaled 172,281 out of the 50,252,552 immigrants to the United States from all over the world. In other words, Africa provided about one-third of one percent of United States immigration through 1981.

Since the definition of the term "refugee" by the United States Immigration and Naturalization Service is not the same as the UNHCR definition, we should note the precise wording of Public Law 96-Sec. 212 (a)(42), as amended in what is known as the Refugee Act of 1980:

The term "refugee" means (A) any person who is outside any country of such person's nationality or, in the case of a person having no nationality, is outside any country in which such person last habitually resided, and who is unable or unwilling to return to, and is unable or unwilling to avail himself or herself of the protection of, that country because of persecution or a well-founded fear of persecution on account of race, religion, nationality, membership in a particular social group, or political opinion, or (B) in such special circumstances as the President after appropriate consultation (as defined in Section 207(e) of this Act) may specify, any person who is within the country of such person's nationality, or, in the case of a person having no nationality, within the country in which such person is habitually residing, and who is persecuted or who has a well-founded fear of persecution on account of race, religion, nationality, membership in a particular social group, or political opinion. The term "refugee" does not include any person who ordered, incited, assisted, or otherwise participated in the persecution of any person on account of race, religion, nationality, membership in a particular social group, or political opinion.

A number of Africans already in the United States as diplomats, students, employees of international agencies, or otherwise have asked for asylum under the following Sec. 108 of the same statute:

(a) The Attorney General shall establish a procedure for an alien physically present in the United States or at a land border or port of entry, irrespective of such alien's status, to apply for asylum, and the alien may be granted asylum in the discretion of the Attorney General if the Attorney General determines that such alien is a refugee within the meaning of Section 101 (a)(42)(A).

(b) Asylum granted under subsection (a) may be terminated if the Attorney General, pursuant to such regulations as the Attorney General may prescribe, determines that the alien is no longer a refugee within the meaning of Section 101(a)(42)(A) owing to a change in circumstances in the alien's country of nationality or, in the case of an alien having no nationality, in the country in which the alien last habitually resided.

Opening immigration to African, as well as European and Asian, refugees has been a domestic, rather than an international, issue brought to the fore by the African refugee crisis. But of greater concern to black Americans than to the OAU, is the fate of those urban refugees whose educational aspirations can best be met in developed countries or whose past political activities make them unwelcome or especially vulnerable in Afrian countries of asylum. The number of refugees to be admitted from each country is set by the President after appropriate consulta-

Table 1.3
African Refugees and Asylees
FY-83 (10/82-9/83) and FY-84 (10/83-6/84)

Country of origin	Approved/granted		Denied		Pending	
Refugees	FY-83	FY-84	FY-83	FY-84	FY-83	FY-84
Angola	10	63	4	122		
Cameroon	0	0	0	1		
Ethiopia	2,592	1,594	725	1,112		
Lesotho	0	11	1	3		
Malawi	1	6	0	0		
Mozambique	11	26	1	4		
Namibia	3	12	6	3		
Somalia	0	0	2	0		
South Africa	14	7	13	54		
Zaire	11	32	5	5		
Asylum cases						
Ethiopia	213	258	576	737	1,410	631
Ghana	14	8	14	32	57	76
Liberia	8	2	52	98	137	85
Somalia	2	31	46	168	214	120
South Africa	12	5	8	5	43	3
Uganda	14	38	60	75	172	102
All Africa	266	353	765	1,135	2,077	1,082

SOURCE: Letter to the author from Doris M. Meissner, Executive Associate
Commissioner, Immigration and Naturalization Service, dated August 24,
1984, Attachments A and B.

tion as provided in P.L. 96-212. The category for all Africa was set at 3,000 in 1984, as in other recent years. This number presumably reflects the level of interest in emigration to the United States, as well as the availability of alternatives in other countries of asylum, among other considerations.

By far the largest group of African refugees seeking admission to the United States comes from Ethiopia (see Table 1.3). Some 213 out of 266 Africans granted asylum in Fiscal Year 1983 were Ethiopian; in the first nine months of FY-84 they constituted 258 of the 353 approved. Similarly, there were 1,594 Ethiopians out of 1,751 African refugees approved for entry in FY-84, and 2,592 out of the 2,642 approved in FY-83.

The figures are not impressive: they make the point that emigration to the United States is not high on the priority list of either Africans (refugees or others) or American policy makers—despite the importance of this safety valve to a number of potential contributors to African development.

WORKING TOWARD POLICY OBJECTIVES

In view of the objectives of initiatives now being espoused by the community of refugee professionals, academics, and bureaucrats—including our own—where do our policies fit? What values do we announce in our policy statements and in our handling of the refugee emergency?

If we made a list, it might look something like the following, in rough order of their importance to us:

1. *Prudence* (i.e., protecting our own selfish interests): We act in ways which will discourage recipients from taking undue advantage of our kindness and generosity, which will leave a role for other donors and perhaps motivate their assumption of a fair share of responsibility, thus limiting the cost of our relief activities.

2. *Humanity,* or responding to suffering with compassionate assistance: We send food for the hungry and devise ways to reach refugee camps when the roads are impassable; we respond dramatically to sudden disasters and mobilize awesome power in real emergencies. (It is more difficult to move us as a people when the need is undramatic or routine.)

3. *Omnipotence*: We (sometimes unwittingly) enjoy the power which comes with our ability to provide for life and to stave off death; we are all too often less scrupulous than we might be about making sure that our decisions and procedures have the informed consent of those upon whom we visit our largesse. When does deciding who-gets-what cross the line that separates helpfulness from officious interference in the lives of others? We try to be wise and fair, but do we who are so often accused of

worshipping power really have enough respect for helpless people (especially those who do not share our state of development or, for that matter, our religions or ideologies) to give proper weight to their priorities and preferences? Do we honestly care about their views? How do we communicate to our policy-makers our sense of the importance of such issues?

4. *Efficiency*: We envision ourselves as able to make things work through good management of resources, yet we have typically put our greatest efforts in the African refugee area into short-run, stop-gap arrangements, when longer-run programs and procedures are clearly indicated. We are coming to recognize the impact of refugees on development in the countries which take them in, but our policies have not assumed the leadership in the current movement to integrate refugee programs into the economic development plans of the host country. Is the short-run need to minimize our national budget inhibiting our ability to take steps which may cost more today but will greatly reduce dependency tomorrow and save our budgets a great deal more in the long run? In short, are we shrewd only within a narrow time span—and reckless regarding the more distant future?

5. *Responsibility*: Our concern for finding the root causes of refugee flows and dealing with them is a logical outcome of experience which demonstrates that this source of human misery shows no sign of abatement. Yet an additional aspect of responsibility is to consider the problem as a whole in all of its ramifications.

Our moral courage sometimes ascends beyond what is politically expedient. As a people, we are capable of sudden and effective action. One of my most dramatic memories of the State Department is of the emergency when Iraq declared war on Iran and failed to supply Somalia with its accustomed fuel for transportation—essential for delivering food to distant refugee camps. In those camps were people whose undernourished bodies could not survive more than three days without food. People in the Department went to work creatively and in three days had identified fuel tankers at sea within two days of a Somali port, and an American oil company with a supply in a nearby African country (red tape had to be cut in two countries to get it exported to Somalia); even helicopters were located in the event that trucks could not make delivery in time. Clearly, we can do the spectacular; we enjoy rising to such a challenge.

But can we do the unspectacular? Can we work patiently with diverse people to build development in an African environment which has little to recommend it? Can we find a way to advance the economic development of both the refugees and their hosts, considering their needs and wishes and working with sometimes diverse donors to produce an effective plan for cooperative action? We have seen our private voluntary agencies work effectively to such ends; can we not align our policies with this spirit?

It is with this less exciting but profoundly real challenge that we need the best of our creative powers, the broadest of our vision, and the deepest wells of our resourcefulness and understanding. We can and we must deemphasize our infatuation with dramatic life-and-death rescues and get at the hard job: economic development with refugees in place while we also grapple with the root causes and try to bring an end to the outpouring of suffering which is inherent in the African refugee problem.

NOTES

1. Edward J. Derwinski, Statement before the Senate Judiciary Committee, September 26, 1983, *Proposed Refugee Admissions for FY1984.* Current Policy No. 517, U.S. Department of State, Washington, D.C., 1.

2. Ibid., 6.

3. A. E. Dewey, Statement at the informal meeting of the Executive Committee of the United Nations High Commissioner for Refugees, Geneva, Switzerland, January 25, 1984. Public Information Series: *Refugee Aid and Development,* U.S. Department of State, Bureau of Public Affairs, 2.

4. Ibid., 1265.

5. Paul Hartling, "Succor for Africa's Refugees," *The Christian Science Monitor,* July 6, 1984, 1.

6. H. Eugene Douglas, Statement before the Senate Judiciary Committee, September 26, 1983, *Proposed Refugee Admissions for FY 1984,* Current Policy No. 517, U.S. Department of State, Washington, D.C., 6.

7. Ibid., 7.

8. James N. Purcell, Jr., *Refugees: Overseas Aid and Domestic Admissions,* Current Policy No. 571, U.S. Department of State, Bureau of Public Affairs, Washington D.C., 1984, 32–33.

9. Douglas, 6.

10. Bradford Morse, *Statement by Mr. Bradford Morse, Administrator of the United Nations Development Programme to the Second International Conference on Assistance to Refugees in Africa,* Geneva, July 9, 1984, 5. (Photocopied typescript)

11. Chester A. Crocker, "Reagan Administration's Africa Policy: A Progress Report," Department of State *Bulletin,* 84: 2082 (January, 1984), 40.

12. U.S. Department of State, *African Refugees: A Time for Solutions; The U.S. Government Role,* Washington, D.C., 1984, 1–5.

13. Karl E. and Alma F. Taeuber, "The Black Population in the United States," in Mabel M. Smythe, ed., *The Black American Reference Book* (Englewood Cliffs, NJ: Prentice-Hall, 1976), 162.

REFERENCES

James N. Purcell, Jr., Statement before the Subcommittee on Immigration and Refugee Policy of the Senate Judiciary Committee, June 20, 1983, *Refugees: A Continuing Concern,* Current Policy No. 496, U.S. Department of State, Washington, D.C., 1983.

George Schultz, "The U.S. and Africa in the 1980s," Department of State *Bulletin,* Vol. 84, No. 2085 (April, 1984), 9–11.

U.S. Department of Justice, Immigration and Naturalization Service. *1981 Statistical Yearbook of the Immigration and Naturalization Service.* Washington, D.C. (1982).

U.S. Department of State. *FY85 and Supplemental FY84 Migration and Refugee Assistance Programs.* Washington, D.C. (1984).

U.S. Immigration and Naturalization Service. *Statistical Yearbook.* Washington, D.C. (1982).

Commentary

Roger P. Winter

There is a system the international community has constructed for protecting and developing solutions for the world's refugees. It is not at all perfect; it depends for its viability on the good faith adherence of governments to internationally-agreed-upon principles. Compared to most international systems, it functions reasonably well.

The international system was originally designed to apply to persons who met the fundamental refugee test of having a well-founded fear of persecution in their homeland because of the individual's race, religion, political opinion, or similar situation. The underlying obligation assumed by governments adhering to internationally accepted principles is that of *non-refoulement*. Essentially this means if the person fled persecution in his homeland, do not forcibly send him back.

Over the last several decades, the nations of Africa north of South Africa have been viewed as more generous than much of the rest of the world when faced with an influx of refugees from neighboring countries. This generous attitude is demonstrated by the legal definition of refugee adopted by the Assembly of Heads of State and Government of the Organization of African

Unity on September 10, 1969. In addition to accepting the international definition of refugee included in the 1967 Protocol on the Status of Refugees, the Convention Governing the Specific Aspects of Refugee Problems in Africa also applies the term refugee to:

> ... every person who, owing to external aggression, occupation, foreign domination or events seriously disturbing public order in either part or the whole of his country of origin or nationality, is compelled to leave his place of habitual residence in order to seek refuge in another place outside his country of origin or nationality.

If the United States accepted a definition this generous, virtually all Salvadorans in this country would be permitted to stay here until things settled down in El Salvador.

At the conference on the Situation of Refugees in Africa, held May 7–17, 1979, at Arusha, the delegates stressed their support for all of the important principles of refugee protection generally accepted by the international community. In its closing statement, the conference:

> stressed the importance of the scrupulous observance of the principle of *non-refoulement* expressed in the various international instruments and notably in Article II paragraph 3 of the OAU Refugee Convention which prohibits measures such as rejection at the frontier, return or expulsion, which would compel a refugee to return to or remain in a territory where he has reason to fear persecution, and recommends that this principle be incorporated, as appropriate, in the national law of African States; [and]

> Condemns the existence and conclusion of agreements of whatever kind concluded between African States permitting the forcible return of refugees to their country of origin, contrary to the principles of asylum as prescribed, *inter alia* in the 1969 OAU Refugee Convention....

Notwithstanding individual breaches of common intent, these principles earned the African continent a constructive, exemplary reputation in refugee protection and treatment. Unfortunately the fabric of refugee protection in Africa shows clear signs of unraveling. This disturbing trend holds great negative implications for individual refugees in Africa and for the international system of refugee protection. As a consequence, counteracting this development should be an integral feature of United States policy towards Africa. With this in mind, I offer the following examples:

DJIBOUTI: In 1982 Djibouti forcibly repatriated a number of refugees to Ethiopia. By 1983 Djibouti had made clear to UNHCR and others that it would renounce its obligations under international refugee covenants and forcibly repatriate *all* Ethiopian refugees unless UNHCR worked out an acceptable repatriation scheme. The resulting program was initiated in September, 1983. The problem here is not the repatriation itself but rather the serious threat of mass *refoulement* that engendered it.

ZAMBIA: Once well respected for its treatment of refugees, Zambia, throughout 1983 and 1984, has repeatedly forcibly repatriated refugees from Angola, Zimbabwe, and Malawi. Refugees have been returned to the border in shackles; some have been killed resisting *refoulement.* Some authorities believe Zambia now has the worst refugee protection record on the continent north of South Africa and that agreements of a more or less formal nature exist between Zambia and contiguous nations to repatriate refugees involuntarily under certain conditions.

UGANDA: Consistent with Uganda's sad recent history of mistreatment of its own citizens, the nation has also been a key factor in refugee matters. Nearly a million of its people are internally displaced or outside the country as refugees. The Ugandan government has the somewhat unique record of having (at least) allowed or (at worst) conducted attacks on Rwandan refugees who had been resettled over twenty years in Uganda. While much of the world considered these refugees to be "firmly resettled," they were displaced and dispossessed along with ethnic Rwandan citizens of Uganda beginning in October, 1982. A total of nearly 100,000 were uprooted through December, 1983.

KENYA AND TANZANIA: In 1983 President Nyerere of Tanzania received the Nansen Award for his and his nation's helpful treatment of refugees. In late 1983 Tanzanian and Kenyan officials arrested and exchanged dissidents, including a number of documented refugees.

In addition, in February, 1984, Tanzania and Uganda agreed that 10,000 ethnic Rwandans expelled from Uganda in December, 1983, would be repatriated. The agreement did not preclude the use of force.

These examples may seem little different from other examples of harsh treatment of aliens, such as Nigeria's expulsion of Ghanaians or the expulsion of Zambians from Zaire which occurred in September, 1984. But these refugee matters are in fact different, not necessarily in human terms, but clearly so in legal terms. The international covenants on refugees are some of the few examples of instances where the international community has established legal, almost moral, standards by which the actions of a sovereign government can be judged with respect to its treatment of its own nationals or the persecuted nationals of other nations. Because of this relatively advanced international consensus on refugee treatment, repeated violations that undercut the effectiveness of these international standards must be of concern to the entire world community. They should also be taken seriously in the formulation of United States foreign policy toward African states.

I do not mean to suggest African states are unique in demonstrating an erosion of high standards of refugee protection. This phenomenon is seen elsewhere in the world and in a pronounced fashion in the developed world. Nevertheless, because of the reputation Africa had gained, this deterioration is widely viewed as discouraging.

Why has this occurred? Frankly, I do not believe there is a simple, definitive answer. Some factors, at least, are clear. One of these, of course, is the constricted economic atmosphere the world has suffered over the last few years. Many of the less developed nations, a condition widely represented on the continent, have suffered mightily during this period. When resources are short, the alien often becomes a target.

However, another factor is that promotion of refugee protection by the developed Western world has become less of a priority than it was a few short years ago. In some cases, donor nations such as the United States may have found their political willingness or even moral position to criticize the restrictive refugee practices of less developed countries undercut by their own restrictive policies.

Development and economic aid, of course, enter the logic of this discussion at a variety of points. It has long been recognized that, since refugees are a matter of concern to the international community, that community has an obligation to share the burden of nations who receive refugees from neighboring states, in order to help enable that nation to live up to the standards of protection and treatment the international community has set. This concept of burden-sharing is obviously of great importance when the country of asylum is poor or less developed. The Arusha conference recognized "that effective implementation in Africa of the principles relating to asylum will be further advanced by the strengthening and development of institutional arrangements for burden-sharing adapted within the framework of African solidarity and international cooperation as defined in paragraph 8 of the Preamble and Article II paragraph 4 of the 1969 OAU Refugee Convention."

The logic here, I believe, is inexorable. Although burden-sharing can involve initiatives other than aid, bilateral and international aid must be viewed as important tools of the international community in both the prevention and ultimate solution of refugee episodes. Aid is also of critical use in maintaining adequate standards of protection while refugees are in asylum.

While the utilization of bilateral aid in these matters is more easily understood, that of international sources is often even more important. The capacities of institutions like the World Bank or International Monetary Fund, however, seem seldom to be brought to bear on refugee matters.

It is easy to understand why such institutions do not wish to take on the role of human rights or refugee monitor of client nations. This simply is not their mandate. However, when a client government actually generates economic disruption of its own economy or that of a neighbor by precipitating a refugee flow, and therefore impinges on matters that are a part of that institution's mandate either in a sending or receiving country, then I believe the institution would be derelict not to take such developments into account.

In this context I am reminded of a conversation I had with a representative of the IMF on the economic disruption caused by Uganda's displacement of ethnic Rwandans in October, 1982. He postulated the theoretical possibility that Uganda could in the long run be better off economically by purging itself of "dissident elements." Notwithstanding that scary possibility, I pointed out that certainly Rwanda, the poor and overpopulated recipient of 44,000 of Uganda's displaced, would not likely be benefited. He remarked somewhat blindly, "Yes, but we (IMF) don't have a program in Rwanda."

There are cases where aid policy can and ought to be used by the international community and bilateral donors to help prevent new refugee flows; to assist with integration of refugees in the nations providing asylum—including longer-term development assistance to both refugees and host country nationals—and to assist with reintegration of refugees who voluntarily choose to return to their homeland for whatever reason.

Nevertheless, while there is much justified talk within refugee-expert circles on the role of assistance in these three ways, I am concerned that its utility in fostering refugee protection in its most basic elements is not receiving the clear focus it merits. The dangers from a humanitarian perspective are such that aid must be utilized as a tool to prevent nations from mistreating citizens to avoid refugee flows; to foster high standards of protection of refugees while they are in asylum; to reinforce the international community's commitment to non-refoulement; and, to use UN-ese, as "a preemptory norm from which no derogation is permitted."

The United States needs to begin to take this issue seriously in Africa. I have great admiration for Eliott Abrams's recent initiative regarding human rights violations in Uganda. However, in general, United States policy over the last few years has shown little awareness of the need to support those African govern-ments that take the high road regarding refugee protection, and to use the carrot-and-stick approach towards others, or of enlist-ing other governments and international institutions in such an effort. What is needed is not crippling punishment of offending governments but, rather, creative use of leverage to support internationally accepted principles.

On a related matter, resettlement from Africa to the United States or elsewhere has always been a sideshow in the overall picture of refugees in Africa. Policymakers of the Western world, with almost undisguised relief, applaud the widely held belief of persons such as President Nyerere, who in his opening address to the Arusha Conference declared that African "refugees are indi-viduals with a right to life in Africa. All need a chance to re-create their lives in Africa, and to regain the dignity of being self-reliant and making a contribution to the development of our continent."

The American people tend to think of the concepts "refugee" and "resettlement in the United States" as inextricably linked. This is not so generally, and really is not the case in Africa. While some African refugees are and should continue to be resettled in the United States and elsewhere, the largest challenge to United States policy regarding refugees in Africa is in assisting African nations to retain or regain a high standard of refugee protection so that the reputation for generosity deserved in the past is equally deserved now. Prevention of refoulement is the linchpin of the whole scheme. Almost everything else is negotiable.

DISCUSSION

Much of the commentary and discussion of this paper revolved around issues such as the growing erosion of the African tradi-tion of asylum; the plight of persons displaced for economic reasons; the repatriation of refugees; and the changing attitude of the United States to granting asylum to the disinherited of the earth.

It was generally conceded that the OAU should take the lead in halting the growing tendency of African states to expel refugees in order to gain favor with the countries from which the refugees came. At the same time the OAU was applauded for insisting that the place for African refugees was in Africa, rather than on foreign continents. The problem which both the OAU and the United States faced was said to be those cases where the "mind-set" of the African refugees militated against accepting asylum in other areas of Africa. Even when so settled, many refugees continued to regard themselves as displaced persons. The insistence of the current United States administration that many political refugees return to their homelands with a change of government, or when the political climate shifted, was judged too inflexible. It was suggested that more attention should be paid to the demonstrated willingness of most African refugees to return home *when conditions were propitious,* before assuming that they have to be forced to do so.

The plight of "economic refugees" such as the Ghanaians expelled from Nigeria, was discussed at length. One discussant cited the general lack of interest, both among African states and the Reagan administration, in such disasters. It was suggested that the absence of a "pogrom-like" atmosphere (such as in the Ghanaian-Nigerian case) prevented the African states from reacting. The attitude of the United States was attributed to our general policy against accepting "economic refugees." It was pointed out that the American private organizations did attempt to help the Ghanaians, but their funds were limited.

The growing attempt of the administration to "privatize" refugee assistance was the subject of much discussion. Questions were raised about the amount of funds available to private groups, the real source of the funds (whether private or government) and whether, here again, the emphasis on the private sector did not represent a general unwillingness to grant official aid to African states. There was also general concern that, from President Carter's time onward, the United States began to view refugee relief in budgetary rather than in humanitarian terms. There was an admission that there were limited funds; more troubling was the fear that the United States was retreating from the tradition that always showed concern for the poor and the destitute.

A number of discussants agreed with the presenter and the commentator that, with the exception of the Ethiopians, relatively few Africans wished to emigrate to the United States. But attention was called to the inability of increasing numbers of other Africans to emigrate to this country. The suggestion here was that the United States should recognize the "old country" status of Africa as a source of immigrants and that it should recognize that many urban and highly educated Africans wish to come here in order to improve their lives as other people do. Nevertheless, given distance, cost, and concern for racial problems, the United States should not fear that the level of immigration from Africa will ever become high.

Finally, the desirability of recognizing and dealing with the impact of refugees on the development plans of their COA was broached. There was a feeling that the growing emphasis on economic aid in contrast to humanitarian concerns was really counterproductive. The two types of aid were viewed as inseparable. Nevertheless, it was suggested that many local aid officials do not readily like to revamp their aid requests. It was much easier to seek a policy directive from Washington if there was really the will to address the plight of refugees when planning economic development in African countries.

CHAPTER 6

UNITED STATES RESPONSE TO AFRICAN EDUCATIONAL AND CULTURAL POLICIES

Marie Davis Gadsden

In the late spring of 1959 when Secretary of State Herter ordered the immediate dispatch of a teacher of English as a foreign language to the Republic of Guinea, I learned once and for all that educational and cultural policies—like almost everything else in foreign policy formation—are political expedients dictated by the priorities and pressures of time, place, personality, and human prejudices. United States foreign policy toward Africa in education and culture has altered imperceptibly since 1959. Explicit policy—such as it is or has been—was then non-existent for Africa as a vital aspect of United States international concern. From the daily schedules at the Presidence with the English translator for President Sekou Toure to the seventeen ministries where the United States TEFL specialist was expected to conduct regular language tutorials, one learned quickly that the United States dealt with Guinea *through* their NATO ally (the French), and that even the United States ambassador—a black diplomat— was at times by-passed by the State Department, as decisions were made directly with the French embassy in Washington and in Conakry. My professional colleague, the president's interpreter, was French, and her daily translation tasks, which it was my duty to edit, provided interesting insights into the reality of the shaping of foreign policy. It was the common and derisive comment of most Frenchmen in Guinea that the United States took its orders from France. It is this introductory bias regarding the reality of United States foreign policy which conditions this cursory discussion of African educational and cultural policies and the United States response.

For the purposes of discussion here, certain assumptions are basic. Education is perceived as encompassing *all* schooling—formal, non-formal, and informal, as well as continuing education. Education is construed to be an indispensable social, economic, and political *investment.* Education has demonstrable impact on sectors other than production: It also influences health, population, culture, and environmental quality. It is, therefore, a commonplace (especially since the publication of Gray Becker's *Human Capital* in 1964) to talk of human development. What in the 1950s began as "manpower" development is now addressed as human development. Dramatic gains in the developing world in the three decades since then include increased life expectancy (42 to 54 years), a doubling of average incomes, and an impressive rise in literacy (from 30 to more than 50 percent). This focus on human capital and human development brings into sharp relief, however, the continuing and widening human disparities between the peoples of developing nations and of industrial nations. While more than 600 million adults in LDCs are illiterate, and one-third of primary school-age children (and nearly 50 percent of the girls) receive no schooling,[1] much remains to be done to achieve the goals of human development espoused at least rhetorically by the fifty or more nations of the continent of Africa. No responsible African official or concerned African citizen questions as the crucial element the *human* factor in African development.

Inextricable from the education context is the cultural milieu in which and for which the education is to be formulated, implemented, and evaluated. In this sense, educational effectiveness and efficiency cannot be measured only in quantitative terms, cost-benefit ratios, or economic investment potential. As Aklilu Habte cites in *Education and National Development,*[2] one must pose the question, "Is the role of education merely economic or does national development imply development in its broadest context—in culture, in language/linguistics, in technology, in the arts, in law, in history, in environmental intelligence or perceptions, in geo–political perspicacity, in research/documentation/archival resources, and in administration/management?"

To explore with any validity or credibility the educational and cultural policies of Africa is to appreciate fully that no concord, no consensus, no authoritative pronouncements on culture or education exist which establish beyond question the policy issues germane to these two critical dimensions of national and continental responsibility. More than a decade ago, a former African diplomat asserted in his introduction to *U.S. Policy Toward Africa* that:

> U.S. policy toward Africa is in a state of flux and thus provides a unique opportunity for the African States to develop initiatives and a joint policy in the interest of the primary aspirations of Africa. This will require concerted action on the part of the African Nations—clear definition of their objectives, resolute planning, and prompt action. Regretably the diplomacy of the African States ... particularly in the U.S., has been relatively ineffectual.[3]

African nations, through the UN, the World Bank, and IMF, and in such bodies as the OAU, are united in their positions against colonialism, racism, and the apartheid status of South Africa. No such clear and consistent policy pronouncements are provided to its corps of foreign service representatives on the complex questions of education and culture. Few of the embassies of African governments in the United States have effectively operational offices to transact, promote, clarify, espouse, or even transmit policies concerning education and culture. If national policies on education and on culture for individual states are not manifest or codified for public dissemination at the independent embassy level, one cannot reasonably expect clear policy consensus and formulation at the OAU level. African embassies often are overworked and understaffed or have no officer responsible for, or experienced in, cultural/educational support activities. Materials, data, and publications for these policy elements may be inadequate or unavailable. Indeed, one of the factors which contributes to the absence of data is that empirical research and statistics and data on joint policy for education are limited, erratic, or non-existent in numerous LDCs in Africa. As a matter of fact, in the science of educational research and comparative education, a primary issue is how universal or general is a policy, a tendency, a methodology. A major problem in validating conclusions about education and culture in African states is the absence of local documentation or critical evidence. Where it exists, it is often a product of, or influenced unduly by, expatriate or Western researchers and their research assumptions. It is instructive here to note that with less than 5 percent of the world's school population, the United States accounts for the majority of the world's empirical research on education.[4] The absence of articulated or definitive policy or African consensus regarding education policy may well be a function of the dearth of empirical educational research from which to draw data appropriate for the formulation of multinational policies acceptable to such a diverse constituency as the corps of independent nations of Africa.

Perhaps the most reliable and generally accepted principles from which to deduce African policy are the five broad bases enumerated by a World Bank officer, Aklilu Habte: (1) expansion of basic education; (2) reduction of educational inequalities; (3) improvements in the cost-effectiveness of the transfer of knowledge; (4) provision of required manpower skills; and (5) development of national analytic capacities in management, administration, and planning.[5]

The first of these principles addresses the initial concern of wider access of primary-age children to formal schooling. With the dawn of independence in the late 1950s and early 1960s, the cry was to provide schooling for every child. Prohibitive school fees, costs of uniforms, books, supplies, and transportation, and often costs for boarding, made even primary education unavailable for many African children. As this quantitative goal was seriously attempted, other aspects of basic education claimed attention: literacy and adult education, the problem of dropouts and repeaters, and the quality of instructional materials and instructors.

The second principle forced consideration of three intransigent issues: (1) education of females, (2) education of rural school children, and (3) training in vocational/technical subjects for those young people who were not destined to follow the academic track to middle, high, and post-secondary school education. As a supervisor of Peace Corps Volunteer teachers in Africa in the 1960s, I can recall visiting numerous classes where one or two girls uncomfortably but bravely pioneered the coeducational model. I also recall how seldom the teaching staff was female. Education was almost exclusively the province of the city or town. Parents made every sacrifice to get a child into school. The parallels were painfully reminiscent of the conditions in education in the first half of this century for rural and urban blacks in my own state of Georgia. African school facilities, materials, and instructors on the government school level presented certain limitations. The elite schools—primary and secondary—for the Africans were church-sponsored: Catholic, Anglican, Protestant, and for a fee. Small surprise that independence brought with it a policy push for equity and equality.

The third principle is critical to policy, to future development, and to economic viability—even survival. Cost-effectiveness in human development—whether in education or in cultural and social terms—is increasingly a factor in approval of funding, in loan transactions, and in assessing priorities for the allocation of limited fiscal resources. All African governments and their ministries of education express frustration, disappointment, and anxiety on the issues of dropouts and repeaters. The efficacy of the instructional cadre, the physical costs for effective transfer of knowledge, and the expense of materials and equipment tax the most creative and responsible governments. With fewer than half of all primary-school-age children in one-third of all the sub-Saharan countries actually in school, with only 40 percent of the African nation's having more than 15 percent of the target age group in secondary school, the need for increased enrollment is apparent. With increased primary and secondary school enrollments, cost-effectiveness is even more a necessity. On average, expenditures on formal education currently amount to 16 percent of total government expenditure; in two-thirds of the countries under discussion for which data are available, schooling budgets account for 4 percent of the GDP (gross domestic product).[6] Thus policies which address the dual problems of repeaters and dropouts are high priorities. With the projected rapid population growth for the balance of this century, progress in universal education will be even more difficult. A study of 27 countries expanding primary education in the 1950s and 1960s documents an average tripling of recurrent costs when enrollments doubled.[7] The obvious accompanying impact of increased primary education enrollment and success is the impact and strain on already taxed secondary school facilities. The colonial legacy of fixed places, difficult reentry if loss of place in secondary school occurs, the traditional curriculum geared to selection-in for university and college levels, and the European models for terminal examination systems compound the policy dilemma of the African officials responsible for the directions, modifications, and sustained development in education. The recent experiences in Kenya and the Ivory Coast are instructive on this point.

Merely maintaining present primary enrollment ratios will demand increasing the number of available places nearly 4 percent annually.[8] African governments already invest "about twice as much as in other developing areas of the world" for primary education, about four to five times as much for secondary education, and five to ten times as much for post-secondary education (percent of per capita GNP). These costs are exacerbated by high repeater and dropout rates—ten pupil-years to complete a six-year primary course and a mere one-third to one-half of the entering primary students completing the six-year cycle. The Berg Report notes that while dropout and repeater rates are lower for secondary and post-secondary levels, they are still substantial.[9] Within the continental scenario, the actual rates obviously vary (very high in the Ivory Coast—ten student-years for one three-year graduate—and low in Kenya and Nigeria). The bottom line is how to develop, implement, and sustain policies to manage intelligently the principal budget factor—recurrent costs, 75 to 90 percent of which underwrites teacher salaries—while simultaneously responding to other educational pressures which demand attention and subsidy also. The relatively high teacher costs for salaries (and often housing and other maintenance aspects) exist in part because of the persisting expatriate teaching cadre, particularly for secondary and post-secondary levels. But the rates are high relative to per capita income also even where the expatriate factor is insignificant or irrelevant. The costs reflect to some degree the market reality: Educated, qualified, experienced professionals remain in short supply two decades beyond the heyday of independence. But public sector pay scales are rigid, tied to educational attainment levels influenced by the modern industrial/technical nations, and tied as well to the traditional scales of the colonial period. Education salary rates are not likely to adjust significantly to market conditions or to the government's relative ability to pay. Thus African governments have few alternatives beyond such policies as increased teacher-pupil ratio, multigrade instruction, double-shift systems, instruction by mass media, and intelligent matching of types of schooling and societal demands within the context of existing physical plants, as well as the existing instructional pool of professionals.[10]

It is relevant to note that expansion in primary education generally facilitates increased basic education access for the rural areas, for the girls, and for the poorest of the urban primary school-age population—male and female. The redistributive tendency at the primary school level stands in sharp contrast to the trends on the secondary and higher-education levels. Here relatively higher costs for public education tend to benefit the middle- and upper-income levels of the school-age population, promoting an ultimate effect of redistribution of income from poor to less poor.

This analysis cannot address adequately the current controversies on the "rates of return to education"; however, no one argues the evidence and reality that low per capita income countries also have literacy rates below 50 percent. All nations categorized as middle-income in the World Bank sampling between 1957 and 1978 showed literacy rates above 50 percent.[11] The explicit connection between educational achievement and economic advancement is equally linked to social and cultural aspects of national life. Numerous studies establish the fact that basic schooling contributes to agricultural productivity, to national growth, to life expectancy or better health, to industrial productivity, and to more intelligent use of the environment (water resources, wastes, forests, soil erosion, and pollution). But most significant of all in human resource development is the indisputable circumstance that *people* create ideas, make decisions, and implement activities. Such activities are either destructive or constructive, intelligent or foolish, innovative or retrogressive, selfish or humane, parochial or global in conception, theory, and impact. Human beings make war or peace, conserve resources or waste and destroy them, expand the frontiers of knowledge or deny and abridge the options for challenging involvement and meaningful change in our way of life and our record of human achievements.

The extent to which African leaders on a national, regional, or continental level evolve, support, and pursue policies consistent with, compatible with, or reflective of the five principles prescribed by the World Bank for Africa, negotiations for sector development vary. These national variables are reflected substantially in the United States response (the analysis to be considered in the latter half of this presentation).

Before turning to the matter of United States response, let us look briefly at cultural policies endorsed by African nations and their representatives. The inextricable impact of culture and education is clear. As formal school policies and structures have evolved, nothing is more paradoxical than the extreme diversity and cultural heterogeneity among the 45 states of the sub-Sahara region and the surprising homogeneity within the region. The similarities are instructive as one explores the cultures and the impact of cultural traditions on policy formation. How are these people homogeneous? Most of those nations are small—small populations, small economies with low average incomes, small industrial or technical labor forces, and a small cadre of professionals. Of the 45 states, 24 have less than five million citizens. The gross domestic product of 44 of the 45 is less than that of Hong Kong. Foreign trade accounts for some 25 percent of the GDP. These are specialized economies—most of them agricultural with about 70 percent of the population in this sector. Fifty percent or more of the agricultural production is subsistence production. Some 80 percent of the populations is rural. The modern wage employment structure absorbs in most countries less than 10 percent of the work force. Exports are limited to two or three primary commodities. The pool of educated citizenry was limited at independence; a national governance infrastructure was almost non-existent. They encompass unusual ethnic diversity. They have persistent political fragility. All emerged from colonialism some twenty to twenty-five years ago—except Liberia and Ethiopia, of course. All except Lesotho and Swaziland are classified as tropical. All have land-extensive agricultural traditions. Almost all nations in the region have high population growth and high fertility rates. These cultures are essentially non-industrial, non-monetary, non-urban, and non-Christian in character. The Lagos plan of action provides insight into the objectives endorsed by the African Chiefs of State at the April, 1980, meeting of the Organization of African Unity. Cultural concerns and priorities are never far from the center of the issues addressed there.

In linking the educational and cultural concerns of African nations, Aklilu Habte asserts that Africans "want education to discover and sustain the fundamental values of their own cultures and subcultures." Habte's philosophy deserves full restatement here:

> Peoples' values are unique. They may, for instance, be deeply religious. They may believe in the importance of the family, in the virtue of true courage, in civility, in the dignity of the individual, and in the wisdom of age and experience. Their historic music, poetry, and painting are similarly unique. But the arts of the nation, and many other traditions, many of them oral, will soon be lost if they are not recaptured in more enduring forms.... Nations want to preserve and develop their identity. Historically and at present, the school is the chosen medium—not the only one of course for the transmission of such a cultural heritage...[12]

Other cultural elements which impinge upon the evolution of appropriate national policy are the traditional rituals, the indigenous religions, the kinship patterns, the folk literature, the tribal medicine and herbal legacy, the rites of hospitality, the festivals, traditional barter and trade and marketing systems, and the close relationship of Africans to nature and their role and function in the universal order of creation.

Clearly, the cultures within the national context will shape the political, social, aesthetic, and religious context of each country. The policy priorities are: (1) to preserve cultural history, artifacts and records; (2) to interpret and correct perceptions about cultural mythology; (3) to explore cultural evidences of the past and relate these discoveries to the present and future; (4) to teach respect for and pride in the past; and (5) to promote understanding for and tolerance of cultural diversity. But the importance of culture as an adjunct of education and national security is easy to establish. The interface of culture and education has not been facile in the new states in Africa. Several reasons account for this failure to integrate education and cultural objectives. Instead of becoming complementary and integrative aspects of national development, these two policy sectors—education and culture—may on occasion conflict and diminish the degree of convergence and congruence. National leaders may perceive education as an instrument destructive to culture. Scientific discovery and modern technology may bring into question the validity of traditional wisdom and folk belief and contribute to conflict between the generations. Economics and educational impacts may diminish the contacts between the educated and the illiterate and result in cultural isolation and/or rejection. Adjustments to two apparently incompatible modes of life can cause psychological stress and even mental illness. Examples of African participants who fail to accommodate to the pressures of minority, racial, social, and community conditions when placed in an American milieu that lacks accustomed cultural supports are not difficult to document. Climate, foods, dress, male-female mores, religion, time, pace, and social codes all combine to challenge the African participant and the United States Peace Corps Volunteer who must cope within the local context and learn to be cosmopolitan and international in value system and social behavior.

Initial policies and programs in LDCs in Africa during the 1960s aimed at expanding educational access, not in altering educational content or character. Physical facilities, books and materials, teachers, and budgets were the focus. Superficial aspects of national culture were introduced into the educational system. Expatriate staff and colonial controls were altered and diminished but not expelled or dislodged. Some of the new content related to culture and local conditions—for example use of local language, introduction of African literature and African history—gained a footing in the African educational establishment. But these changes did not alter significantly such fundamental aspects of the inherited systems as: (1) school calendars; (2) prescribed textbooks; (3) official language of instruction; (4) instructional methodology; (5) structure of cycles; (6) examination techniques; (7) form and function of the ministries; or (8) the mission and philosophy of national public education. The impact of national politics and culture did foster assertion of self-reliance, pride in local languages, determination to establish national identity, and a Pan-African consciousness and euphoria about independence.

Following the quantitative goals of the 1960s, the qualitative objectives of the 1970s evolved. The April, 1980, report of a review of 35 such plans in 17 countries documented a concern for (1) social equity; (2) development of science teaching; (3) improvement of efficency of the school system—internal and external; (4) relevance of educational content, methodology, examinations; and (5) building national capacity for educational research and for educational management.[13]

Clearly, these qualitative objectives of the 1970s reflected dominant cultural impact in these areas: "relevance," the use of local languages, and the institutionalization of educational development. Cultural import is best demonstrated by the position that relevance "derived from the function of education in identifying and sustaining the historical, cultural, and religious traditions of a country and fulfilling its needs as a modern, changing entity." This position forced a rethinking of the fundamental nature of education to inject it with a "national character" which combined "authenticity and modernity"—elements perceived of as "an effective combination for rejecting, at the level of institutions and at the level of content, imported patterns and ready-made formulae."[14] Further, the African ministries of education extended the concept of relevance to encompass the educational needs of diverse population groups *within* each nation (especially women, migrants, ruralists, ethnic units), as well as the relationship between national life and culture and the external world.[15]

In short, the cultural policies included both attention to such traditionally and easily recognized cultural elements as dance, music—song and instrumental—painting and sculpture, textiles and traditional dress, archaeology, and languages, as well as the study of ethnic societies and their structures, coinage, writing systems, and religions. Unfortunately, much of the pioneering effort in this cultural arena had been initiated by expatriate professionals and much of the African heritage in the arts, anthropology, and archaeology was the domain of non-African researchers. Western museums often retained more of the precious legacy of African cultural artifacts than did the African states themselves, and efforts to recover some of these priceless artifacts were launched during this era of national consciousness-raising. The cultural policies could not take precedence, however, over the basic needs policies which had of necessity to focus on governance, food, housing, health, water and sanitation, education, transport, and employment. Because education is fundamental to the resolution of the problems in all of these other basic areas, educational policies are more tangible and specific than are the cultural policies enunciated.

Cultural policies are implicitly incorporated in related national policies which are the inevitable responsibility of the national leadership of African states. Factors which alter and significantly modify culture are urbanization policy, environmental policy, national and intra-Third World trade, rural development and industrialization, migration, refugee policy, transnational enterprises, appropriate technology, transportation policy, and communications and media policy. Every one of these factors impinges upon traditional values, cultural survival or transition, and social behaviorism and coding. "The role of non-material basic needs, both as ends in their own right and as means to meeting material basic needs that reduce costs and improve impact, is a crucial aspect of the basic needs approach" and policies.[16] Non-material needs accompany and interface with material needs and do not depend significantly on allocation of scarce resources or state subsidy. Any intelligent definition of and approach to basic needs, however, will factor into its content a wide spectrum of human needs which money cannot buy or which material goods simply cannot satisfy. The basic-needs approach comprehensively conceptualized is relatively more cost-effective than other approaches because it builds upon linkages between sector programs which impact upon each other and because it employs capital saving techniques.[17] It is in the non-material needs aspect that cultural issues and problems significantly reside. Policy formulation for meeting basic needs which ignores this fact does so to the detriment of cultural values and security or survival.

With this overview of African policy positions on education and culture, let us refocus our analytical lens and examine the United States response to African policies in these two critical sectors. It is somewhat misleading to describe as or even imply that United States foreign policy in education and culture is a *response*. United States foreign policy in all sectors emanates from internal national priorities and political, economic, and social pressure groups. It would also be terribly naive to assume or to posit a consistent, integrated, and multisector conceptualization of national foreign policy with short-, medium-, and long-range objectives. The careful, well-researched study by Immanuel Wallerstein in 1975, "Africa, the U.S. and the World Economy: The Historical Bases of American Policy," is as pertinent today, as it was during the mid-1970s. The perspective which Wallerstein recreates as the fundamentals of United States foreign policy from 1789 to 1975 is one which makes American economic interests and historic diplomatic linkages central to the existence and development of national policy and United States foreign policy initiatives or projects.[18] If one searches for United States policy positions on Africa, the record is arresting. As Wallerstein points out, an examination of the basic documents in the 1940s provides not one single reference to Africa, and for the 1950-1955 period only one reference, and that was to Libya for a defense facilities agreement.[19] John Foster Dulles made the American position explicit when, on June 1, 1953, he declared in a speech to the nation that

> ... our NATO alliances with France and Britain require us to try to preserve or restore the old colonial interests of our allies. .... It would be a disaster if there were any break between the U.S., Great Britain and France. However, without breaking from the framework of Western unity, we can pursue our traditional dedication to political liberty.[20]

Then the United States policymakers felt compelled to keep intact the essential relationships with NATO partners, even when doing so contradicted our national democratic principles. This compulsion is no less a priority today; it therefore continues to influence United States-Africa foreign policy. That was true at our embassy in Conakry, Guinea, in 1959. Despite the emergence to independence of 51 states, the implications for United States-Africa foreign policy remain the same. NATO solidarity and economic stability take precedence over ideals of democratic process and decolonialism or neocolonialism. When Vice President Nixon proposed to President Eisenhower in his report of April 7, 1957, that the State Department create a Bureau of African Affairs, it was the reality of African political independence which prompted his recommendation. When such a bureau became a reality on August 20, 1958, the Eisenhower administration was reluctant to name a separate ambassador to each newly independent nation. This deference to European allies was symbolically altered by President Kennedy when he decided to give each state its own United States ambassador and scheduled official meetings with as many of the new heads of states as possible. Thus the symbolic United States policy changes toward Africa gave the hope of substantive policy change. In 1984 Africa is still relatively speaking *not* a priority region in United States foreign policy. Policy is still more symbolic and pragmatic than consistent with traditional democratic principles or national ideals.

Nonetheless, there are explicit United States policy positions which make clear our interests and involvements in Africa. Official United States educational and cultural policies are best documented by the programs, funding, and directions supported by three federal agencies, though the policy evidence and implications extend beyond these three federal units. The Department of Education (DOE), the U.S. Information Agency (USIA), and the Agency for International Development (AID) carry the onus for educational and cultural interaction or response to African states. The AID policy paper, *Basic Education and Technical Training,* endorses "the development of human resources (or human capital) as vital to the growth of overall productivity and the efficient use of physical capital" on the grounds that people "shape and energize a nation's development."[21] The AID priorities in education link explicitly the issues of agricultural productivity, population, health, and a skilled labor force.

In responding to African LDC policies to improve education and training systems, AID proposes to focus on (1) increasing efficient use of resources, (2) sustaining and raising the qualitative and quantitative results of education and training investments, and (3) enhancing the efficacy of education and training systems in supporting the social and economic development goals of a nation.[22] AID will encourage direct community involvement in the establishment and maintenance of schools and the cooperation of private sector employers in the implementation of technical/vocational training programs. United States policy on basic education supports:

- Improving the efficiency of *existing* education systems—formal and non-formal—as a whole

- Expansion of existing systems contingent upon assessment of the adequacy of the system and specific measures to resolve problems of the existing systems

- Concentration of assistance in states which encourage private and public schools

191

- Decentralization of education management, diversification of school sponsorship, and local participation

- Priority given to improvements in retention rates, promotion and efficiency measures at each level of schooling rather than to increasing initial enrollment figures

- Increasing education opportunities for rural, poor and female children

United States policy for vocational education and technical training emphasizes:

- In-service training with a strong, direct role for employers in implementing their own programs

- For small- and medium-scale enterprise development, pre-service training for the new labor force and for the existing labor force needing retraining for new occupational areas, and in-service training for the existing work force

- For the informal sector, non-formal approaches using local PVOs, community organizations, and producers' associations as direct resources for training in such basic functional skills as literacy, numeracy, merchandising, management of small credit loans, simple bookkeeping and such basic business and entrepreneurial skills

- Providing opportunities for women to participate in training programs

These policy positions are accompanied by a series of four stated constraints: (1) policy, (2) organization and management, (3) technology, and (4) resources.[23] The AID policy constraint focuses on "systemic reform" of the entire education establishment. Discussion of "return to private sponsorship of schools" which were nationalized is a possible dialogue element. Such dialogue is encouraged by giving priority to "policy-relevant assessment, analysis and research" and to "education researchers, policy analysts, administrators, and key technicians in general participant training programs." The second constraint encourages "decentralization of administration and financing of local school systems," involvement of private sector employers in technical skills training programs in both "the sponsorship and implementation," and extensive reliance on private sector suppliers for "production and distribution" of educational materials and supplies. AID proposes to make organization and management central to its efforts to support "strengthening the capacity and quality of the existing education systems." The third policy constraint addresses research and development efforts in the use of "radio and other media (e.g., rural satellites, video and audio recorders) which contribute to cost effective extension of education and training service." The AID criteria includes feasibility "for application in the typical school or training setting" and "technical and administrative capacity to make effective use" of such technologies. Finally, the resource constraints factor in (1) resource mobilization, (2) efficient use of available resources, and (3) the availability and reliability of external resources. The AID policy paper cites as critical intangibles such factors as local leadership and administrative structures "which facilitate full participation in local decision-making and resource mobilization."

A careful analysis of the policy paper, *Basic Education and Technical Training*, should be accompanied by a thoughtful reading of the AID policy paper, *Recurrent Costs*, particularly with reference to the comparative data on education expenditures. Both documents consider the implications and results of "inappropriate policies on the part of donors or LDC governments."[24] Waste, mismanagement, and inefficiency are elements which affect the development, implementation, and support of present and future policies.

Policy statement and analysis aside, let us now shift to United States programmatic and funding realities. "The Summary of Programs by Country and Appropriations" in the Congressional

Presentation FY 1985 lists *seven* African states receiving funding in 1982: Ghana, Lesotho, Liberia, Malawi, Sierra Leone, Swaziland, and Tanzania. In 1983 it documents *four*: Lesotho, Malawi, Swaziland, and Zaire. In 1984 it records *seven*: Botswana, Cameroon, Guinea Bissau, Lesotho, Liberia, Swaziland, and Tanzania. In 1985 it includes *eight*: Botswana, Cameroon, Guinea-Bissau, Lesotho, Liberia, Somalia, Swaziland, and Zimbabwe. These data (in thousands of dollars) do not include funds allocated for Africa Regional funding or Southern Africa Regional funding, which are cited separately:

	Southern Africa Regional	Africa Regional
1982	3,000	12,890
1983	3,050	14,868
1984	3,000	13,513
1985		12,150

The FY 1985 programs promote the "integration of agriculture production with education." The Yaounde Conference sponsored by the Africa Bureau of AID in July in Cameroon demonstrated this integrative initiative. An impressive array of African educators, agriculturalists, and economists convened to consider "Agricultural Education: A Catalyst for African Development." A number of the African states represented at the conference, however, are not among the FY 1985 roster of states proposed to receive United States funding for education and human resources development activities. The official position is candid and unequivocal: "The financial contribution of the U.S. to education and human resources development activities in developing countries is small, whether compared to the magnitude of the problem or to the programs of other donors."[25] A recent ranking places the United States eighteenth among industrialized donor nations in its fiscal contribution for such foreign aid.

The AID picture does not, of course, convey the complete United States position for it does not reflect cultural and educational initiatives funded by USIA and DOE. These programs carry the cultural aspect of foreign policy more explicitly than does AID. The Council on International Exchange of Scholars (CIES) and the International Education Division of the Department of

Education handle the Fulbright Exchange Program. DOE has five areas for grants: Group Projects Abroad Program, Foreign Curriculum Consultant Program, Faculty Research Abroad, Seminars Abroad, and Doctoral Dissertation Research Abroad. Other federal departments include elements which clearly are of educational significance; these departments have international dimensions which embrace specific education and technology features in health, labor, transportation, commerce, and defense. Projects developed through these departments cut across the education and culture sectors, but are not explicitly documented in a fashion to make inclusion in this brief analysis meaningful or quantitatively valid. Another feature of the United States education and culture sectors abroad is the binational commissions now active and established in 42 countries, but these are not relevant in Africa. The 11E contract with USIA for the Exchange of Students Program and for the Hubert H. Humphrey North-South Fellowship Program services LDCs, some in Africa.[26] The latter project brings mid-career professionals from LDCs to the United States.

Likewise, the official United States response is often linked to private sector initiatives through private voluntary organizations, religious missions or organizations, charitable agencies, and community-action groups. Indeed, a significant percentage of AID project activity in African education is the result of cooperation between American PVOs, philanthropic organizations or foundations, and interdenominational and international church bodies. These private sector development initiatives often predate official United States foreign policy interests in Africa and, therefore, have traditional, locally based networks which have a long record in educational and cultural relations.

The intractable problems of refugee populations—victims of war, drought, or political displacement—have also had an impact on the education and culture sectors of African states. Kenya, Cameroon, Tanzania, Botswana, Zaire, Zambia, and Sudan are examples of countries which were severely pressured by the influx of refugees needing support in health, education, housing, employment, and security, as the very fabric of their culture was being torn by civil or guerrilla conflict or by protracted wars. The United States public and private response to such human crises has not equalled the American response to Asian or European (for example, Poland) or Middle East (for example, Lebanon, Israel or Egypt) crises. There has been, nonetheless, some response—private and public—which has had impact on the educational and cultural sectors. The refugee projects of the Phelps-Stokes Fund or of AAI, IIE, and other such PVOs have been largely in education and have been funded through AID and/or the State Department. African governments have been mutually cooperative in these refugee programs in education, often providing field experience and re-entry permits for students on completion of their studies in the United States or in other countries of Africa. Such education initiatives have been supported for Somalis, Ethiopians, Ugandans, Namibians, South Africans, Zimbabweans, and Equatorial Guineans. These have been both degree and certificate programs and have aimed at repatriation or employment in Africa for the participants.

It is fair to note also that other United States funding which may support the educational and cultural sectors of African states may be derived from multilateral and multinational programs which are supported by agencies to which the United States government is an official contributor. Thus, some element of United States response is represented by the UNESCO, World Bank, IMF, and other such operations which include the two sectors in their project activity. Although this is an indirect response, it is still an aspect of United States official action in support of the educational and cultural sectors of the LDCs approved for subsidies by these organizations.

The final area of official United States involvement in Africa which deserves mention is the Peace Corps, for which Africa is the area of largest operation. Education has always been a feature of Peace Corps support in Africa, though it has diminished dramatically as a project area across the continent. As teachers, 37.9 percent of the volunteers are in the classroom in Africa. Here the emphasis has shifted from teaching to teacher training, relevant curriculum development, and technical/vocational instruction. In collaboration with USAID, the Peace Corps is involved in a Teacher-Text-Technology (TTT) initiative through the State Department and American educational institutions.[26] The countries which are a part of Peace Corps education efforts include Liberia,

Table 2.1
International Expenditure Comparison Index, 1977:
Functional Categories of Expenditures

	General Public Services	Defense	Education	Health	Agriculture	Transport and Communications
Bangladesh	Low	Low	Low	Average	Average	High
Bolivia	Average	Average	Average	Low	Low	Average
Botswana	Average	Low	High	High	High	n.a.
Burma	Average	High	Low	Low	High	n.a.
Burundi	Low	High	Average	n.a.	Average	n.a.
Cameroon	High	Average	Average	Low	Low	High
Chad	Average	High	Average	Low	Average	Low
Costa Rica	Low	Low	Average	Low	Low	High
Dominican Rep.	Low	Low	Low	Average	Average	Low
Ecuador	Low	Average	Average	Low	Average	n.a.
Egypt	Low	Low	High	Average	High	Low
El Salvador	Average	Low	Average	Average	Low	Average
Gambia, The	High	n.a.	Average	High	High	n.a.
Ghana	Average	n.a.	High	Average	Average	Average
Guatemala	Low	Low	n.a.	Low	Low	n.a.
Honduras	High	Low	Average	High	Low	n.a.
Jamaica	Low	Low	High	High	High	Average
Jordan	Average	High	High	High	High	High
Kenya	Low	Average	Average	Average	Average	Average
Lesotho	High	n.a.	High	Average	High	n.a.
Liberia	High	Low	Average	High	Average	Average
Malawi	Average	Low	Average	Low	Average	Low
Mali	Average	High	High	Average	Low	Low
Morocco	High	High	High	Average	n.a.	n.a.
Nepal	Low	Average	Low	n.a.	Average	n.a.
Nicaragua	Low	Low	Low	Low	Low	n.a.
Niger	High	Low	High	Average	Low	Average
Pakistan	Low	High	Low	Low	Low	Average
Panama	High	n.a.	Average	High	Average	Average
Peru	Average	Low	Average	Low	Average	n.a.
Philippines	Average	Average	Low	Low	Average	High
Rwanda	Low	High	Low	Low	Low	High
Senegal	Average	Low	Average	Low	Low	Low
Sierra Leone	Average	Low	Average	Average	Low	Low
Somalia	High	High	High	High	High	Low
Sri Lanka	Low	Low	Average	Average	Average	n.a.
Sudan	Low	Average	Low	Low	High	Average
Swaziland	Average	Low	High	Average	High	n.a.
Tanzania	Average	Average	Average	High	High	Average
Thailand	Low	High	Average	Low	Average	Average
Upper Volta	Average	High	Average	Low	Low	Low
Yemen	Average	High	Low	Low	Low	Average
Zambia	High	n.a.	High	High	High	High

SOURCE: Alan A. Tait and Peter S. Heller, "International Comparisons of Government Expenditures: A Starting Point for Discussion," IMF, Discussion Memorandum, DM/81/53, July, 1981.

Each index runs from zero to four hundred. Any value less than 75 was recorded as "Low," values between 75 and 125 were recorded as "Average," and values greater than 125 were recorded as "High."

197

Table 2.2
United States Information Agency

GRANTS TO FOREIGN NATIONALS

Country	University Study		Advanced Research		Teaching or Educational Seminars		University Lecturers		Practical Experience and Training		Hubert H. Humphrey Scholars		Foreign Totals Cumulative	
	1949-1981	1981-1982	1949-1981	1981-1982	1949-1981	1981-1982	1949-1981	1981-1982	1954-1981	1981-1982	1978-1981	1981-1982	1981-1982	1949-1982
Angola	23	2			8									23
Benin	10	5	2										2	20
Botswana	16	2	3	1							1		6	25
Burundi	28		7	1	3						4	3	6	45
Cameroon	44		1		3		4	1			1	1	3	58
Canary Islands														1
Cape Verde					5	1							1	6
Central African Rep.	10		1		15	1	1						1	27
Chad	3	1	1		4		1							9
Congo	8	1	2	2	2	1		3			1		4	20
Djibouti	3										2			5
Equitorial Guinea	1													1
Ethiopia	82	1	10		2		3					1	1	98
Gabon	2				4		1							6
The Gambia	10				2								1	15
Ghana	177	6	45	9	22		10	1	1		2	1	17	278
Guinea	1		1	1	6	1					6	1	2	12
Guinea-Bissau	1		1	1	1						2	1	1	4
Ivory Coast	21	4	23	3	15		4	2			2	1	6	69
Kenya	270	3	22	1	15		1	2			2	2	8	323
Lesotho	14	14	2		2		1					5	19	20
Liberia	108		4	1	41		1		18		6		1	197
Madagascar	7		4		6									17
Malawi	26		2		14			2			4	3	3	51

Table 2.2 (continued)
United States Information Agency

GRANTS TO FOREIGN NATIONALS

Country	University Study 1949-1981	University Study 1981-1982	Advanced Research 1949-1981	Advanced Research 1981-1982	Teaching or Educational Seminars 1949-1981	Teaching or Educational Seminars 1981-1982	University Lecturers 1949-1981	University Lecturers 1981-1982	Practical Experience and Training 1954-1981	Practical Experience and Training 1981-1982	Hubert H. Humphrey Scholars 1978-1981	Hubert H. Humphrey Scholars 1981-1982	Foreign Totals 1981-1982	Foreign Totals 1949-1982 Cumulative
Mali	5		3	1	30	3						2	5	43
Mauritania	10	1	2		7								2	21
Mauritius	6		3		1		2							12
Mozambique	33		1											34
Namibia	16		1											17
Niger	2		5		17		1				1	1	1	26
Nigeria	175	2	89	12	14		19	2	2		1	1	16	316
Rwanda	11		6	1	14			1			1	1	2	34
Senegal	9		15	1	14	1							3	43
Seychelles														
Sierra Leone	51		17		8		3				2	2	2	83
Somalia	99		19		3		5		7		1	6		99
South Africa, Rep.	289	28	19		3						1		34	358
St. Helena													3	
Swaziland	13	8	19		24		2	1			7	3	18	19
Tanzania	175	5	6	4	5		4	2			2	4	9	247
Togo	13	2	16	2	6		1	1			2	2	5	36
Uganda	176		1	1	10	1	1					2	1	206
Upper Volta	1		16	2	25		2		2			1	1	14
Zaire	34	5	19	2	13		1	1	2		5	3	11	95
Zambia	111	9	6		14				6		4	3	14	168
Zimbabwe	95		6		14									115
Multicountry														
Totals	2,189	98	375	49	375	11	62	19	36		59	49	208	3,316

Table 2.3
Academic Grants Awarded 1949-1981 and 1981-1982

GRANTS TO U.S. CITIZENS

Country	University Study 1949-1981	University Study 1981-1982	Advanced Research 1949-1981	Advanced Research 1981-1982	Teaching or Educational Seminars 1949-1981	Teaching or Educational Seminars 1981-1982	University Lecturers 1949-1981	University Lecturers 1981-1982	U.S. Totals 1981-1982 Cumulative	U.S. Totals 1949-1982 Cumulative	Foreign, U.S. 1981-1982 Cumulative	Foreign, U.S. 1949-1982 Cumulative
Angola			2				3			2		26
Benin			1				2	1	1	9	2	29
Botswana			1				1	1	1	2	7	27
Burundi	1						12			17	7	62
Cameroon	7				5		14	2	2	24	5	82
Canary Islands	1									1		2
Cape Verde		1									1	6
Central African Rep.	1				2		2	2	3	6	4	33
Chad							3			4		13
Congo			2		1		3	3	3	8	7	28
Djibouti												5
Equatorial Guinea											1	1
Ethiopia							32	1	1	33	1	131
Gabon							5			6	1	12
The Gambia					1					1		16
Ghana	6		11		5		48	1	1	71	18	349
Guinea					2		6			8	2	20
Guinea-Bissau											1	4
Ivory Coast	5		1				11	2	2	14	8	83
Kenya	1		12	2	3		21	1	3	44	11	367
Lesotho	1		2	1			11			14	1	34
Liberia			2		8		68	5	6	85	25	282
Madagascar					1		4			5		22
Malawi					2		10			14	5	65
Mali					2		4	2	2	6	5	49

Table 2.3 (continued)
Academic Grants Awarded 1949-1981 and 1981-1982

GRANTS TO U.S. CITIZENS

Country	University Study 1949-1981	University Study 1981-1982	Advanced Research 1949-1981	Advanced Research 1981-1982	Teaching or Educational Seminars 1949-1981	Teaching or Educational Seminars 1981-1982	University Lecturers 1949-1981	University Lecturers 1981-1982	U.S. Totals, Cumulative 1981-1982	U.S. Totals, Cumulative 1949-1982	Foreign, U.S. Cumulative 1981-1982	Foreign, U.S. Cumulative 1949-1982
Mauritania			1							1	2	22
Mauritius												12
Mozambique							2			2		36
Namibia												17
Niger					10		8			8	1	34
Nigeria	73		15		1		48	7	7	153	23	469
Rwanda			1	1			8			11	2	45
Senegal	5		1	2			15	2	4	25	7	68
Seychelles										2		2
Sierra Leone	3		1		2		10	2	2	19	4	102
Somalia			2		3		4			9		108
South Africa, Rep. of	7		1		3		19			30	34	388
St. Helena					3		1			1		1
Swaziland					1		5	1	1	6	4	25
Tanzania	6		7				26			46	18	293
Togo	1		2		7		5	1	1	9	10	45
Uganda	7		24				23	2	2	61	7	267
Upper Volta					5						1	14
Zaire	1						22	2	2	25	13	120
Zambia	1		12		13		34	1	1	60	15	228
Zimbabwe			1		1		4	1	1	7	1	122
Multicountry			1				10			10		10
Totals	126	1	102	6	82		503	40	47	860	254	4,176

Malawi, Rwanda, Tanzania, Togo, Swaziland, Mali, Sierra Leone, and Burundi. This represents a decrease from a high of 24 African states in the first two decades of Peace Corps operations in Africa. Then every state had a major education project. The shift is consonant with the priorities of United States administration at the present time.

In the final analysis education and culture will remain the handmaidens of other development sectors which are major priorities in economics, trade, and health services; agriculture, health, communications, management, and administration will continue to capture attention. Only to the degree that the goals in these areas cannot be achieved without integration with the educational and cultural sectors will these stepchildren in the development arena appear relevant. Quantitative measures will continue to outweigh qualitative data; economic success will continue to be measured in GNP and GDP—indices which do not clearly factor in human capital.

EDUCATION AND HUMAN RESOURCES DEVELOPMENT

In FY 1985 both new and ongoing programs totaling $46.2 million, which would include the integration of education with agricultural production, will help expand Africa's human resource capacity. AID Education and Human Resources Development focus in Africa will be devoted to:

1. Improving the efficiency and effectiveness of primary school systems. There will be emphasis on improving production of appropriate teaching materials and use of innovative technologies of instruction, including radio, as a means of overcoming the traditionally poor quality of instruction offered in rural areas. The Rural Information System project (669-0134) in Liberia, for example, is using the radio to broadcast educational programs to the rural population, 80

percent of whom are relatively isolated. In FY 1985 assistance is being requested to improve the quality of primary school instruction in Liberia, under the new Improved Efficiency of Learning II projects (669-0166).

2. By improving the quality of the non-formal educational programs, AID will help African countries in their effort to develop literacy and numeracy skills sufficient to bring presently illiterate adults into the development process. Also included will be skills training for small-scale enterpreneurs and farmers to increase their productivity. This will aid them in becoming viable participants in the private sector. The ongoing Lesotho Basic and Non-Formal Education Systems project (632-0222) is working on reorienting basic education to meet basic development needs and improving the educational system's capacity to educate and train persons in subjects that support rural-based income and employment.

3. Support will be provided to strengthen selected indigenous institutes to develop their capacity to provide instruction and to undertake research, policy analysis and planning in the Human Resource sector. Particular emphasis will be given to national and regional institutes that offer training and other support services in the areas of management and development administration.

4. Participant training activities such as the African Manpower Development Project (698-0433) provide training opportunities for Africans to study in the United States or in Third World countries. Training will focus at the upper levels of indigenous organizations both in the public and private sectors and on those technical and managerial skills where there is particular shortage of manpower. In addition, development management improvement will be emphasized across all sectors. For example, within the Sahel

account, the Sahel Manpower Development Project (625-0960), all long-term United States participants must agree to enroll in two courses in management.

Table 2.4
Summary—FY 1985—
Education and Human Resources
(In Thousands of Dollars)

	Total	Grants	Loans
Bureau for Africa			
Cameroon	10,500	3,600	6,900
Guinea-Bissau	500	500	—
Lesotho	3,003	3,003	—
Liberia	3,300	3,300	—
Somalia	2,000	2,000	—
Swaziland	3,000	3,000	—
Zimbabwe	11,708	11,708	—
Africa Regional	12,150	12,150	—
Total for Bureau	46,161	39,261	6,900
Bureau for Asia			
Bangladesh	250	250	—
Indonesia	3,250	1,250	2,000
Nepal	1,243	1,243	—
Philippines	300	300	—
Sri Lanka	200	200	—
Thailand	10,600	—	10,600
So. Pacific Regional	2,000	2,000	—
Asia Regional	4,400	4,400	—
Total for Bureau	22,243	9,643	12,600
Bureau for Latin America and Caribbean			
Belize	2,240	2,240	—
Bolivia	50	50	—
Costa Rica	7,710	7,710	—
Dominican Republic	7,275	3,275	4,000
Ecuador	1,330	1,330	—
El Salvador	22,000	22,000	—
Guatemala	8,785	8,785	—
Haiti	300	300	—
Honduras	11,245	11,245	—
Jamaica	5,971	1,971	4,000
Peru	190	190	—
Panama	7,020	7,020	—
Caribbean Regional	6,300	6,300	—
Rocap	5,000	5,000	—
LAC Regional	12,890	12,890	—
Total for Bureau	98,306	90,306	8,000

REFERENCES

1. The World Bank, *Poverty and Human Development* (New York: Oxford University Press, 1980), 2.

2. Aklilu Habte, "Education and National Development," IMF, *Finance and Development,* (June 1982), 20–23, Reprint 1983.

3. Frederide S. Arkhursy, ed., *US Policy Toward Africa* (New York: Praeger Publishers, 1975), 7.

4. Stephen P. Heyniman and William A. Laxley, *The Effect of Primary-School Quality on Academic Achievement across Twenty-Nine High and Low Income Countries,* World Bank Reprint #268 from *The American Journal of Sociology,* Vol. 88, No. 6 (May 1983), 1164.

5. Habte, 9.

6. Elliot Berg, et al., *Accelerated Development in Sub-Saharan Africa* (Washington, D.C.: The World Bank, 1981), 81.

7. Ibid., 113.

8. Ibid., 82.

9. Ibid., 83.

10. Philip N. Coombs and Jacques Hallak, *Managing Educational Costs* (New York: Oxford University Press, 1972).

11. Poverty and Human Development, 17.

12. Ibid., 10.

13. Wade D. Haddad, et al., *Education Sector Policy Paper,* World Bank, (April 1980), 19–20.

14. Resolution adopted in Lagos, Nigeria, at the 1976 Conference of African Ministries of Education.

15. Haddad, 20.

16. Paul Streeten, "From Growth to Basic Needs," *Poverty and Basic Needs,* World Bank (September 1980), 8.

17. Arkhurst, Chapter 2, 11–37.

18. Ibid., Note 10, 36–37.

19. U.S. Department of State, *American Foreign Policy: Basic Documents, 1950–1955* (New York: Arno Press, 1971), Vol. 2, 2173–74.

20. AID Policy Paper, *Basic Education and Technical Training,* Washington, D.C. (December 1982), 1.

21. Ibid., IV, 4.

22. Ibid., 11–12.

23. AID Policy Paper, *Recurrent Costs,* Washington, D.C. (May 1982), 7, 11, 16, 19.

24. *Congressional Presentation* — FY 1985 — Main Volume (AID), 60.

25. Board of Foreign Scholarships, *Fulbright Program Exchanges,* Washington, D.C. (December 1982), 20–21.

26. *The Peace Corps in 1983: A Year of Achievement,* Washington, D.C., U.S. Peace Corps, 12 and 14.

Commentary

Calvin H. Raullerson

All of the data that we have been able to assemble in the academic and technical assistance research community confirm the importance of education and training as a key to the development process. The priority given to education in Africa is revealed by some gross statistics on institution-building in Africa since 1952. Student population has quadrupled from nine million in 1950. The number of university students has grown from 70,000 in 1950 to more than 350,000 today. Other figures suggest the enormity of the task ahead. While university enrollment has grown in the above dimensions, university-aged Africans have increased by more than four million in the past fifteen years.

Dr. Gadsden has offered a creative challenge in reminding us of the cultural realities and constraints for both the United States and Africa. I want to supplement her presentation with another practitioner's observations and concerns. The real problem solving in this arena is finding innovative solutions that are in our mutual interest, are supportive of real African development, and are not couched in a punitive giving mode.

We are forty years into the groundswell of African independence. The scarcity of trained manpower remains a critical problem. Reliance on expatriate trained manpower is still high. This is especially so in those responsibilities that require university-level education. There is an urgent need for viable policies that address such critical areas as employment generation, income generation, small enterprise development, health, and energy-related concerns. The enhancement of the quality of life in the rural areas is another area of concern. Urban bias in technical assistance needs to be balanced by greater consideration of the enhancement of the quality of life in the rural areas.

The problem-solving in these areas must be done by Africans, trained mainly in their own institutions, bringing to bear the qualities of their own environment and culture. The qualities of a nation's people reflect its progress. Better-trained and better-informed farmers mean as much to productivity as do new techniques and machinery. Human beings everywhere are the source of policies, actions, innovation, and opportunity.

Education and training provide the technical, scientific, and professional skills necessary for the production and movement of goods and services. The public and private sectors require entrepreneurial and administrative skills. Equally important are the skills, knowledge, and attitudes of the masses of ordinary workers, small farmers, and traders.

There is no definitive answer or policy on what determines the quality of human resources. Practical experience is important. Knowledge and attitudes that children acquire from their families and from society at large are another ingredient. There are also many different kinds of formal education and training: general primary and secondary school schooling, technical and vocational schooling, general and specialized higher education. All of these impart specific skills, enhance the ability to learn, and mold perceptions of work and change.

There is no clear evidence regarding either the contribution of human resources to production and growth or what determines their quality. However, in all countries better-educated people tend to earn more, to a degree that makes educational spending, especially for primary education in developing countries, an attractive investment.

However, knowledge, skills, and attitudes are not the only factors that affect economic performance. A healthy and well-fed labor force is more physically and mentally energetic than one

209

that is sick, hungry, and susceptible to a lower life expectancy. A healthy work force gets more work done and is more innovative. The linkage of education, health, and nutrition to rapid growth is often measured inaccurately as well. Development also depends on factors such as the availability of natural resources and physical capital with which all resources are used. Even with these caveats the development of human capital remains a critical priority for Africa.

The development of human capital has been affected by cultural and environmental factors. Most African nations have a diversity of cultures and languages. The process of nation-building has been difficult. New institutions of national integration are in conflict with loyalty to indigenous institutions and customs. National boundaries are unnatural and often separate ethnic groups. This has led to conflict, economic repercussions, a tendency to short-term political goals, displacement of large numbers of people, and inordinate attention to military concerns.

Institutions created in the colonial era have not been necessarily relevant to national realities in the post-colonial period. National institutions as well as educational institutions were based on colonial agendas and not on African needs and realities. Institutions of local government, education, health, and rural reconstruction appropriate to African objectives have been slow to develop.

The colonial experience also placed most Africans outside the modern economy. The continuing prevalence of subsistence farming among most African farmers, the accumulation of the most productive farm lands by colonial powers, the lack of infrastructure, the slow pace of capital flow into African countries—all provide a tension and inequity between the traditional African environment and the pace of development.

There is also a cultural problem for the United States on the horizon. The prospects for the world between now and the year 2000 look frustrating. We have been the most powerful nation, but now there are events in both the developed and developing world that we cannot control. This is threatening to us, and it is revolutionary, not in a conservative/liberal sense, but because it provides a framework through which change can be made. A part of the threat is our need to make transition from a traditional view of the world to that of an interdependent world system. Interdependence will increase in both political and economic aspects. There are complications that grow out of this for us and the rest of the world in increasing tensions, conflicts, and resource constraints. The increasing interplay of political and economic variables will present a world to which we will need to apply new approaches and accommodations. The key question in this transition is not whether it is going to happen, but who is going to manage the dynamics. Another vital concern is how long we will be able to resist the reality of this new mode and its operational implications. In development assistance one key question will be the terms of the partnership in this interdependence. Do we, for example, continue to plan and program as a senior partner, or do we encourage an equal sharing of the partnership?

Our value system has traditionally been based on the tenets of survival, justice, economy, self-fulfillment, and self-respect. It has focused on individualism, our concept of property rights, the limited state, competition to satisfy consumer desires, and scientific specialization. The concerns of the individual have been accommodated to interest-group pluralism.

Domestically we have seen, over time, some modification of this kind of ideology. We have shifted from equality of opportunity to equality of results. We are moving from the theory of the contract to concern with consensus. The concept of the limited state has evolved into the active planning state (though that is being held in some question now), and science has shifted to holistic concerns and the recognition of the interdependence of its disciplines.

The real world we face presents a picture of uncertainty: demographic and geographic realities in a world of resource scarcities; ecological concerns in the wake of land degradation and inefficient land-use management; traditional institutions in conflict with current realities. Even our traditional behavior patterns of rugged individualism—a John Wayne to come out of the West and save the day—have undergone significant change.

Internationally, we need to preach what we practice and then to do some fine tuning as we look to development needs: fine tuning through development education; new programming modes and techniques; innovation in management. Development assistance is a risk-taking business, and we need to take chances. We need to be alert as to where we have a choice and where we do not. There is a great danger that as a nation and as development assistance actors we will close up, become fearful, and relate assistance to compliance. The management implications of this new era are bound up in our need to run an institution not only to meet the status quo, but also to manage a period of revolutionary change—change that is not necessarily from one political system to another, but to a new dynamic in the world with new techniques of problem-solving that confront our current realities. The global patterns of interdependence center around a number of major issues and dynamics: population, food production, energy, environment, trade, human rights, and the north-south dialogue in which we are bound to face confrontation, adaptation, and integration.

The rate of change in the scientific, political, and economic spheres will continue to accelerate. Concurrent with this, ecological factors will become more important in both the developed countries and the less developed countries. The assumption of interdependence clearly identifies this. We will probably desire to influence policy change and development decisions in the less developed world rather than merely transfer resources. The quality and dimension of our development effort will depend on the LDC's perception of the importance of growth with equity, our willingness to enhance the partnership relationship in direct assistance, and in coordinated multilateral and private approaches to assistance.

The dynamics of the world indicate that high technology advance, past, present and future, is not likely to affect the developing world as much as it will the developed world. There will be continued slow growth largely because the decisions of development continue to rest primarily with the developed world. The key need, then, is for innovation and experimentation. Implied in this is the need for us to recognize that the implementation of our programs must be close to the felt needs of the developing world. In short, we need to involve our partners in Africa and elsewhere in the planning and implementation of development assistance to a greater extent than we have in the past.

If we are to cooperate in helping developing countries achieve their share of the world's goods and if we are to eliminate poverty at home, we must realize that neither increased resources nor better technology are sufficient, though they are clearly necessary.

The crucial element is style: It has to be done in a human style. When we meet despair anywhere, it is in part a consequence of powerlessness. There is an important ethical issue that we need to consider: How do we achieve the benefits of development without destroying people's capacity to act freely? This quality of life that we are attempting to achieve is not the same for all the peoples of the world. It is certainly not, in the final instance, an abundance of goods. One should question whether the word "assistance" does not smack of charity, paternalism, or some other attitude demeaning to the recipient. Perhaps "technical cooperation" is a preferable term implying an equitable exchange and not a unilateral conferral of knowledge upon inferior recipients. When one examines words such as "assistance," one could go on to question the attitudinal baggage conveyed by the word "development"—coined by those from developed areas to characterize efforts by others which often implicitly presume to be aimed at imitating their own accomplishments and achieving their own status.

More important than the words are the attitudes and sensitivity of the individual development actor, who must come to the knowledge that there exists an inherent structural paternalism in the very relationship between one as "helper" and the other as "recipient," between "developed" and "underdeveloped."

Another dynamic is that in the transfer of technology from one society to another, the "how" is as important as the "what." We need to recognize the values of the recipient, and we need to recognize that development assistance, particularly because much of its verbal baggage comes out of the West, needs to be done in a human style and in a way that maximizes the freedom and dignity of the individual. Sensitivity, awareness, and understanding are all characteristics that must mark the person who presumes to engage in the highly complex act of helping another—an act that becomes even more complex and more demanding if it be between humans of different cultures or different economic levels.

This is the ethical dimension—to expand the recipient's freedom, his area of choice—to master the means that will enable him to say, "I did it, and my doing made a difference." Such mastery depends more than anything else on what one African writer has called the donor's "aptitude for understanding and manner of loving." This is the challenge of our mutual ability to cope with change, and the cultural implications of the "helping hand."

DISCUSSION

Central to the discussion of Dr. Gadsden's paper and Dr. Raullerson's response to it were the issues of United States attitude toward the educational and cultural needs of Africa and the style with which these needs are addressed. Dr. Gadsden's view—to wit, that people must realistically understand that the United States approach to education and culture in Africa (as to every other aspect of African life), in contrast to that of Europe, will always be marginal—was not challenged. Nevertheless, the question was raised as to whether this bias in our national thinking should not be challenged. Is a Eurocentric position really in our national interest?

Attention was called to the lack of coordination between the various agencies involved with our policy in the areas of education and culture. It was suggested that this lack of coordination vitiated the United States' marginal (or as Dr. Gadsden termed it, "symbolic") policy toward Africa. One discussant said that the attention given to education and culture in the Lagos Plan of Action did indicate that the Africans are determined to overcome the lack of planning in those areas. Moreover, the attention they were paying to the cost-effectiveness in these two domains represented a new point of departure which the United States should recognize and applaud. However, there was pessimism that much could be done about short-term policy planning procedures when only longer-ranged planning (for example, until the year 2000) would effectively deal with African needs.

Many participants in the discussion were disturbed by the growing importance of the buzz-word "privatization," and its implications for United States policy toward Africa. It was claimed that, while this concept may have a great deal of utility in the United States, it may be ill-adapted to the reality of Africa, where there is very little private wealth. Another discussant criticized the paternalistic connotations of the concept, implying as it did that the United States is really laying down the law as to how the Africans should plan their lives. The concern voiced was that the realities of contemporary Africa called for more coordination than in Western societies. The necessities of nation-building and the need to deal with ethnicity and other cultural differences often called for the type of planning unnecessary and unknown in developed countries. Nevertheless, one observer claimed that funds mediated through the private volunteer organizations, whether of private or government origin, can be used more flexibly than those provided government to government.

The element of style in United States educational and cultural policy (meaning that it is not what the United States did or did not do, but the way that it was perceived) was commented upon by a number of discussants. Here again, it was suggested that the notion of privatization, especially in education and culture, contributed to the impression that the Africans were really dependent upon outsiders and that they were being shunted to the private sector because United States government funds were not now available. It was pointed out that neither the United States nor other donors recognized the importance of the counterpart contributions of African states. The Peace Corps program was cited as an indication of what the Africans always provided in order to accommodate those who wished to help them. There was the further suggestion that much of the attempts of outsiders to help Africans foundered not on *what* to give, but on *how* to give what was available. Finally, disappointment was expressed that there was not greater recognition of the contribution of a sound educational and cultural policy to United States foreign relations.

CHAPTER 7

UNITED STATES POLICIES TOWARD SOUTH AFRICA AND NAMIBIA

Gwendolyn M. Carter

Any attempt to analyze United States policies toward South Africa and Namibia on the eve of an election is a hazardous enterprise. Moreover, southern Africa is in flux and what seems appropriate at this point may well not be so later. Nonetheless, the Democrats spelled out in their platform eight specific ways in which they would have "reversed" what they call "the Reagan administration failed policy of 'constructive engagement'" and "strongly and unequivocally opposed the apartheid regime in South Africa."

With the avowed aim of hastening "establishment of a democratic unitary political system in South Africa," the Democratic platform pledged "scrupulous enforcement of the 1977 U.N. arms embargo," including enforcement of restrictions on the sale of "dual use equipment." The platform also reimposed export controls in effect during the Carter administration which the Reagan administration had considerably relaxed. Going much further than this, however, the Democratic platform pledged, among other sanctions, to impose bans on "all new loans by U.S. business interests to the South African government" and also on all new investment and loans to the South African private sector until there was "substantial progress toward the full participation of all the people of South Africa in the social, political, and economic life in that country."

The Democratic platform also proposed banning the "sale or transfer of sophisticated computers and nuclear technology" to South Africa and stopping "the importation of South African gold coins," both sanctions which had been discussed in detail in the Democratic-controlled House of Representatives Sub-committee on Africa.[1]

Striking directly at one of the most unsavory features of South African life, the Democrats compared the house arrests of political opponents of the South African government to the harassment of the Sakharovs, and demanded the release of Nelson Mandela, described as "leader of the African National Congress," his wife Minnie, and "all other political prisoners."

Regarding Namibia, the Democrats said they would demand compliance with U.N. Security Council Resolution 435 of 1978 which spelled out the necessary steps for Namibian independence. Moreover, they pledged "effective sanctions against South Africa unless and until" it granted Namibia independence.

The Republicans naturally claimed credit for the March, 1984, Nkomati agreement establishing working relations between South Africa and Mozambique and for what they called improved American relations throughout southern Africa. In their platform the Republicans pledged that they would "continue to assist threatened African governments to protect themselves," probably by providing arms, and would "work with them" for two specific purposes: to "protect their continent from subversion"—presumably from the East—and to "safeguard their strategic minerals," possibly an oblique reference to the Cape Route and to what used to be considered South Africa's role in protecting it.

Concerning Namibia, the Republicans maintained that they would continue what they termed their "vigorous efforts" to achieve its independence. Naturally, they linked this goal with "the expulsion of Cubans" from what they termed "occupied Angola."

Rather surprisingly, nearly half of the short section on Africa's share of the platform was devoted to asserting the Republican "commitment to the rights of all South Africans," which was followed by the statement that "apartheid is repugnant." Thereafter, there was a more general statement that "in South Africa as elsewhere on the continent, we support well-conceived efforts to foster peace, prosperity and stability."

What was more striking in the Republican platform, and in its reaffirmation in the convention address by Jeane Kirkpatrick, former United States Ambassador to the United Nations, was their attack on the foreign policy of the Democratic Party and its execution by the Carter-Mondale administration. At the start of its foreign policy section— "America Secure and the World at Peace"—the Republican platform rejected what it called "the notion of guilt and apology which animates so much of the foreign policy of the Democratic Party," and earlier maintained that the Democratic Party "asserts the rhetoric of freedom but in practice it follows a policy of withdrawal and isolation."

Kirkpatrick echoed the theme. "We need friends and allies," she said, "with whom to share the pleasures and the protection of our civilization. We cannot, therefore, be indifferent to the subversion of others' independence or to the development of new weapons by our adversaries or of new vulnerabilities by our friends," to which she added: "The last Democratic administration did not seem to notice much, or care much or do much about these matters. . . ." It was not only an unjustified barb but a dangerous one, striking at the basic consensus that should undergird the country's foreign affairs.

The very fact, however, that American policies toward South Africa and Namibia were considered to be of major importance in 1984 reflects not only the striking developments that have taken place within southern Africa during the past decade but also substantial changes in the political thinking and values both of American public figures and the general public. While there has long been a general abhorrence of the overt racial discrimination that characterized South African life and policies, this basic attitude has now become intertwined with issues of strategic concern, East-West tensions, the international role of the United Nations, and many others.

Two decades ago the issues of southern Africa seemed remote to most Americans, as well as to the government. The United

States complied with the United Nations-sponsored arms embargo against South Africa in the early 1960s and supported a variety of resolutions condemning apartheid. There was little, if any, general discussion on the issues or positive use of American power, or even of its potential influence on situations in southern Africa. There was a ritual opposition to colonialism and apartheid but little concern. Indeed, President Nixon's first term was marked by a strong bias toward southern Africa's white regimes as providing the necessary basis of stability and "constructive change" in the region.

This negative attitude in the early days of the Nixon administration toward promoting change in southern Africa, and particularly within its white regimes, went so far as to lead it to lift partially the arms embargo against South Africa, and to oppose rather than support United Nations resolutions critical of apartheid. Most strikingly, the Nixon administration yielded to domestic pressure and acquiesced to the 1971 Byrd amendment that enabled the United States to import Rhodesian chrome in violation of the United Nations-mandated economic sanctions imposed on Rhodesia following Ian Smith's illegal unilateral declaration of independence on November 11, 1965.

GROWING INSTABILITY IN SOUTHERN AFRICA AND KISSINGER'S FAILURE TO STABILIZE IT

The mid-1970s, however, provided to the Nixon and Ford administrations alarming evidence of growing instability in the white-controlled states of southern Africa. Of particular concern was the intrusion of Soviet and Cuban arms and personnel into the civil war in Angola. At the same time, the African nationalist onslaught on the Ian Smith regime in Rhodesia was growing in intensity. The Portuguese were yielding control in Mozambique, and in 1976, South Africa's largest peri-urban African township, Soweto, erupted in protest at apartheid restrictions. Moreover, the startling success of the Arab oil boycott raised overall concern regarding the West's continued access to the rich mineral resources of southern Africa should they come under the control of unfriendly Soviet-oriented states.

As events moved quickly in Angola, then-Secretary of State Henry Kissinger sought to block the Soviet and Cuban intrusions seeking to gain control in the Angolan civil war for the Marxist-oriented People's Movement for the Liberation of Angola (MPLA). However, the Tunny resolution in the Senate prevented him from taking the overt military actions he desired. Subsequently, the Clark amendment in the House forbade direct or indirect assistance to Angolan factions. South African troops, invading Angola from the south with tacit American approval, failed to change the situation and were forced to withdraw. The MPLA was widely recognized as the legitimate government of Angola—although not by the United States—but was forcefully opposed by the Union for the Total Independence of Angola (UNITA).

During his remaining time as secretary of state in the Nixon and Ford administrations, Kissinger sought to establish a containment policy governing the rest of southern Africa, most notably in Rhodesia and Namibia. Engaging in shuttle diplomacy with the tacit support of the South African government, Kissinger succeeded in persuading Ian Smith to accept a constitutional framework which would establish majority rule in Rhodesia within the next two years. These provisions proved unacceptable, however, to the Zimbabwe Patriotic Front, led at that time by Joshua Nkomo and Robert Mugabe, and also to their supporters, the presidents of the Front Line States (Angola, Botswana, Mozambique, Tanzania, and Zambia).

Kissinger also sought, with little success, to persuade South African leaders to withdraw their forces from Namibia as demanded by Security Council Resolution 385. Despite South African protestations, Kissinger had little confidence in the constitution-making potential of the recently established Turnhalle Conference composed of representatives from the eleven ethnic divisions into which South Africa had divided the territory. Thus, although Kissinger had seized the initiative once more in United States-southern Africa relations and prepared the way for new policies by the incoming administration, there was no peace either in Rhodesia or in Namibia when Kissinger turned over the office to his Democratic successor in 1977.

NEW POLICIES UNDER THE CARTER ADMINISTRATION

The Carter administration had good reasons for adopting a more liberal and Africa-oriented policy toward southern Africa than Kissinger had pursued. President Carter himself had strong humanitarian feelings that made apartheid repugnant. Moreover, his party's support by liberal academics, church groups, and black Americans had contributed substantially to its narrow victory at the polls. In addition, African nations (most notably Nigeria, which had replaced South Africa as the United States' largest African trading partner) commanded increasing international attention. Thus constructive policies favoring African interests rather than reflecting fears of Soviet encroachment in southern Africa seemed appropriate in the mid-1970s and also proved popular, at least in the early years of the Carter administration.

President Carter appointed Andrew Young United States Ambassador to the United Nations. Young, a distinguished black internationalist with a background as an effective congressman from Georgia (1973–77), indicated his intention of supporting United Nations policies in southern Africa, particularly in Rhodesia. With strong administration support, Congress was quickly persuaded to repeal the Byrd amendment, thereby registering the new American commitment to aid in bringing Rhodesia to an acceptable independence.

In his 1980 article in *Foreign Affairs*,[2] Andrew Young maintains that the repeal of the Byrd amendment "helped create" a new atmosphere of "considerable trust" with both the British and the Africans. Thereafter, there was what he called a "free-flowing exchange of information" between the United States and Great Britain on the one hand, and with the Zimbabwean Patriotic Front, the Front Line States, and Nigeria on the other. African-

Western talks over the next three years led to the Lancaster House negotiations out of which came Zimbabwean independence.

Throughout these and other negotiations, the Carter Administration's respect for the Front Line States led to support of their initiatives rather than continued attempts to force them to follow American leads. Behind this latter posture was the belief that regardless of their particular ideology, the policies of independent African states would not threaten American interests unless the East-West conflict was brought specifically into the situation, as it had been over Angola.

In its role in the Rhodesia-Zimbabwe negotiations, as well as in other African situations, the Carter administration studiously avoided the friendly posture toward South Africa that had marked the preceding Ford-Kissinger period. The most dramatic example of its distinctive posture toward South Africa came during the meeting on May 19 and 20, 1977, in Vienna. During that meeting Vice President Mondale addressed Prime Minister Vorster with no uncertainty about the American goal of full political participation by all South Africans. While it was after the meeting that Mondale affirmed that his words meant "one man, one vote," there had never been any doubt about his basic meaning, nor Vorster's strong reaction against it, nor its impact on African thinking both inside and outside South Africa.

Despite its obvious distaste for South African policies, the Carter administration was slow to take any punitive action against that country. Several possible measures, like discouraging new investment and bank loans, were considered, but even the milder move of denying tax credits to investors was not adopted. Carter and Young appear to have shared a belief, for which they had very little evidence, that economic interactions between the United States and South Africa could have a beneficial effect. Fortunately, in March, 1977, the Reverend Leon Sullivan announced that twelve American companies had adopted a code of fair employment and non-segregation practices in South Africa which the government could applaud.

In October, 1977, a crackdown by the South African government on black consciousness organizations, the Christian Institute, and the major newspaper edited by an African, *The*

World, followed the security police killing of Steve Biko, South African black consciousness leader.

These actions led the United States to join with its Western allies in support of a Security Council decision on November 4, 1977, that mandated an embargo on South Africa's acquisition of arms and related materials. Although a voluntary embargo already existed, the decision was psychologically significant since there had never before been a mandatory embargo against a United Nations member.

THE NAMIBIAN SITUATION

The second major southern African issue with which the Carter administration was concerned was the future of Namibia. Taken from Germany during World War I and officially declared a mandate under the League of Nations thereafter, Namibia had been treated as virtually a fifth South African province after that war. Moreover, after World War II South Africa was the only country to refuse either to grant independence to a captured territory or to place it under the more rigorous United Nations trusteeship system. On the contrary, South Africa increasingly extended its own discriminatory legislation to Namibia, treating it as if it were part of its own territory.

Judicial redress was sought before the World Court in a long, drawn-out case which ended in 1966 without a decision. The General Assembly, with the United States voting in the affirmative, then revoked South Africa's mandate through Resolution 2145 on the ground of maladministration and resolved to take over the administration of Namibia itself until the territory reached independence. Subsequently, the International Court of Justice in an advisory opinion issued on June 21, 1971, reinforced the Assembly's action by declaring that since South Africa's presence in Namibia was illegal, it was under an obligation to "withdraw its administration immediately" and thus end "its occupation of the territory."

South Africa, however, refused to yield and began a long-range program of reorganizing the administration of the territory into white and ethnic African divisions. Representatives from these entities were then formed into the so-called Turnhalle Conference, as already noted, which on August 18, 1976, produced a short statement of principles suggesting "independence" by the end of 1978. The South West African Peoples' Organization (SWAPO), the exiled nationalist movement headed by Sam Nujoma, was never included in these discussions despite the fact that it was recognized as the authentic representative of the Namibian people by both the Organization of African Unity and the United Nations.

Confronting this situation, the Carter administration took the lead in organizing the so-called Contact Group composed of representatives of the five Western Security Council members—the United States, Great Britain, Canada, France, and West Germany—working closely with the Nigerians and with representatives from the Front Line States. Chaired by the American representative, Donald McHenry, the Contact Group undertook personal negotiations early in 1977, meeting in Pretoria with Prime Minister Vorster and other high-level South African figures. Subsequently, they conducted their own investigations in Namibia itself. Both in South Africa and in Namibia, the Contact Group made it clear that a Turnhalle "constitution" would in no sense be acceptable.

Following a seemingly endless series of meetings among all parties concerned with Namibia, Prime Minister Vorster agreed on April 25, 1978, to a United Nations-sponsored transfer of power in Namibia. The Americans and the British pressured SWAPO to agree as well. A plan for a United Nations civilian and military operation in Namibia, paving the way for elections leading to Namibian independence, was unanimously approved by the Security Council on September 29, 1978, and embodied in Resolution 435. It was sponsored by the five members of the Contact Group, including, of course, the United States, and by Gabon, Mauritius, and Nigeria.

By that time, however, Vorster was already objecting to the size of the United Nations force that the Secretary-General had suggested would be necessary to prepare for electing the government of an independent Namibia. In the light of subsequent developments, none of which have yet brought Namibia close to independence, it is worth noting that the Cubans in Angola were never mentioned during any of these exchanges.

The Carter administration was sensitive to the harsh conditions, as well as to the restiveness of the massive African majority in South Africa. It also recognized the growing importance of Nigeria, with its huge oil reserves (making it second only to Saudi Arabia for American imports) and its determination to play a role in international affairs affecting Africa. Since that time, neither factor has played so important a role in determining America's South African and Namibian policies, but their impact has not been forgotten.

THE REAGAN ADMINISTRATION

With the electoral victory of Ronald Reagan in November, 1980, American policies toward southern Africa changed substantially. The Carter administration had at least urged the South African regime to open negotiations with accepted leaders of its black majority and to move toward more evenhanded policies affecting all its people. Jesse Helms, Barry Goldwater, and Strom Thurmond, strong critics of Carter's Africa policies, headed key committees in the Republican-controlled Senate. Reagan himself was believed to hold similiar views. Thus a strong tilt toward the white regime in South Africa could be expected.

In an article entitled "South Africa: Strategy for Change," printed in *Foreign Affairs,* Winter 1980– 81, Chester A. Crocker, an academic who became assistant secretary of state for African affairs, gave notice that he envisaged southern Africa as both "a changing area" and one of East-West rivalry in which the United States must compete with what he called "our global adversary" if we were to influence and shape its destiny.

Crocker maintains that he did not underestimate the potential power of black nationalism to become ultimately a major force within South Africa. However, not surprisingly, he stressed the importance of the political and military white dominance that Prime Minister Vorster was organizing under his own leadership. Crocker thus gave notice that he was determined to work with that force through what he called "constructive engagement" to secure American economic and security interests in southern Africa.

Crocker hardly mentioned Namibia in his article although the Geneva Conference on Namibia was under way in January, 1981, even before the inauguration of the Reagan administration. It had been organized to handle South Africa's charges that the United Nations bias toward SWAPO made it impossible to enforce the procedures that had been drawn up to implement Security Council Resolution 435. Reagan's refusal even to send an observer to the conference undercut whatever possibilities it might have had.

Crocker and his staff were far from being unaware of possibilities latent in the Namibian issue. They believed that South African disengagement from Namibia might be bargained against the withdrawal of the Cubans from Angola. At least the former seemed more likely if the latter took place.

Crocker opened his initiative late in March, 1981, and by the end of the summer the Contact Group had approved an American plan for negotiations it was then felt might possibly lead to a final settlement in Namibia. The plan involved three stages: (1) an agreement on basic principles that would protect minority rights after independence, (2) procedures to establish a body that would draw up a constitution, and (3) implementation of these arrangements through a United Nations force.

By February, 1982, South Africa and SWAPO had agreed on a statement of constitutional principles, and in July, 1982, the Contact Group announced that stage one was completed. But by this time the Cuban issue dominated all discussions.

On September 12, 1982, President Reagan sent a personal letter to African heads of state expressing his own commitment to the linkage principle. It precipitated a bitter diplomatic struggle. The Front Line States rejected the notion of linkage and the Angolans launched wide-ranging efforts to swing African and Eastern opinion behind support for a continued Cuban presence in Angola. Paradoxically, the Cubans probably became still more entrenched in Angola because of the reverberations from the linkage proposal. At least the Americans had failed to indicate any official support for UNITA, although that had seemed possible at one point.

The key to the policies directed by Crocker and his deputy, Frank Wisner, has been their belief that Soviet military aggression in southern Africa will increase, and, less convincingly, that Cuban forces in Angola are a focal point. Speaking in Munich on November 9, 1983, Wisner described American policy toward Namibia in simple — indeed oversimplified — terms. He endorsed Resolution 435 as "the best, indeed the only way of obtaining" Namibian independence. In the American view, however, this goal is linked in turn to protecting the security of South Africa itself by removing the Cuban troops from Angola.

To many observers the argument is flawed by failure to recognize both South Africa's massive military strength, acknowledged by Crocker himself, and by the apparent Cuban need to concentrate on supporting the MPLA government against the substantial forces and military acumen of its rival UNITA. Though based in the southern part of Angola, where its ethnic roots exist, UNITA, well-supplied with South African arms, seems able to launch attacks against MPLA facilities in areas well beyond that base.

Questions may be raised as to how the presence of Cuban troops in Angola most affects American policy in Africa: Is the effect of Cuban troops there of most concern in our policies toward Namibia and South Africa? Does the presence of Cuban troops relate more to our policies in middle Africa, falling within the broad dimensions of American-Soviet rivalry within that continent? Or is the issue an extension of the long-continued tension over Cuba's proximity to the United States and its influence in other nearby island territories such as Grenada? All these factors may well interrelate to cause the Cuban issue to appear more threatening than any one aspect of the situation might suggest. At least the Reagan administration tried twice, though unsuccessfully, to abrogate the Clark amendment, thereby removing restraints in the use of American troops in Angola.

By placing the security of South Africa so firmly in the center of American policy in southern Africa, the United States played into the hands of the Vorster administration. Not surprisingly, the two regimes agree in their distaste for the Marxist orientation of the governments in both Angola and Mozambique. That orientation has led to continued American non-recognition of the MPLA regime in Angola and to the withdrawal of the American ambassador from Mozambique for a considerable time following a dispute over the presence of CIA personnel. From the South African point of view, however, the danger posed by these two regimes was their hospitality to the exiled African National Congress, the long-established standard bearer of African nationalism dedicated to turning South Africa into a non-racial state.

The United States lent a supportive hand to South Africa's negotiations with Mozambique. The result was the Nkomati Accord early in March, 1984, pledging that each side would refrain from providing sanctuary and aid to the opponents of the other. Mozambique has lived up to its pledge and has ejected all but a very few active members of the African National Congress (ANC). Combined with a comparable earlier agreement between South Africa and Swaziland, which was publicized only relatively recently, the Nkomati Accord has noticeably hurt the ANC, although not in any sense irreparably. There is little if any indication, however, that South Africa has lived up to its pledge to sign the Accord restraining the Mozambique Resistance Movement (MNR), whose devastating attacks on and inside Mozambique had been the reason that country felt forced to sign the Accord.

In an unusually long and comprehensive interview with Jonathan Steele and Victoria Brittain, printed in *The Guardian* (London) on July 20, 1984, Crocker claimed that the United States had "helped to define an agenda of change, negotiations and development" within which "all the major players" in southern Africa were participating. Citing particularly the Nkomati Accord between Mozambique and South Africa, he maintained that "the illusion that armed struggle will solve South Africa's problems has been dealt a body blow."

As for change inside South Africa, Crocker claimed in an interview printed in the airmail edition of *The Star* (Johannesburg) of June 25, 1984, that it was already under way though he admitted that "it had not led as yet to results satisfactory to any of us, you or me." Challenged to describe "specific proposals"

Americans are making to help the South Africans "formulate a consistent programme of action for change," Crocker first mentioned channelling funds "directly" to black South Africans "to promote black advancement particularly in the field of education." In the second place, Crocker took credit for encouraging "the constructive involvement" of American and other firms in "removing racism from the economy and the job market," presumably through the Sullivan principles. The Republican administration, however, has vigorously opposed the Democratic proposal to impose penalties under the Export Administration Act on American firms that do not adhere to those principles.[3]

The final point made rather ambiguously by Crocker in his interview in *The Star* was that there were "limits" to the American relationship with South Africa "in the absence of significant movement away from a system that is based fundamentally on legally entrenched racism."

Challenged to estimate whether the Mozambique-South Africa agreement had put "the liberation movements" on the defensive, and to comment on the future for SWAPO and the ANC, Crocker made a sharp distinction between the two organizations. SWAPO, he emphasized, is an important party to the Namibian negotiations and has support from the Front Line States and "others as well, internationally." The ANC, he suggested, was like "other exile movements such as the PAC [Pan-African Congress]," and is thus apparently to be disregarded in any negotiations.

This offhand attitude toward the African National Congress, the oldest and most popular opposition movement in South Africa, seems unfortunately to be characteristic of the attitude of the Reagan administration. It was challenged during hearings in the Subcommittee on Africa referred to earlier, and more particularly and in detail through a substantial scholarly article by Professor Thomas G. Karis of City University, New York, entitled "Revolution in the Making: Black Politics in South Africa," in the Winter, 1983–84, issue of *Foreign Affairs*.

Professor Karis points out that the African National Congress "has become a well-organized liberation movement with wide-ranging international connections" and is "now enjoying a broad-based resurgence of support for its program of resistance to the white South African government." Although its mobility within southern Africa has undoubtedly been hurt by the implementation of the Nkomati Accord, one result seems to have been to reinforce its links with and bases in other countries in southern Africa and to strengthen those within South Africa itself. This underestimation of the importance of the African National Congress in the current South African situation may be one of the Reagan administration's more important misjudgments.

The counter side of the Reagan administration's downplaying the role of the African National Congress is its conviction that, as Wisner stated in the discussion in the Subcommittee on Africa on September 14, 1983, "revolutionary change is under way in South Africa." He hastily added that, of course, repression continued which would naturally be verbally condemned. But when Howard Wolpe, chairman of the subcommittee, asked why that condemnation should be taken seriously when at the same time the United States was moving toward "an expanded closer relationship," there was no reply.

On June 23, 1984, Lawrence S. Eagleburger, Under Secretary of State for Political Affairs, delivered a comprehensive speech to the National Conference of Editorial Writers in San Francisco. He maintained that "we stand against injustice, and therefore must reject any legal and political premises and consequences of apartheid." Going still further, he declared that "by one means or another, South Africa's domestic racial system will be changed," but without specifying in what ways, and whether they would improve the conditions and opportunities of South Africa's huge African majority.

Eagleburger also declared that American and South African interests were "best served by encouraging the change that is now under way in South Africa." He presumably meant the representation being provided the Coloureds and Indians under the new constitution, which he said it would be "arrogance" to disregard. He made no mention, however, of the fact that both the Coloured and Indian chambers are strictly limited. Under the new constitution, they may deal only with matters affecting their own communities, while on any issue of general concern, all three chambers vote together thereby affording the white majority complete control. Moreover, the fact that Prime Minister

Vorster has become President Vorster, with a guaranteed five-year term and enhanced authority, further tips the balance toward continued white control.

What needs to be faced by the United States (regardless of which party is in power) is that a progressive and devastating denationalization of South Africa's African population is in process with the apparent aim, however it may be concealed, that ultimately there will be no African citizens in that country. Has the United States the will and the leverage to stop this appalling process, and exert its influence so as to improve the conditions of life, economic opportunities, and above all the security and stability of South Africa's black majority? The Democrats have spelled out a series of possible sanctions if any American administration has the will to make use of them.

Even if an American administration would formally condemn the South African government's arbitrary arrests and imprisonment of its opponents and critics, and particularly its extensive use of torture, there might well be some effect. The United States has little hesitation about doing so if the offender is an Eastern regime. Surely, the forcible removal and resettlement of whole African communities that have long had legal rights to where they live is more than reason enough to protest in ways the South African government can hardly ignore. Unfortunately, one is left with words rather than deeds, and even the words rarely ring true.

Finally, let me put forward what I hope American policies toward South Africa and Namibia will be someday, and what I fear will happen if those policies are not established and followed.

What is needed in southern Africa is a consistent policy supported by both American political parties and worked out in conjunction with our Western allies and with the SADCC countries and South Africa itself. The Namibian issue ultimately may be worked out by South Africa and SWAPO, even if the United States continues to insist that Cuban withdrawal from Angola must be part of the arrangement. How much better if the United States would reconsider its insistence on Cuban troop withdrawal (they have long been north of the line originally proposed) and allow the parties most concerned to work out their own *modus vivendi*. Otherwise, I fear still greater violence and little change except more suffering by those who have never known much else.

The major problem for southern Africa is clearly South Africa itself, with its unacceptable racial policy on the one hand and its dominant military power on the other. There is always the danger that its military police power will be used to block internal or external policy that seems to threaten Afrikaner supremacy at home or its own explicit hegemony within the region.

There seem only two possibilities of securing basic change in the structure and practices that result from apartheid and all that flows from the principle of racial domination. One is by internal violence supported by any other willing states. The other is by external persuasion backed up by any sanctions necessary to be convincing. If the discussions can be kept secret, there is more chance of some success in persuading the South African regime to move steadily toward a more open society. At least it seems worth a try.

REFERENCES

1. Hearing on the Internal Political Situation in South Africa before the Subcommittee on Africa of the Committee on Foreign Affairs, House of Representatives, Ninety-Eighth Congress, First Session, September 14, 1983.

2. Andrew Young, "The United States and Africa: Victory for Diplomacy," *Foreign Affairs: America and the World* (1980) 648–666.

3. Hearing on the Internal Political Situation in South Africa in the Subcommittee on Africa, House of Representatives, September 14, 1983, 82ff.

Commentary

Peter Duignan

I am less concerned than is Dr. Carter with the platforms of the Democrats and the Republicans. These as usual are full of sound and fury and signify little or nothing. Once elected, a candidate is likely to pay little attention to the platform or to feel bound by it. At least that has been the case in most elections. But it is not at all obvious to me why the Democratic Party should be committed to "a democratic unitary political system in South Africa." After all, there are confederal democracies such as Switzerland, and there are federal states that leave a wide measure of independence to provinces, such as in Canada.

Sanctions and boycotts have failed in the past to move the South Africans; they will probably fail to move them in the future, so revamping export controls and adding more sanctions to reduce loans as the Democrats suggest seems to me sterile and a return to failed policies. The means to be used cannot achieve the ends desired, so why pursue them?

The difficulties of applying moral judgments to diplomacy are many. Few governments outside of Western Europe and North America are democratic. Few governments are moral or just or rule for the benefit of their people. If the United States stops

talking to South Africa and imposes further sanctions and boycotts on that country because of its racist policies, we will have
to stop talking to half the nations of the world who oppose their
minorities, their political opposition, their religious bodies, or
persons who own property. And, to be consistent, the United
States would be obliged to apply equal doses of sanction and
boycott to most dictatorships in Africa.

Perhaps for a while we should impose a self-denying ordinance
on moral judgments on relations between states. Diplomacy, like
politics, is the art of the possible, and if we use our leverage
toward an unachievable end we will create a mess.

The Democrats may see a parallel between the arrests of political opponents in South Africa and in the Soviet Union, but most
students of the Soviet Union would be shocked at such a comparison, either in terms of the numbers involved, or of the conditions
of arrest of Sakharov in comparison, say, to the Reverend Mr.
Naude. Yet the Democrats call for economic sanctions against
South Africa of a kind not advocated against the Soviet Union.

I would hardly characterize Nixon's administration as having
"a strong bias" toward the white regimes of southern Africa.
During the Nixon era, United States offical disapproval of South
Africa relented only slightly. Whereas the Africanists in the State
Department looked to increased pressure on the "white minority
regimes" in southern Africa, the National Security Council and
the Defense Department argued in favor of a cautious South
African-American rapprochement. The new policy, expressed in
a National Security Study Memorandum (NSSM 39, 1970), derived from four assumptions: (1) The whites in southern Africa
would retain power for a considerable time, especially in South
Africa, where military power could easily curtail internal or
external African opposition to white rule. (2) Increasing industrialization in South Africa would improve the condition of the
blacks, thereby leading to greater internal stability. (3) The
United States was likely to effect internal reforms in South Africa
by maintaining friendly relations with Pretoria, rather than by
issuing empty threats that would merely make the whites more
obdurate. (4) The Nixon administration could not afford to
penalize American businessmen in the name of a policy that was
not working in the first place. This in effect is what happened and

has proven to be a realistic policy. Kissinger erred only in thinking the Portuguese could hang on.

Nevertheless, Nixon was far from being a traditional conservative. While pledging himself not to interfere in the "internal affairs" of any African nation, in 1970 he committed himself to outspoken censure of South Africa and Rhodesia in a manner inconceivable thirty years earlier, and in a fashion appied to no other government:

> There is no question of the United States condoning, or acquiescing in, the racial policies of the white-ruled regimes. For moral as well as historical reasons, the United States stands firmly for the principles of racial equality and self-determination.

The United States, according to the President, believed in peaceful rather than warlike change. But the United States abhorred "the racial policies of the white regimes"; the real issue was to find a means of changing them without drifting into the vortex of violence and counterviolence.

The MPLA according to Dr. Carter is "widely regarded as the legitimate government of Angola, although not by the United States." But it is not clear what her definition of legitimacy is. The MPLA was not elected to power, and does not represent the majority of the people of Angola; the MPLA stays in power only because of Cuban troops and Soviet and East German arms and officers. The Portuguese handed over the succession not to the MPLA but to a tripartite government constituted in January, 1975, by agreement between the Portuguese and the MPLA, UNITA, and the FNLA. All of these three were regarded as "the sole and legitimate representatives of the Angola peoples."

With the MPLA's victory in 1975, Angola moved into the international limelight. Some American academics have called for United States recognition of the Marxist-Leninist regime at Luanda, as have liberal politicans who considered such recognition justified by both self-interest and equity. But it is not in the United States' interest, or in the interest of the Angolan people, to recognize the MPLA government. For the present, the MPLA is an anti-Western group that looks on the Soviet Communist Party as a model. According to its own statements, the MPLA is not simply a radical African nationalist group, as claimed by academics and even by such United States government agencies as the Agency for International Development. The MPLA, which in 1977 became a Marxist-Leninist vanguard party dedicated to the pursuit of "scientific socialism" and world revolution, does not seek to pursue a neutral foreign policy. The MPLA firmly sides with what it calls the "socialist camp" in the global struggle against the forces of world capitalism.

Operating as the self-styled "vanguard of the proletariat," uniting workers, peasants, and intellectuals in a country overwhelmingly dependent on backward farmers, the party believes in the Leninist principle of "democratic centralism" and looks to the transformation of Angola into a socialist state. The MPLA's influence is weak among dissident ethnic groups such as the Bakongo in the north and the Ovimbundu in the south. By 1979, almost half of the Central Committee were military professionals. In 1984, some fifteen to twenty thousand Cubans were still deployed in Angola.

Admittedly, the MPLA permits the Gulf Oil Company to operate on Angolan soil, but this is only common sense—a substantial portion of Angola's revenue comes from Gulf Oil's operations. Similarly, the Soviet Union and its allies have consistently asked for and received Western credits and infusions of technology and managerial expertise. That does not mean that they are not Communist governments or that Angola would not, in time of international tension, stop selling oil to the West. The Soviet Union, however, considers these commercial relations instruments in the international class struggle, which they intend to win. Going beyond Lenin's predictions, capitalists now compete among themselves for the privilege of selling, on easy credit terms, the very rope by which they will be hanged.

In terms of international morality and civil rights, Angola's record has been deplorable. It is a police state complete with reeducation centers and German-trained secret police. There is widespread persecution of practicing Christians; whites have fled or been forced to leave. The MPLA is a minority party that rules through terror and Cuban troops; it represents only one-third of the people. The other two-thirds are represented by the National Front for the Liberation of Angola (FNLA) and the National Union for the Total Independence of Angola (UNITA), which holds large parts of the country. Free speech, a free press, and the right to vote—the same freedoms that the United States sought to establish in Zimbabwe through international embargo—are absent in Angola.

There is as yet no sign of improvement. Food shortages are everywhere; the Benguela Railway has not operated since 1975 because of guerrilla activities; and exports, except oil from Cabinda, have dwindled. Angola has joined the long list of countries whose bright hopes in a revolution have been dispelled by post-revolutionary reality. The United States should not recognize the MPLA as the legal government of Angola but should arm and train the FNLA and UNITA to force the MPLA to form a coalition government. It should also encourage the Cubans, East Germans, and Soviets to return to their homelands.

While FRELIMO, which controls Mozambique, has maintained somewhat more independence from the Soviet Union than has the MPLA, it is still a self-proclaimed Marxist-Leninist party and is an admitted member (as is the MPLA) of the international Marxist-Leninist movement. The United States should encourage FRELIMO to leave the Soviet camp, to refuse all facility or base rights to the Soviets, and to practice, as it is now, a form of détente with South Africa.

As Dr. Carter shows, the Carter administration repudiated the agreement concluded between Kissinger and Smith over Rhodesia and refused to accord recognition to a moderate and racially-mixed government in Salisbury. The Carter team used harsh language in condeming South Africa. Above all, the administration took it for granted that the United States had the right to interfere in South Africa's affairs, and that black political rights within the Republic of South Africa could only be satisfied within the framework of a unitary state through the institution of a universal franchise, defined by Vice President Mondale as "one man, one vote, with each vote equally weighted."

The liberal members of the Carter administration, however, labored under severe constraints in that American (and also British) public opinion would not back a tough line against

South Africa. The Foreign Policy Association, an influential liberal American group, completed an opinion study of its members and found that 51 percent of them wanted to work closely with South Africa to maintain stability. Only 10 percent wanted to sever ties with Pretoria if the South Africans were to continue with their policy of apartheid. A nation-wide Harris poll proved even more discouraging from the liberal standpoint. While the majority of Americans disapproved of South African policies, more than 76 percent of the respondents considered that Americans had no more right to interfere in their internal affairs than had South Africa the right to impose their views on Americans.

The 1978 elections strengthened conservatives within both the Democratic and Republican parties, leaving American liberals on the defensive over domestic and foreign matters. The Carter administration became increasingly convinced that the United States required South African cooperation in dealing with the Namibian and Rhodesian questions. The Carter administration in fact depended, in part, on South Africa's good will over Rhodesia. Smith had been brought to the negotiating table by South Africa's unwillingness to continue pouring money into the Rhodesian war. Increased pressure on South Africa, it was believed, would strengthen the *verkramptes* (hard-liners) within the National Party as against the *verligtes* (enlightened ones); it was argued that Americans would gain more concessions from the Afrikaners by using the carrot rather than the stick. The administration then began to use more diplomatic language in dealing with the South Africans. No attempt was made to suspend United States trade with South Africa. For all practical purposes, the policies pursued by Carter and his predecessors came to differ more on matters of emphasis than of substance. As Ambassador Young put it in a Senate hearing, "there is really no clear break [with the Kissinger policy]. . . . It is more an evolution of that policy." So in the end the Carter policy looked much like the Nixon-Kissinger policy. When Reagan came to power he simply continued the Nixon-Carter approach but took a globalist view of the regime's problems.

I see the Reagan administration and Chester Crocker's policy of constructive engagement in a somewhat different light than does Dr. Carter. This is not because of political loyalty—I am a

Democrat and not a Republican—but because I helped draft the Reagan southern Africa policy and believe it to be a sound one.

Before Reagan, United States policy in southern Africa had been ambivalent and inconsistent, alternating between cooperation with South Africa and support for black nationalism and attacks on apartheid.

In spite of the United States' vital interests in South Africa, it has hesitated to promote these interests by allying with South Africa. Washington saw the costs as too high in terms of black African and world opinion. Fundamentally, the United States has been, and is, committed to forcing reform in South Africa, ending apartheid, and gaining independence for Namibia.

The Carter administration initially supported human rights issues in order to win black American support, but then muted its criticism when it realized the United States needed Pretoria's cooperation to settle the Rhodesian (Zimbabwe) and Namibian issues peacefully. Reagan has done the same thing to achieve peace in the region and to free Namibia.

After President Reagan was inaugurated in 1981, the State Department argued for further concessions to South Africa in order to end the stalemate in Namibia. Washington announced a new policy of constructive engagement that had both regional and global ramifications; it sought peace and reform in southern Africa and it sought to force the Cubans out of Angola.

Constructive engagement, according to an administration spokesman appearing before the Subcommittee on Africa of the House of Representatives in 1982, has as its objectives: (1) fostering movement toward a system of government by consent of the governed and away from the racial policy of apartheid and political disenfranchisement of blacks; (2) continued access to the strategic minerals on which the United States and other members of the Organization for Economic Cooperation and Development are dependent; (3) assuring the strategic security of the Cape sea route, through which pass vital United States oil and mineral supplies from the Middle East and South Africa; and (4) regional security in southern Africa against the Soviet-Cuban threat.

There are five components to the United States approach to the southern African region: (1) internationally recognized independence for Namibia; (2) internationally supported programs of economic development in all the developing countries of the region; (3) negotiations to force the withdrawal of Cuban troops from Angola; (4) détente between South Africa and the other states of the region; and (5) peaceful evolutionary change in South Africa away from apartheid and toward a system of government based on consent of the governed.

The United States has also been negotiating bilaterally with South Africa on Namibian independence, as Dr. Carter shows. The major new element in the negotiations is the requirement by both Washington and Pretoria of withdrawal of Cuban forces from Angola. The United States believes this is necessary to get South Africa to give up Namibia and to initiate constructive changes within South Africa itself away from apartheid. This reflects the new global outlook of the Reagan administration, which sees Cuba as an integral part of the Soviet drive for world dominance.

President Reagan has indicated that his administration regards apartheid as repugnant to basic American values, but that as long as South Africa appears to be attempting to move away from its racist system of government, the United States should be helpful and encouraging. Constructive engagement therefore is dependent on reform within South Africa, the attainment of internationally recognized independence for Namibia and peace between South Africa and its neighbors.

Constructive engagement has produced some positive results in my view. Washington, however, will be unable to continue its present policy in the face of severe African hostility without registering even more success.

In South Africa, in spite of some reforms and new openings to Indians and Coloureds, there has been no new legislation to end discrimination since 1980 and blacks are still without the vote. There will have to be more movement for change. There is some evidence that further changes are planned, for example, on the Mixed Marriages and Immorality Act. Still, constructive engagement may have had some influence in reforms in South Africa. It was United States diplomacy which helped Angola and Mozambique to sit down and negotiate détente with South Africa.

African leaders had increasingly condemned United States efforts on the grounds that they were ineffective or that the United States practiced a form of closet collaboration with Pretoria. Yet alternative plans promise no solution either. The sad truth is that external pressure has failed and will continue to fail to produce major reforms until the internal conditions for change develop. Only Pretoria can help the United States continue its policy of constructive engagement by making bold domestic reforms and by cooperating on Namibian independence. If this is not done, then we will see a new United States policy—either distancing itself from South Africa or returning to diplomatic harangues and increased sanctions. After the Nkomati Accord and the Angolan Accords, the states of southern Africa appear, in effect, to have adopted the United States position towards South Africa.

The external campaign against South Africa has generated some pressures for change. It has helped awaken black consciousness and has revived the liberation struggle. There is no evidence that the anti-apartheid movement will lessen its pressure to isolate South Africa and to reduce the amount of assistance South Africa receives. While international opinion cannot force significant changes or defeat South Africa—only internal subversion and external assaults can do that—it can isolate South Africa, deny it goods and services, and thus raise the costs of continuing the apartheid system.

Unreformed, South Africa will never again command the friendly respect that it enjoyed in the United States when Prime Minister Jan Smuts was at the helm in Pretoria (1939-1948). The United States' commitment to racial equality and to human rights is now too strong to tolerate apartheid. South Africa will have to make more significant reforms and share power with blacks, Indians, and Coloureds before Americans will accept an alliance—and this is true no matter how important the Cape Route is, how much the West needs South Africa's strategic minerals, or how strong the Soviet-Cuban presence becomes. South Africa's anti-Communism, or its value as a military base during wartime, will not prove sufficient to overcome hatred of apartheid during a time of peace.

Political and economic warfare against South Africa, however, will not liberalize that republic or improve the lot of its black people—only internal reform and economic development can do that. The United States should seek to cooperate with a reform-minded Pretoria insofar as collaboration is in its strategic interest. The West should seek to support moderate forms of government in Namibia rather than aid its declared enemies. Similarly, it should consider recognition of Angola only after all foreign troops—Cuban and East German—and Soviet military experts have left. This would force the MPLA to form a coalition government with the two guerrilla organizations that now oppose it from the bush. Such a withdrawal should be a necessary condition for diplomatic relations with the United States.

Dr. Carter describes the object of the ANC as "turning it [South Africa] into a non-racial state." I have a different analysis. ANC believes that South Africa should first of all experience a national democratic revolution, to be achieved by a coalition between the proletariat, the progressive elements of the peasantry, the petty bourgeoisie, and the national bourgeoisie. The national democratic revolution itself will form a steppingstone toward socialism. The ANC is closely linked by ties of leadership and doctrine to the South African Communist Party. In the event of an ANC victory, the ANC would no doubt go through the same transformation from a progressive "organization" or "popular front" to a unitary Marxist party as MPLA and FRELIMO have done and as all other Communist-dominated fronts have done elsewhere.

In March, 1984, Mozambique signed a non-aggression agreement with South Africa, the first concluded between South Africa and its post-colonial neighbors. Under its terms, South Africa ceased support for the so-called Mozambique National Resistance Movement (MNR), and Mozambique no longer made its territory available to the ANC. At the time of writing, the precise implications of the treaty still remained to be elucidated. As far as Mozambique's Marxists were concerned, did the treaty imply coexistence as between contrasting social systems? Or did the treaty merely entail peaceful coexistence between differing state systems—the Soviet doctrinal interpretation? Was the treaty an African equivalent of the Nazi-Soviet pact of 1939? How would

FRELIMO militants regard this arrangement? Would the signatories end by violating the treaty terms in a clandestine fashion?

On the face of it, however, the South Africans had won a major victory. An avowedly Marxist-Leninist regime had committed itself to ending effective support for its revolutionary comrades. If the treaty were to be faithfully observed, its conclusion would vindicate South Africa's "outward" strategy. The arrangement conceivably might form a milestone in the evolution of future relations between Marxist-Leninist and Western countries in general. The new compact, on the face of it, certainly seemed to bode ill for the ANC and for those of its foreign well-wishers who hoped to intensify the armed struggle against South Africa. The revolutionary solidarity that the ANC had established with FRELIMO appears to have ended. Critics of South Africa will not be allowed, and the ANC will no longer be encouraged.

Mozambique also had other reasons for signing the Nkomati Accord: (1) Mozambique's disastrous economic situation; (2) Mozambique's need for economic ties to, and economic assistance from South Africa; (3) the ANC's inability to make much headway in its guerrilla campaign; (4) the effects of South African counter-raids on Mozambique; (5) South Africa's as yet unchallengeable military strength within the southern African context; and (6) Mozambique's dependency on South African communications.

It is not clear why the Nkomati Accord should have strengthened ANC and "reinforced its links and bases in other countries in South Africa." Which countries? Zimbabwe has not provided, and cannot afford to provide, bases owing to Zimbabwe's logistic dependence on South Africa—the same goes for Botswana, Lesotho, and Swaziland. Angola has arrived at an accord with South Africa over SWAPO. And even a SWAPO-run Namibia would not offer a good base for the ANC.

Early in 1984 the ANC had to rethink the strategy of what it called national liberation, having lost apparently the use of all privileged sanctuaries in the adjacent countries. The ANC had been shut out from Mozambique, Swaziland, and Lesotho. (Botswana and Zimbabwe had never sanctioned military action against South Africa from their territories.) The ANC's ally, SWAPO, had lost the use of its bases in southern Angola through a new agreement in 1984 between Angola and South Africa. In all probability, South Africa's military and diplomatic success will strengthen black consciousness as against militant Marxist-Leninist groups, and persuade the masses that military action at present is futile. Peaceful efforts will probably take the place of violent action although this does not preclude the occasional outburst of urban violence such as we have seen recently.

Commentary

Walton R. Johnson

As the conference organizers anticipated, Professor Carter's paper on United States policies toward South Africa and Namibia is thorough and authoritative. To facilitate further consideration of the topic, therefore, I have chosen to make three observations.

Constructive engagement is the catchword which describes the southern African policy of the Reagan administration. My first observation is that constructive engagement has been changing over the past four years in substantial and fundamental ways, raising the question of whether a coherent policy actually lies behind this glib phrase.

Chester Crocker's original argument for constructive engagement, published in *Foreign Affairs,* Winter, 1980–81, stressed that the West must "... engage credibly in addressing a complex agenda of change" in South Africa. He wrote "... too often our focus is on the wrong issue: the ultimate goal, instead of the process of getting there. The dismantling of apartheid and the creation of a new nonracial order is not going to take place through a sudden dramatic act, or result from one concession in one deal." The innovative feature of constructive engagement, he continued, is its insistence on serious thinking about the sequencing and interrelatedness of change in South Africa.

This early version of constructive engagement offered a formula for a bilateral policy toward South Africa which had changed to a nonracial order as its principal objective. It was seemingly intended to counter those who argued for a bilateral policy of divestment, withdrawal, and sanctions. However, as Professor Carter's paper has made clear, constructive engagement in 1984 is a regional policy, not a bilateral one, and its principal objective appears to be the security of the South African state, not orchestrating change in apartheid.

In our deliberations here we would be well advised to debate whether constructive engagement is in fact a coherent, well-formulated policy and, if it is, why there have been such significant shifts in focus, meanings, and objectives.

The second observation is on the impact of recent American policy. As regards South Africa, Professor Carter has correctly noted that our policy has "played into the hands" of the Botha government. As the regional power, South Africa has long sought to use its economic and military strength to forestall successful challenges to apartheid. This can best be done by replacing the former colonial states of Angola, Mozambique, and Rhodesia with "client" independent states. South Africa's "outward-looking policy" of the 1960s and her proposal for a "constellation of states" in the 1970s were attempts to lure its majority-ruled neighbors into such a client relationship.

With few exceptions, the African governments in the region have pulled in the other direction. They have striven to reduce their dependence on South Africa and to avoid becoming permanently locked into its sphere of influence. With regard to economic linkages, the formation of the Southern African Development Coordination Conference (SADCC) is a manifestation of these regional efforts. Politically, the independent nations have vigorously and vocally opposed apartheid and have offered assistance to its opponents.

Thus, until recently South Africa's strategy of establishing a regional Pax Pretoria had been partially thwarted. However, many observers maintain that the new policies in Washington have encouraged Pretoria to be more aggressive in its attempts to dominate the region and to dig its heels in even more with respect to domestic change. Indeed, the South African Defense

Force (SADF) has been wreaking havoc in virtually every country in the region. The African governments refer to these activities as a deliberate campaign of destabilization by South Africa. The South African government denies complicity in some of the events and calls the others "preemptive" or "retaliatory" measures required for its own defense.

It is beyond dispute that devastating economic, military, and political subversion is occurring in a manner which is moving steadily toward the Pax Pretoria that hardliners in South Africa have long sought. Illustration of this movement is found in the much-lauded Nkomati Accord. This agreement has been presented as a voluntary pact between sovereign states—a pact which reduces regional tensions and fosters regional cooperation. In reality, however, it seems as though the Mozambicans were simply bludgeoned into submission. For the past ten years, with support from the South African and Rhodesian governments, the Mozambique National Resistance (MNR) has been fighting in all parts of Mozambique except the immediate environs of Maputo. FRELIMO's military resources have been severely stretched and its small coffers have been drained. The country's frail economic infrasructure has been steadily chipped away, often with active and direct South African military involvement. In addition, Maputo has been the victim of several preemptive and reprisal bombings by South Africa's air force. Considering the fact that Mozambique has been experiencing a crippling multi-year drought as well as this destabilization, in the opinion of many, Maputo had no alternative but to capitulate to South Africa's demands at Nkomati.

So far, South Africa has openly imposed its will on Swaziland and Mozambique. Similar strategies for implementing a regional Pax Pretoria are being pursued with regard to Namibia, Angola, and Lesotho. There is even considerable evidence of South African destabilization in Zimbabwe. At this meeting we should ask ourselves: To what extent is Washington implicated in these events? Are these events congruent with our long-term national interests? Are our policies having the desired impact?

The third observation has to do with future American policy. The need to pursue certain specific objectives in our relations with South Africa has been well argued in *The Report of the*

Study Commission on U.S. Policy Towards Southern Africa. Adding to the commission's list, I call your attention to the following of Professor Carter's statements. She asserts, "What needs to be faced by the United States, regardless of which party is in power, is that a progressive and devastating denationalization of South Africa's African population is in process with the apparent aim, however it may be concealed, that ultimately there will be no African citizens in that country." In 1978 the South African government appointed a commission to enquire into, and make recommendations on, the feasibility of independence for the Ciskei. In 1980 the commission, chaired by George P. Quail, unanimously reported that the Xhosa did not support Ciskei independence. The renunciation and cessation of the bantustan program is a *sine qua non* for the achievement of a unitary, non-racial state in South Africa. An urgent order of business for American policy, therefore, must be to help bring a halt to the denationalization process.

In addition, the United States should broaden its examination of specific action plans which could implement positive change in South Africa and support those parties which are willing to execute them.

In sum, America's future policy toward South Africa should emphasize specific and concrete measures which can be employed by the government of South Africa to rapidly propel the society in the direction of a democratic unitary state based on one-person, one-vote. Given United States interests in orderly change in South Africa, short time tables should be set for the implementation of these measures, and the United States should be prepared to exercise strong sanctions should Pretoria not be willing to move swiftly and unambiguously. And, as part of a new forward-looking policy, American officials must maintain serious and visible dialogue with representatives of the African population, especially the African National Congress and the Pan-Africanist Congress.

DISCUSSION

The major themes in this discussion were the background of United States policy toward both South Africa and Namibia, and the implications of this policy for Angola and Mozambique. There was disagreement with the view that NSSM 39 was correct and realistic in recognizing the permanence of white power in South Africa and the need to compromise with it. Rather than likening this realism to the Nazi-Soviet pact, as one commentator suggested, NSSM 39 was viewed as more akin to the Munich pact between Hitler and Chamberlain with its pious: "Peace in our time!" It was asserted that this error of many past administrations led inexorably to the type of thinking which produced the almost-unworkable policy of constructive engagement. Moreover, it was claimed that this line of policy resulted in the Nkomati Accord, which, while seemingly curbing the ANC, will ultimately lead to a disaster for the United States policy in southern Africa. This statement was countered by the observation that whatever the feeling of some other discussants, Samora Machel wished a rapprochement with South Africa, and that the accord with South Africa was signed in the national interest of his country, which was beset by guerrilla attacks, drought, famine, and mismanagement.

There was disagreement about the relationship between constructive engagement and the Cuban presence in Angola. One discussant stressed that one should not forget that constructive engagement was initially not designed with Angola in mind, but to bring about change in South Africa by use of the carrot and not by the unproductive stick. As such, this American policy was deemed basically naïve, because it did not take into consideration the determination of Afrikaners to hold onto power by all the means at their disposal. Then, by extending this policy to all of southern Africa, in keeping with its global approach to the Soviets, the Reagan administration was said to have attempted to link problems which should have been tackled separately. It was argued that possible collusion between the United States and South Africa against the MPLA forces in Luanda may have led to the introduction of Cuban troops into the region. There was disagreement as to whether the United States was responsible for halting the South African invasion of Angola and the possibility of their going "all the way to Lagos." But it was suggested that the Cubans should not really be viewed as Soviet surrogates in Angola. Moreover, to link the Cuban presence in Angola to both the Namibian and internal South African issues was viewed as a mistake.

The view of one supporter of constructive engagement was that the Nkomati agreement strengthened the black consciousness movement in South Africa because it demonstrated the limitations of militant Marxist-Leninist initiatives in the area. The challenge and rebuttal to his remarks was that such a reading of the situation indicated a profound misunderstanding of the nature of black resistance to the South African regime. It was admitted that there were doctrinal differences between the black consciousness leaders and the ANC, but this had nothing to do with Marxism-Leninism, and everything to do with whether South Africa will be a multiracial nation where the power of the black majority will be muted, or a black country where the rights of the non-black minority would be protected. It was asserted that in spite of the ANC's difficulties, its leaders are becoming folk heroes in southern Africa and that they will be able to perform occasional sabotage, thereby disproving the ability of South Africa and its allies to seal that region off from the rest of the continent.

Attention was called to the ways in which constructive engagement increased the ability of South African whites to denationalize the Africans and get away with it. The people of Ciskei allegedly overwhelmingly voted against separation, preferring some form of "condominium" in the future. This did not stop South Africa from denationalizing them. Today South Africa denies any responsibility for the severe economic hardships in the area and one of the worst infant mortality rates in the world. It was suggested that the policy of constructive engagement locked the United States into acquiescing to that kind of harm to the African majority in the region. Such a development was deemed dangerous to the United States, and it was concluded that our policy should be revamped.

TOWARD AN AFRO-SPECTIVE POLICY

Elliott P. Skinner

The United States should now look beyond constructive engagement and formulate a more coherent policy toward Africa, not
only because that controversial policy has so far failed to fulfill
its promises in South Africa, but because it has once again revealed our seeming inability to deal *specifically* with Africa and
its problems. This call for an Africa-specific (or Afro-spective)
policy is due to the recognition that the United States has always
hesitated to view Africa with our national interest firmly in mind.
We have always refused to look Africa fully in the face.

The approach suggested here is made with full recognition
that Africa is a very dependent region within the global system,
and that the United States has a need to place its emphasis on
those areas of greatest importance to us. It is also acknowledged
that we have age-old allies whose needs must be met, and that an
Afro-spective United States policy might entail a modification of
such alliances. An Afro-spective United States policy must also
face the complexity of a continent of many small and weak states
beset by manifold problems. Nevertheless, to be successful or
meaningful, a United States policy toward Africa must be prepared to deal with the realities of that continent, with its prob-

lems, its fears, and its hopes, and help to develop all the potential that it possesses. The result could be a policy that gives priority to what is in our national interest, and in the interest of most of the peoples on the African continent.

For understandable historical reasons, the people of the United States have resisted dealing specifically with Africa and its peoples. Viewing that continent from the vantage point of the complexities surrounding the status of blacks in colonial America, the emerging United States wanted little to do with Africa. The early United States respected European dominance in Africa, but preferred to let others deal with African issues which had not been taken over by the metropolitan powers. It was only with greatest reluctance that the United States faced the issue of dealing with the emerging independent states of Africa, and often our policies were instructed by the interests of our European friends and allies. With the advent of the cold war, our policy toward African states was designed to prevent the Soviet Union from having an undue influence on that continent, and to preserve the power and prestige of the retreating European powers.

In seeming contrast to Britain and France, which accepted the logic of African international sovereignty and designed policies to deal with this, the United States designed a policy in southern Africa based on the permanancy of Portuguese rule, of continued white domination, and the fear that African nationalism would lead to Soviet Communism. The fall of the Portuguese empire shattered that dream, led to the independence of Zimbabwe, and left South Africa confronting the need to change the status of Africans within its borders. Instead of facing courageously the reality in South Africa, the United States accepted a policy of constructive engagement clearly designed to protect the interests of the white South African minority, hoping thereby that this group would change its commitment to a frankly racist policy of apartheid. The fear of Soviet Communism was seen as legitimizing the continuation of this Eurocentric policy. Ignored was the reality of the African demographic majority which sooner or later must gain power in South Africa. Moreover, in pursuit of this will-o'-the-wisp, and insisting that the South African whites were our allies in the struggle against Soviet Communism, the United States extended the implications of constructive engagement to the continent as a whole. This policy can never succeed. The time has come to stop trying to fine-tune or calibrate an incoherent policy, and the time has come to develop an Africa-specific policy that is in our national interest.

The need for a policy that went beyond constructive engagement was clearly recognized during the course of the conference whose papers, commentaries, and discussions form the major portion of this book. The dreadful economic plight of much of Africa, in the Sahel, in the Horn, even in southern Africa, impressed itself on the American people. The swollen bellies of Ethiopian children disturbed our evening meals, inducing college students to skip meals and send money to Africa instead. An embattled U.S. AID administrator was quizzed by an angry Congress and a skeptical media, to explain United States economic aid policy toward Africa. President Reagan felt the need to explain to the American people that the United States would help to alleviate hunger and misery, even in Marxist-Leninist Ethiopia.

What passed relatively unnoticed was that Africa's economic plight had long been recognized by the United States. Secretary of State George Shultz, an economist, stated in February, 1984, that:

> Declining African markets and growing regional insolvency are a significant drag on global recovery, with a particular impact on Europe. In short, the West cannot afford—and we will not sit idly by and watch—the accelerating decline of Africa's economy.

Recognition of the relationship between Africa's economic decline and its drag on global recovery is all to the good, and it is understandable why Africa's economic problems do have a particular effect on Europe. What is troubling, however, is that here again Africa's plight is interpreted in terms of its impact on Europe. Shultz's statement is not any different from statements made after World War II when Africa's economic needs were ignored by the Marshall Plan since it was taken for granted that their metropoles would take care of them. But this is 1985, and most of the African states have been sovereign for almost a generation. While it is still a fact that most or all of the African countries are still dependent upon Europe economically, is it not time for the United States to start planning for an economic future when this will not be so?

Unless there is a determined change in our economic policy toward African countries which has taken for granted the primacy of European trade in the area, American businessmen will not be encouraged to trade with Africa. Both we and the Africans insist that trade is preferable to aid, and Africans welcome trade with a vibrant American economy, if only to gain access to sophisticated technology. This development might encourage American businesses to create joint offices in the major African countries, where they could pool their technical staffs, use interpreters in common when the need arose, and aggregate the small business community in such a way as to make it profitable. These procedures would also enable American businesses to benefit from some of the funds the United States allocates to multilateral organizations in Africa. A more determined trade policy in such large countries as Nigeria where the United States does have a balance of payment deficit, might do much to build markets for American industries and help those states to develop economically. One benefit from such a policy would be that American companies could diversify their activities in Africa to states other than South Africa, where the profits are increasingly seen as not worth the political hassle.

An Afro-spective United States economic policy toward Africa would place the burning and potentially disturbing problem of conditionality in a more effective framework. Today, many African economic planners are concerned that the United States pays little attention to their economic plans but tries to place conditions on the little aid it does provide. A clear statement that the United States is prepared to take seriously such African initiatives as the Lagos Plan of Action, and the Southern African Development Coordination Conference (SADCC) could clear the air. Of course, the United States should insist that such plans be thoroughly discussed, and that perhaps some aspects of the World Bank/Berg Report be incorporated in them. The result of such a discussion might even result in the Africans' accepting many of our ideas of conditions under which aid is offered, or our accepting their views of our conditions.

Some way should be found for the United States to offer aid to the African states while taking African opinions into consideration. The plan of the Reagan administration to initiate a five-year, $500 million aid program beginning with $75 million for Fiscal Year 1985, to be allocated to countries that undertake certain policy reforms, is highly reminiscent of previous policies which failed. It is quite possible that a free market approach to farming will reduce the dependence of African countries on outside food. Almost all of the colonial governments' earlier food-producing plans, such as the "Office du Niger" in Mali and the "Groundnut Scheme" in Tanganyika (Tanzania), failed, and so have those promulgated by the independent African states. In fact, one disturbing problem is the relative ignorance of how to increase food production in Africa. However, the solution is not for the United States to attempt to take an economic initiative without involving the Africans. If the past is any guide, such expatriate planning is very risky. It might be better to engage the Africans in an Africa-specific economic venture in which they will be the ultimate beneficiaries.

There is no escaping the awesome reality that as a global superpower, the United States must be able to project its military power into Africa if and when the strategic need arises for it to do so. Past experience shows that from the shores of Tripoli to the Suez Canal and Red Sea, United States military forces must be prepared to defend the national interest in Africa as elsewhere. What the past shows as well is that many problems which led to United States intervention were caused in part by African instability, and not Soviet adventurism. Because of our overwhelming concern with the Soviets, African states, including South Africa, and even European imperial powers, have been able to manipulate the United States to come to their rescue when they felt that their primarily parochial interests were threatened by non-Soviet forces. The Horn, Central Africa, North Africa, and now southern Africa come readily to mind as areas where this has happened.

261

An Afro-spective United States strategic policy would bear in mind that the changes in military technology in recent years have given us new ways of dealing with the African reality. There must be new ways of thinking about such African strategic questions as sea lanes, launching pads, protection of resources, and the use of African terrain as sites for warfare by surrogate forces. Our contemporary concern with the presence of Cuban troops in Angola as an example of the use of African terrain by surrogates in superpower conflict is a case in point. But this conflict must be viewed against the backdrop of why the Cubans went there, and how their presence became linked to our own Euro-centric African policy. There is every indication that the African states are as eager as the United States to get rid of outside military forces whose presence only complicates their difficult parochial problems.

The United States should profit from the clear fact that most African states do not welcome foreign bases on their territories, and get rid of them as soon as conditions permit. There is also a growing feeling that even European powers such as France, with residual military commitments to African states, are finding it increasingly difficult to honor these. Is this not the time for the United States to support the Organization of African Unity as the strategic instrument in an Afro-spective policy? That organization has survived against major odds and has attempted to deal with African problems, even military ones. It has not been successful in many of its operations, but is it not the kind of entity which, if supported, would be able to rally the Africans around a policy which is in their interest, and also in our own?

An Afro-spective policy designed to encourage the OAU to take a more active role in mediating our strategic concerns on the African continent applies with equal force to African regional issues, and those posed by social and political conflicts within individual African states. Whether or not the United States' quarrel with Qadaffi created a problem for the ability of the OAU to meet in Tripoli or to deal effectively with the Saharawi problem is now moot. Much to our consternation, the North African states, appealing to sentiments which have little meaning to us, and specifically not involving our major adversary, the Soviet Union, are attempting to resolve problems in their region. We have also not been successful in mediating among the states in the Horn of Africa because it is clear that the ethnic issues there have confused and confounded both ourselves and the Soviets. Our previous alliance with Ethiopia did not solve that country's problem with Eritrea or Somalia, and it is unlikely that the Soviets could help Marxist-Leninist Ethiopia or the other states in the region to resolve the primordial issues facing them. Would it not be better if the United States could encourage the OAU to help the local states deal with their problems? After all, the problems there are basically African in character, and may have to wait for an eventual African solution.

Much to the displeasure of some and to the satisfaction of others, Tanzania helped resolve the problem posed to Africa (and its reputation in the world) by the excesses of Amin in Uganda. Thus, a local problem which at one period did call for the intervention of an outside state was resolved without involving superpower confrontation. South Africa is not Uganda, but our definition of the situation there as involving superpower rivalry has so far frustrated the ability of the presidents of the Front Line African states to help resolve the problems there. Ironically, the Western allies of the United States, the so-called Contact States, have at times found themselves in greater agreement with the Front Line presidents than with us about how to resolve the issue of Namibia. More instructive have been the occasions when both the white South Africans and the black Africans in the region despaired of our presence as they tried to wrestle with their problems. Are these not signals that our insistence on the global implications of problems of southern Africa may be counterproductive?

There was a strong feeling among the participants at the conference that the United States neither has the resources nor the acquiescence of our citizens to resolve most of the local problems which plague the Africans. This does not mean, however, that American opinions about local African problems do not count, since in this interdependent world local issues do have a tendency to escalate unless adequately dealt with. The interest generated by the United States in human rights has now become global, and has taken on a life of its own—often to our own embarrassment. Therefore, the opinion of the United States does

263

matter, especially when harmonized with those of regional and continent-wide bodies. An Afro-spective policy would encourage us to attempt to mobilize local initiatives to solve problems which, if escalated to global proportions, would not be in our national interest, or in that of the Africans.

Much to the agony and frustration of most people, the level of pain and suffering in southern Africa has increased in the wake of the promulgation of our policy of constructive engagement. Designed largely to protect white privilege in South Africa, this policy has vitiated United Nations efforts to decolonize Namibia, and has exacerbated the problems of the Angolans and Mozambicans. That constructive engagement is detrimental even to the hope that it could aid the United States to counter potential Soviet threat in the region was amply demonstrated when Botswana, long an anti-Communist state, complained that South African pressure was forcing it to think in terms of approaching the Soviet Union for help. The Nkomati Accord between South Africa and Mozambique, hailed by members of the administration as a positive demonstration of success against Soviet penetration of the region, is also unravelling. So alarmed did we become that continued South African support to the MNR was destabilizing the government of Samora Machel that we agreed to furnish non-lethal military aid to him.

It seems clear that the United States' ability to help move Namibia toward independence will be frustrated unless we decouple this process from the Cuban presence in Angola, thereby removing a source of contention between ourselves and most of the African states. The issue of the Cuban troops in Angola should then be taken up with the OAU and with those important African states which have voiced objection to foreign troops on the continent. This policy would also please those American businessmen who have satisfactorily worked with the Angolans and would help to resolve an impasse which is not in our interest or in that of the Angolan people.

Reports from South Africa itself have demonstrated once again that, regardless of what the ruling powers claim, they are not immune to global pressure. Rather than support the bluster of the Afrikaners that they alone have the right to mediate the pace of change while the situation continues to fester, the United

States can be a positive catalyst for change, and if need be, facilitate change. For well-known historical reasons, the United States is more a mirror image of South Africa than almost any other nation in the world. Therefore, it is simply not true that we do not understand that country. The truth is that we and they understand each other all too well. Fortunately for the whites in South Africa, they possess most of the skills needed by a modern society if it would survive and prosper in the contemporary world. Moreover, peoples of European descent still have the power and prestige to ensure the survival of South African whites if need be. A truly Afro-spective policy would induce the United States to encourage South Africa to institute a program of "comprehensive reform." The aim would be to afford all those who live in South Africa to have an equal voice in planning its future. The formula that the South Africans develop will only serve if it enables them to live comfortably with the other people of the planet. Nothing else will work.

The United States should have less difficulty devising an Afro-spective educational and cultural policy toward Africa. As one of the first truly modern multiracial and multicultural societies in the world, the United States has a long, troubled but rich experience of providing education for peoples from different backgrounds. This experiment is still in process, and so is the debate about it. But there are many lessons that the Africans can learn from us. As the situation now stands, it is to the United States, rather than to Europe, that contemporary Africans turn in their drive to catch up with the flow of history and technology. Even the current debate in the United States as to whether the state, local communities, or individual parents should determine and control the education of their children, will be instructive to Africans who, after all, can and must examine all external models against the backdrop of their own realities.

For historical reasons, the United States now possesses a cultural patrimony that has more in common with African cultures than that which they and we received from the cultures of Europe. Moreover, as the United States' culture reflects more faithfully the true mix of this society, the easier it will be for Africans to relate to a culture which demonstrates the modern possibilities of their own Africanness. An Afro-spective policy toward Africa will build on this now natural foundation in the interest of our nation, which has so much to give to the world. Not to expend the money and effort in the realm of education and culture is truly not in our national interest.

Finally, personal and group traumas attending decolonization and nation-building (not to mention wars, pogroms, and natural catastrophies) are not unknown to a United States whose ancestral populations included peoples with similar experiences. Out of this has come a tradition of hospitality and succor to the wretched of the earth. There is therefore deep concern that the United States has been finding it increasingly difficult to help refugees and displaced persons. Faced with one of the largest groups of refugees in the world, the African states and the OAU have supported the policy that African refugees be settled within the continent. An Afro-spective policy would applaud this African initiative, and support those COAs whose slender budgets are strained to provide hospitality to their neighbors. But there are also Africans who, affected by the pushes and pulls of both local and global factors, elect to immigrate to the United States. Those persons should be able to take advantage of the "old country" status given to those regions of the world which have contributed to the mosaic of peoples whose ancestors built the United States. Given distance and anxiety, many Africans may not be willing to emigrate from their countries. But an Afro-spective policy would welcome those who seek to improve their lives and those of their children by immigrating. Hopefully they too would contribute to the national interest of the United States.

POSTSCRIPT

There was an increase in bloodshed and death due to rioting, communal strife and industrial strikes on the eve of our conference. In retrospect, it appeared to be full confirmation of the almost unanimous conclusion of conference participants that constructive engagement was the wrong approach for dealing with the entrenched minority in South Africa. Not only did constructive engagement fail to engage the Botha regime in a process of reform, but as some of the participants in the conference indicated, the South Africans appeared to have been confirmed in their intransigence when faced with a rather naïve United States policy. Alarmed over the deepening chaos in South Africa, black Americans sat-in at the South African Embassy in Washington; organized a Free South Africa Movement; increased their campaign for divestment and banning of the sales of the krugerrand; and called upon Congress to impose sanctions on Pretoria.

These actions appeared in tandem with the decision of the Nobel Peace Prize Committee to grant its 1984 award to Bishop Desmond Tutu, a man who was endeavoring to help his country resolve its problems by peaceful means. President Reagan's attempt to convince the bishop that constructive engagement was far from bankrupt was bound to fail, especially since it took place at the same time as the United States was feeling constrained to recall its ambassador to South Africa in protest against that country's attack upon Botswana and on the installations of Gulf Oil (the American company) in far-off Cabinda, Angola. Black South Africans knew their white countrymen too well to believe that anything short of global pressure for change would succeed.

While many participants in the conference predicted disaster in South Africa, very few of us foresaw the speed with which the situation there would deteriorate. The shooting of hundreds of blacks and Coloureds by the police and the burning of persons regarded as quislings by the rioters inexorably led to the declaration of a state of emergency by the government. No one was surprised when Bishop Tutu took his life in his hands and braved angry demonstrators to save the life of a police informer. President Botha's contemptuous rejection of the bishop's offer to meet in an effort to reduce the conflict, was surely indicative of why constructive engagement could not have worked. Botha's stubborn decision to maintain a hard line after Reagan's national security affairs adviser, Robert C. McFarlane, had told South African Foreign Minister Roeloff (Pik) Botha in Vienna of increasing opposition in the United States to the lack of progress in South Africa, shocked the United States officials, the Congress, and the world. Botha's behavior would not have surprised those participants at the congress who had warned that it would take more than Reagan's repugnance with the policy of constructive engagement to bring about change in South Africa.

It is still too early to tell whether the decision of President Reagan to counter the threatened sanctions against South Africa by the congress by signing an executive order authorizing milder sanctions will send the right signal to Pretoria. What certainly would have impressed the participants at the conference was the President's rather belated and certainly reluctant admission that he found that:

> The policies and actions of the Government of South Africa constitute an unusual and extraordinary threat to the foreign policy and economy of the United States and [I] hereby declare a national emergency to deal with that threat. . . .

If this means that President Reagan is now prepared to go beyond what he is now calling "positive constructive engagement," then this would be in keeping with the recommendations of many of the participants at the conference. If, on the other hand, this is only a band-aid being applied to a rather serious problem, then the future might well be disastrous for both the United States and South Africa.

An Afro-spective policy towards South Africa would recognize what the Reagan office is perhaps only now realizing—namely, that there is no substitute for a program of "comprehensive reform" in that country. Despite the modern predilection towards "one man, one vote," the suggestion that only the people of South Africa can plan their future is a perceptive one. At the same time, there must be recognition that the interconnectedness of the contemporary world and its cultural, economic, political, and social imperatives should condition what the South Africans do. Any failure on our part to speak out and bring these conditions to the attention of all South African leaders, especially the white minority, will only lead to disaster. The factors and forces which led Chester Crocker to develop the policy of constructive engagement, and for President Reagan to promulgate it, are still with us. Any formula that the South Africans develop for their society will only serve well if it enables them to live comfortably with each other as well as with the other peoples of the planet.

Authors and Commentators

Dr. Robert S. Browne, Senior Research Fellow, African Studies and Research Center, Howard University.

Dr. Gwendolyn M. Carter, Professor of Political Science, University of Florida.

Dr. Peter Duignan, Director of African Studies, Hoover Institute on War, Revolution and Peace, Stanford University.

Dr. Richard E. Feinberg, Vice President, Overseas Development Council; Adjunct Professor of International Finance, Georgetown University, School of Foreign Service.

Dr. William J. Foltz, Professor of Political Science and Director of the Yale Center for International and Area Studies, Yale University.

Dr. Marie Davis Gadsden, Deputy Director, National Association for Equal Opportunity/AID Cooperative Agreement.

Dr. Walton R. Johnson, Professor of African Studies, Rutgers University.

Dr. Morton A. Kaplan, Professor of Political Science and Director of the Center for Strategic and Foreign Policy Studies, University of Chicago.

Dr. William H. Lewis, Professor of Political Science and Director, Security Policy Studies Program, George Washington University.

Dr. Calvin H. Raullerson, Vice President, African-American Institute.

Dr. Robert I. Rotberg, Professor of Political Science and History, Massachusetts Institute of Technology.

Dr. Elliott P. Skinner, Franz Boas Professor of Anthropology, Columbia University; Conference Chairman.

Dr. Mabel M. Smythe, Associate Director, African Studies, Northwestern University.

Dr. Roger P. Winter, Director, U.S. Committee for Refugees.

Dr. I. William Zartman, Director, African Studies Program, School of Advanced International Studies, The Johns Hopkins University.

SESSIONAL CHAIRMEN

David Carliner, Esq.
Partner, David Carliner, P.C.

Dr. Richard L. Rubenstein, President, The Washington Institute for Values in Public Policy; Distinguished Professor of Religion, Florida State University.

Neil Albert Salonen, Director, The Washington Institute for Values in Public Policy; President, International Cultural Foundation.

Index

Page numbers in **bold face** refer to sections written by the subject. Numbers in parenthesis refer to footnotes which appear on the indicated page.

Nihize, Saul 135
Nikomati xix
Nimieri, Jafar 95
Nixon, Richard M. xi-xii, xx (4), 48,
85, 190, 222, 238-239, 242
Nkomati Accord 132, 139, 231, 233,
245, 247, 251, 253-254
Nkomo, Joshua 223
NMR xix
NNSM 5
North Africa 261
North Korea 58
NSSM 238, 253
Nujoma, Sam 74, 227
Nyerere 168, 171

O

OAU 19, 32, 57-58, 66, 94, 144-147,
157, 171-172, 179, 185, 227,
251-266
OAU Refugee Convention 166, 169
OE 194
Ogaden Province (Ethiopia) 61, 100
Oman 60
OPEC 14, 18, 26, 30, 33
Orange River 103
Organization for Economic
Cooperation and Development 243
Oujda 96
Ovamboland 121-122
Ovimbundu 240
O'Flaherty, J. Daniel 67 (1)

P

PAC 232
Pakistan 197
Pan-African Congress 232
Panama 197, 205
Paris 96
Pax Pretoria 250-251
Peace Corps Volunteers 181, 187,
196, 202, 215
Peking 85
Pelt, Adrian 67 (5)
Persian Gulf 60-61, 85
Peru 197, 205
Phelps-Stokes Fund 196
Philippines 197, 205
Poland 196
Polisario 140
Port Lyautey (Kenitra) 83
Portugal xiii, 48, 54, 59, 65, 100-101,
123-125, 138, 222, 239, 258
Pretoria 227, 243-245, 252, 268
Purcell, Jr., James N. 151, 162 (8),
164
PVOs 148, 192, 195-196

Q

Qaboos, Sultan 60
Qadaffi 8, 80, 94-96, 109-111, 140,
261
Quail, George P. 252

Upper Volta 197-201
USAID 31, 191, 194-196, 249

Valkinier, Elizabeth Kridl 70 (33)
Varter 224
Vietnam ix, 49-51, 58, 79
Vorster 225-230, 234

W

Wallerstein, Immanuel 189
Weddei, Goukkduni 95
Weinberg, A. M. 69 (32)
West Germany 98, 140, 227
Wheelus Field (Libya) 56, 73
Whitaker, Jenifer Seymour xiv, xx (8)
Wilhelm II 54
Williams, G. Mennen 84
Windhoek 123
Winter, Roger P. 165-171, 271
Wisner, Frank 230
Wolpe, Howard 233
World Bank 169, 179-180, 183-184, 196, 250
World Court 226

X

Xhosa 251

Y

Yaounde Conference 194
Yemen 95, 197
Young, Andrew 6, 236, (2), 224-225, 242
Young, Harry F. 24 (6)
Youssef, Sidi Monhammed Ben 83

Z

Zaire 8-10, 54, 73, 84, 103, 158, 168, 195, 198-201
Zambezi 103
Zambia 167-168, 195, 197-201, 223
Zartman, I. William 69 (23), 107-113, 271
Zimbabwe 6, 65, 73, 101-117, 126-128, 167, 194, 196, 198-201, 205, 223-225, 241, 243, 247, 251, 258
Zulu 75